REMEDIES FOR THE
"I DON'T COOK"
SYNDROME

REMEDIES FOR THE
"I DON'T COOK"
SYNDROME

JANET PETERSON

EAGLE GATE

© 2001 Janet Peterson

All rights reserved. No part of this book may be reproduced in any form or by any means without permission in writing from the publisher, Deseret Book Company, P. O. Box 30178, Salt Lake City, Utah 84130. This work is not an official publication of The Church of Jesus Christ of Latter-day Saints. The views expressed herein are the responsibility of the author and do not necessarily represent the position of the Church or of Deseret Book Company.

Eagle Gate is a registered trademark of Deseret Book Company.

Visit us at www.deseretbook.com

Library of Congress Cataloging-in-Publication Data

Peterson, Janet
  Remedies for the "I don't cook" syndrome / Janet Peterson.
    p. cm.
Includes bibliographical references and index.
  ISBN 1-57345-940-2 (paperback)
  1. Cookery. I. Title.
  TX714.P4623 2001
  641.5—dc21

2001001308

Printed in the United States of America   72082-6796

10 9 8 7 6 5 4 3 2

*To my family, who are my reason to cook:
Larry, Scott, Anna, Andrew, Stephanie, David,
Brinley, Benjamin, Amanda, Tom, Megan,
Greg, Jeff, Vicky, and Brent*

CONTENTS

ACKNOWLEDGMENTS/*ix*

PURPOSE/*xi*

INTRODUCTION/*1*

COOKING TERMS/*13*

BASIC PANTRY SUPPLIES AND SHOPPING CHECKLIST/*17*

KEY TO SYMBOLS/*22*

SOUPS/*23*

SALADS/*43*

BREADS/*79*

BEEF/*101*

CHICKEN/*121*

FISH/*149*

PORK AND HAM/*165*

GRILLING/*175*

VEGETABLES/*205*

RICE, PASTA, AND LIGHT SUPPERS/*237*

DESSERTS/*259*

COOKING RESOURCES/*311*

BIBLIOGRAPHY/*317*

INDEX/*319*

ACKNOWLEDGMENTS

From the moment I proposed this cookbook to Jana Erickson, Eagle Gate imprint manager at Deseret Book Company, she has been enthusiastic and encouraging. It is her expertise that has brought *Remedies for the "I Don't Cook" Syndrome* to publication. I express thanks to Christine Neilson for carefully proofreading the manuscript as I prepared it for submission, and to Janna DeVore for skillfully editing the cookbook.

I also wish to thank the many good cooks who have generously shared their recipes and insights on the importance of families eating together. Heartfelt appreciation goes to Kathy Crawford, Betty Draper, Nancy Hughes, Kathleen McGuire, Pat Menlove, Nancy Simpson, Marjorie Tall, and Kathryn Wade, who not only provided exceptional help for this project but who have also nurtured me through life's projects.

When I began collecting recipes and researching the effects of families eating or not eating together, I had only a general notion that dinnertime does matter. After more than a year of reading, conversing, and observing, I am convinced that dinnertime *does* matter and that eating together is as significant in strengthening families as many other endeavors, including family home evening, scripture study, and family activities. The current trend of saying, "I don't cook" and then relying on takeout and fast food is harmful to families and the physical and emotional well-being of children. It is my hope that users of this cookbook will gain new insights into the purpose of dinner and will enjoy preparing and eating these simple and delicious recipes.

PURPOSE

The purpose of *Remedies for the "I Don't Cook" Syndrome* is to:

- Encourage families to eat dinner together at home.
- Demonstrate what happens when families do eat together.
- Provide good, simple recipes that have ordinary ingredients and few cooking steps.
- Suggest ideas that will help gather families, both nuclear and extended, together and make dinnertime enjoyable.

The recipes in *Remedies for the "I Don't Cook" Syndrome* have been gathered from family, friends, and other good cooks. Each recipe has been tested by my family and deemed worthy to include in this book. A few recipes were created by the contributors, but most of the recipes have been adopted by the contributors—having been handed down from a mother or grandmother, enjoyed at a Relief Society social, found in a newspaper or magazine, or hastily written on a piece of scratch paper. They have been shared for this cookbook because they have become the family favorites of those who contributed them.

Most of the recipes in this cookbook are for families of four to six people. The recipes can be adjusted for smaller or larger groups. Planning leftovers and freezing extra food for later meals are options when recipes serve more people than needed.

The number of servings for a recipe is approximate, as ages and appetites of family members vary widely.

Low-fat alternatives can be easily implemented into these recipes by using low-fat ingredients such as mayonnaise, cheese, or margarine.

While microwave instructions are given for some recipes, directions for conventional cooking are given for most of them. Those who prefer microwave cooking can adapt the recipes to their specific microwave ovens. (Generally, microwave for one-fourth the time given for a conventional oven; increase time by thirty-second increments.)

INTRODUCTION

"I DON'T COOK"

How many times have you heard someone say, "I don't cook" and really mean it?

Whether they are newlyweds, young families, families with busy teenagers, empty nesters, or singles living alone or with roommates, for many people eating a home-cooked dinner with their families has become as rare as mom-and-pop grocery stores.

When the stylist cutting my hair one afternoon told me she didn't cook, I assumed it was a catchphrase that meant she cooked only every now and then. As our conversation continued, however, I learned that she really meant, "I don't cook." What, I asked, did she and her husband do for dinner? She replied that they stopped at one of two favorite fast-food restaurants on alternate nights. (Power bars eaten on the way to work were considered breakfast.)

One family put their home on the market to sell. When a realtor brought a couple to look at the house, they showed particular interest in the kitchen. It was large, beautifully decorated, and immaculately clean. Mrs. Prospective Buyer exclaimed that she had never seen a stove in such mint condition—was it brand new? Hesitant, the homeowners looked at each other and didn't answer until the husband prodded his wife, "Come on, Dear, tell them the truth. It's not new. It's never been used." What food was processed in this kitchen was most often take-out warmed in the microwave.

For years one grandmother has bragged, "I don't cook." Her grandchildren cannot recall ever having eaten a dinner she has prepared, although she has served them snacks of mini-pizzas and bakery cookies. She has missed an enormous opportunity to bond with her extended family.

The "I Don't Cook" Syndrome has become epidemic.

WHAT HAS HAPPENED TO DINNER?

"The word *dinner* once conjured up images of warm, delicious smells emanating from the kitchen as everyone gathered around the table not just for nourishment but for family conversation as well," stated Michael and Mary Eades, coauthors of *The Protein Power LifePlan*. "Dinner in this fast-paced world has often become a catch-as-catch-can proposition, grabbed on the run from whatever fast-food haven lies in your traffic pattern or the one the kids seem to prefer. It too often comes in recyclable polyfoam boxes or paper bags, eaten between stoplights on the way to or from this practice or that meeting."[1]

Consumer Reports notes that "On average, Americans dine out 18 times a month, spending $1 billion a day in the process—the equivalent of $812 per year for every man, woman, and child. In fact, Americans spend three times as much on food outside the home as they did a generation ago."[2] One industry-watcher quoted in the magazine's report stated, "Dinner houses have become the nation's dinner table."[3]

Mary Matthews, a high school psychology teacher, gave her students a homework assignment to eat dinner with their families for one week and then record their experiences. Matthews had discovered that it wasn't just her students who were missing out on family meals. "According to the Food Marketing Institute, only forty percent of American families eat together and then no more than a couple of times a week,"[4] she writes. Based on her research, Matthews has initiated a statewide campaign, "Table Talk: Strengthening Families at Mealtime," to encourage Washington families to eat together.

It seems that the proclamation, "I don't cook" has become equated with other choices, such as, "I don't do windows" or "I don't ski" or "I don't play the piano." Eating, however, is not optional, and the concept that fleeing the kitchen is liberating is a false one that comes with increased expenses and health risks. Even those would-be chefs who do not feel confident in the kitchen and feel they lack culinary talents can learn cooking skills quite easily through reading, observation, classes, experimentation, and practice.

The time and effort spent in preparing satisfying and nutritious meals is one of the best investments a family can make. "If you respect the importance of meals in your home," says Cheryl Mendelson, author of *Home Comforts: The Art and Science of Keeping House,* "you gain a cornucopia of advantages that are acknowledged so rarely as to count among the best-kept secrets of our day. In addition to saving you money, cooking at home can help you be healthier, happier, and more secure, and it provides a wonderful way for you to be with your family."[5]

The blame for disappearing home-cooked dinners does not lie only with the family cook, who may be very willing and able to prepare a tasty and nutritious dinner. When dinner's on the table, where are family members? Often at work; at school; at the gym; at meetings; involved in sports, dance, or music lessons; hanging out with friends; or at the mall.

Our fast-paced and over-programmed lives can exact a high toll on a family's happiness, security, and closeness. Today, it is even more critical that we connect consistently and effectively with those whom we share our lives and with whom we love most dearly—our families. Eating dinner together regularly provides more than good nutrition; it enables family members to share their days with each other, relax, laugh, discuss issues, socialize, and strengthen familial relationships. It's true that "The table is a meeting place, a gathering ground, the source of sustenance and nourishment, festivity, safety, and satisfaction."[6] Perhaps we've become too lax in making dinner a consistent part of family life. Attitude, encouragement, invitation, and, sometimes, insistence can bring families together at mealtime.

One father wrote that showing up for dinner was not an option in his home: "We've done our share of things wrong as a family, but one of the things we did right was to insist that the evening meal be a family event. I cook these meals myself and I go to a great deal of trouble over them. We eat good food and we eat it together. My children, who can sometimes seem thankless, have often said how much they appreciate these efforts, and my daughter, who is now away at college, tells me all the time how much she misses dinners."[7]

THE BENEFITS OF DINNER AT HOME

Families, no matter their size or makeup, must be fed. A good dinner never just magically appears on the table. Cooking dinner does take some time and energy in planning, shopping, preparing, and cleaning up. Nevertheless, the benefits of families regularly eating dinner together in the surroundings of their own homes are significant. The cumulative effects are compelling reasons to make dinner a family event. Habitual dining practices of eating out, ordering in, skipping, or snacking may satisfy the needs of the moment but, in the long run, are detrimental to families as a whole and to their individual members.

- *Costs Less*

Multiply the average of $812 spent annually per person on eating out, and it doesn't take a CPA to tell you that's costly, especially for a family with children. Restaurant prices in recent years have risen slightly faster than inflation, making it even more expensive to eat away from home.[8]

Even if families can afford to eat out frequently (or have meals catered), money is probably the least important factor in the cost of not eating at home. Loss of nutrition, private family interaction, and time (driving to and from and eating at a sit-down restaurant take time) are less tangible but more significant costs.

By choosing to cook at home, a family can save considerable money. Restaurants, after all, are in business to make money, and diners pay for their labor, facilities, and profit margin.

As Michael and Mary Eades put it: "If you don't cook, it's time you learned at least the basics, because for the money you absolutely can't beat the quality of nutrition you can provide for yourself at home. . . . you'll get more cluck for your buck and be certain of what it is you're getting when you develop a habit of eating more meals at home."[9]

- *More Nutritious*

Commercially prepared foods are notoriously high in sugar, starch, and fat, although some restaurants do list low-fat items on their menus. *Consumer Reports* quoted one restaurant-industry analyst who said, people "talk thin and eat fat." Likewise, the magazine found that "fewer than one in ten readers said the availability of low-fat, low-calorie fare was important in choosing a restaurant. A Department of Agriculture study says that away from home, people opt for foods with more fat and less fiber, iron, and calcium."[10] Current restaurant trends present "gargantuan portions" so that diners simply eat more when they eat out. Consuming excess food causes weight gain and other health problems. *Consumer Reports* also noted, "In our years of reporting on restaurants, we can't recall such an array of belly-busting servings across a broad spectrum of chains."[11]

"We really are what we eat, and if we eat well, we'll feel good, and you have to feel good to do anything well," says Marjorie Tall, a grandmother.[12] Home cooking allows a family to select healthy ingredients, tailor meals to suit its own particular nutritional needs and tastes, serve portions appropriate to age and activity level, and monitor methods of preparation.

- *More Variety, Better Quality*

Restaurants and chains offer a number of menu items, and numerous themed restaurants serve foods that satisfy an array of palates, from Middle Eastern to Caribbean to cowboy grub. But most eating establishments nevertheless serve foods that please the general public.

By cooking at home, a family can eat any kind of food it chooses and not be limited by what's on the menu. The family cook can season foods as she wishes and prepare ethnic foods that suit the family's fancy.

Quality of food varies among fast-food outlets, chain restaurants, and dinner houses. Some menu items are consistently well prepared and tasty, while others are poorly done and bland. And spending a lot of money on going out to eat does not necessarily ensure high quality in a meal.

"Quality in, quality out" can be completely controlled in the home kitchen. Selection of ingredients, recipes, and preparation methods is up to the family cook. While not every dinner prepared at home would merit five stars, and some are downright failures, a practiced cook can consistently prepare excellent meals with food of known quality.

- *A Collaborative Effort*

In most homes, wives and mothers are generally the cooks. That women usually wear the chef's hat doesn't mean that other family members cannot cook all or part of the time. One business executive who retired in his forties volunteered to cook and has found immense enjoyment and creative satisfaction in doing so. His family lauds his grilled salmon as perfect. Another man, whose wife was in graduate nursing school, was asked by a friend who had stopped by around dinnertime, "Do you cook every night?" His reply, "Only on the nights I want to eat."

Depending on age and circumstance, children, teenagers, and young adults can help prepare dinner. How will children—the next generation of nurturers—learn to cook if they're not given practice time in the kitchen? Now, with a family of her own, Michelle Beran remarks: "I gained kitchen confidence helping Mom. And she's inspired me to make dinners for my own family special by presenting great food and having good conversation."[13]

One year, our family devised a schedule so that each person—the younger children with mother's assistance—prepared dinner one night a week. We enjoyed a lot of delicious meals—as well as a few unusual ones—became more appreciative of each other's efforts, and helped our children overcome their "kitchen klutziness."[14] Many families routinely and successfully collaborate in the kitchen.

Working together can also facilitate communication. Well-known writer and poet, Emma Lou Thayne, who also happens to be a mother of five daughters, described their combined culinary efforts: "My daughters and I had all come back to the kitchen that had warmed and fed us for thirty years. . . . The air of tomato and bouillon and pepper corns and basil, chocolate and butterscotch ran us all together that day and into the night. . . .

"All our lives we'd bumped bottoms in the kitchen, trying to do fifteen things at once. For dinners when they were little, for parties when they were bigger, for birthdays, holidays, after-school days, before-boating days, we'd been that committee getting ready. In the noisy commotion, we had learned of each other's deepest concerns and lightest considerations. We'd stirred and mashed and cubed and browned our way through tests and boyfriends, hairstyles and testimonies.... The kitchen and being busy allowed an ease not common to other grounds....

"In any kitchen anywhere for the rest of our lives, we'll be doing it by committee, the six of us. Just as I will season with my mother's dashes of nutmeg and my grandmother's sprinkles of sage, they'll carry into their cupboards and onto their stoves and tables the festive know-how of having learned, bottom to bottom, in a crowded kitchen."[15]

- *A Creative, Satisfying Endeavor*

My neighbor Sharon Martin exclaimed, "I love to cook for my family!" And she meant it. "I love to choose the freshest ingredients," she wrote. "Almost always the simplest and freshest work best! I love to see the color of various fresh leafy, green, yellow, red, and multi-colored vegetables and fruits. It makes me happy! I love to make fresh-baked bread, sometimes adding in herbs, sometimes nuts or dried fruits. There's nothing like the aroma of bread or cookies or muffins baking in the oven! I love to go to markets where I can experience a whole array of different fresh fish and seafood. I don't always know even what they are, but I still love to see such a variety of God's given fare!...

"Now I will go and think about what the Lord has provided our family with—an abundance of good fresh food and an abundance of love and care for each other, which is always shared around the dinner table. I feel it is so important for the health of our bodies and probably, even more importantly, the health of our spirits, in just sharing the day with the ones we love."[16]

Cooking doesn't have to be viewed as a chore or a mere interruption between the afternoon and the evening's agenda. After a day of childcare, working, driving, housework, meetings, or other endeavors, for many people cooking is a complete change of activity. It can be a respite from the outside world. Puttering in the kitchen can be a creative, sensory, experimental, rewarding, fun (sometimes humorous), relaxing, or shared experience.

- *An Act of Love and Service*

Pillsbury's familiar slogan, "Nothin' says lovin' like somethin' from the oven," suggests an often-overlooked aspect of home-cooked meals. When the family cook prepares meals for the family, a message that "you're worth my time and energy" is conveyed. "The emotional comfort of home cooking for children is something every parent discovers," observes Cheryl Mendelson. "Sharing meals with the children in the privacy of your home, meals that you have prepared, reinforces your authority and beneficence in their eyes and helps increase their trust and pride in you and your abilities. You have the skill and knowledge to offer them good things; you take time and trouble for them."[17]

It is not just children who need such attention. When a couple became empty nesters, and the wife more or less quit cooking, the husband lamented that even though the house was not full of children, he was still just as hungry each night—and didn't she care about him, too?

Of the many services parents render to their children to provide them with a secure home and to help them develop socially and emotionally, few endeavors can equal that of consistently gathering family members around the table for dinner, serving appealing food, engaging in enjoyable conversation, and nurturing familial relationships. Adult relationships benefit from such efforts also. Artist-entrepreneur Mary Engelbreit (whose husband does the cooking in their home) says, "There is nothing more nurturing to family and friends than a meal that is lovingly prepared and presented."[18]

- *Emotional Nurturing and Security*

Many people recall the security and emotional warmth of dinners at home during their growing-up years. A daughter reflected on her experience: "I have fond memories of always enjoying dinner at home when I was growing up. There was fun conversation between my parents, two sisters, brother and me. . . . and Mom served delectable food. . . .

". . . . Purple Plum Pie is one of Mom's specialties. A big slice of this sweet-tart pie still takes me back to those carefree days at home."[19]

Basic human needs do not change even though life in the twenty-first century, with all its innovations, technology, and affluence, is much different than in previous eras. Mendelson writes: "Good meals at home satisfy emotional hungers as real as hunger in the belly, and nothing else does so in the same way. They promote affection and intimacy among those who share them. Characteristic, familial styles of cooking and dining, foods that 'taste like home,' are central to each home's feelings of security and comfort and to its sense of itself as a unique and valuable place. Cooking at home links your past and future and solidifies your sense of identity and place. When a home gives up its hearth, which in the modern world is its kitchen, it gives up its focus. (The word 'focus' is Latin for 'hearth.') And the people who live there lose theirs too."[20]

Connecting with loved ones consistently at the dinner table enhances emotional health. "When we haven't the time to listen to each other's stories, we seek out experts to tell us how to live," says doctor Rachel Naomi Remen. "The less time we spend together at the kitchen table, the more how-to books appear in the stores and on our bookshelves. But reading such books is a very different thing than listening to someone's lived experience."[21]

- *Strengthens the Family*

In addition to family scripture study, family prayer, family home evening, and other events that bring the family together, eating together as a family will strengthen familial bonds, perhaps as much as any other kind of activity.

Shauna Frandsen evaluated how eating together unified her family: "As a child growing up on a farm in Holladay, Utah, I had the privilege of eating three meals a day with my family, which included two parents, three siblings, and two grandparents. We all woke up early and ate breakfast together. My father and grandfather worked on the vegetable farm all morning and came home for lunch with us. As we grew older, we too did small jobs on the farm. It was unthinkable to miss supper each evening as a family. Our conversations were interesting as the children spoke only English; our grandparents spoke only Japanese; my parents did much interpreting during the dinner conversation.

"As a mother of young adult children today, I still value family dinnertime together, but it does not come as easily as it did for my mother. Many outside activities and obligations pull our entire family in different directions. Nothing interferes with our Sunday dinner, but the weekday meals together are a bonus. When we do gather together, it is literally the best part of the day. I long for the three daily family meals I experienced in my childhood. I attribute the strength of my family to those relationships centered around the dinner table."[22]

As a teenager, Liz Doxey sought to know how to strengthen her family and found that dinner was the answer. "I was seventeen years old when my mom died. I was quickly faced with the role of mother to a household of males. I always knew that my mother made a difference in our household, but I never realized the depth of it. It was now my turn to be the mother, and I didn't know where to start. First off, we were teenagers. We didn't need a mom, right? I quickly learned that mothers are always needed, and women are central in family life.

"Right from the start I knew something was missing in our family life, and I needed direction. My brothers didn't seem to notice. I knew in my heart it was up to me to keep us together and lead us in a positive direction. Naturally, growing up in a religious home, I thought we should read the scriptures together or pray together more often. That seemed like the most logical direction. I decided to pray about it even though I thought I already had the answer.

"It didn't take long for the answer to my prayers to come, but I was so surprised by the feeling I had in my heart. I couldn't get it out of my head that we needed to have regular family meals and that I needed to learn how to cook. Was that supposed to keep our family together?

"Was that the answer? The feeling wouldn't leave, and I knew I had received my answer. I began looking through cookbooks and asking neighbors for recipes. Everyone was so helpful and encouraging. The meals weren't elaborate or fancy, but the time together was priceless. We discussed our day, upcoming events, the future. I know to this day, a seventeen-year-old girl's prayers were answered. Having regular meals together kept us connected when the rest of the world was pulling us apart. I cherish those times we had together and now hope to pass on the importance of regular family meals to my own children."[23]

- *Profound Influence*

Preparing meals isn't simply about assuaging hunger. Janette Hales Beckham, former Young Women general president, began to plan dinner with more in mind than what to fix when she discovered that the dinner table becomes an altar. She knew that what happened around her kitchen table would profoundly and lastingly influence her children's lives. "Now that my children have grown," she said, "I think of my kitchen as a symbol of the right place. I realize that it was in a family setting that I came to understand Planning with a Purpose long before I was in the Young Women program. You've all heard us ask the question in the Young Women program, 'What do we want to do?' when we really want to ask ourselves, 'What do we want to have happen?' For me I was more likely to ask on a hot summer day, 'What are we going to have for dinner?' I'm sure that most everyone would relate to that question on a hot summer day.

"Along with the demands of mealtime, I also started to realize that my own children were gone from home more and more. I remember reading one day these words: 'A table surrounded by eager, hungry children ceases to be a table and becomes an altar.' All of a sudden the question for me became, 'What do I want to have happen in the lives of my family during this brief time we are together each day?' I started to plan mealtime with a purpose. . . . I started to think about Ann, Tom, Jane, Karen, and Mary rather than whether or not the hamburger was thawed. I wondered if they were fortified and strong enough to make decisions and live by the values our family and the Church had tried to teach. The evening meal became an important time. It's interesting to me now that my children are raised and grown, the one thing they love is to come home and sit around our kitchen table and talk, laugh, and reattach to those close family feelings."[24]

Author Jaroldeen Edwards, in her wonderful book about celebrating life, tells a touching story that illustrates perfectly the nurturing involved in planning a meal. She writes:

"My daughter Julia, who is expecting her tenth child, makes seven school lunches every morning. It is a job she has disliked so much it was hard for her to get out of bed, because the chore of making sack lunches is the first chore she faces every day. . . .

"Lunches were a chore for Julia that made every morning less than joyful until the Sunday that her eight-year-old son came home from church and had the following conversation with his mother.

" 'What was your Primary lesson about today?' his mother asked.

" 'Oh, you know,' young Weston said in an offhand way. 'It was that story that everybody knows. You know. The one about the time Jesus was walking around the Sea of Galilee and all these thousands of people came walking after him, and they listened to him for most of the day, and then it got hot and late and they were all tired and hungry and there wasn't any food at all.

" 'Except for this one little boy, and his mother had remembered to pack his lunch, and so he had some loaves and fishes, and Jesus took them and fed all those people.'

"My daughter told me this incident, and there were tears in our eyes. *His mother had packed his lunch.*

" 'So you see, Mother,' Julia said, 'I have learned to like making lunches now, because I realize that when I'm feeding my children, I am feeding the five thousand—and more. It makes me think of all the hundreds of people my children's lives will touch through the years, and I am making that possible by nourishing them as they grow up.

" 'Lunches are a whole new experience since I have thought of that unknown mother in Galilee who made a lunch for her little boy, and her son gave it to the Savior, and the Savior fed five thousand people with it.' "[25]

We cannot foresee the long-term, positive effects of nurturing our families at the dinner table. It is, after all, not just bodies that are being fed but souls.

When the resurrected Christ appeared to his disciples at the sea of Tiberias, he invited them to eat with him.

"Jesus saith unto them, Come and dine. . . .

"Jesus then cometh, and taketh bread, and giveth them, and fish likewise. . . .

"So when they had dined, Jesus saith to Simon Peter, Simon, son of Jonas, lovest thou me more than these? He saith unto him, Yea, Lord; thou knowest that I love thee. He saith unto him, Feed my lambs.

" . . . Feed my sheep" (John 21:12–13, 15–16).

Can we do no less than to feed his lambs and his sheep?

NOTES

1. Michael R. Eades and Mary Dan Eades, *The Protein Power LifePlan* (New York: Warner Books, 2000), 370.
2. "Where to Eat," *Consumer Reports*, July 2000, 11.
3. Ibid.
4. Mary Matthews, "Table Talk: Strengthening Families at Mealtime," pamphlet, March 2000, 2.
5. Cheryl Mendelson, *Home Comforts: The Art and Science of Keeping House* (New York: Scribner, 1999), 37.
6. Laurie Colwin, as quoted in Sarah Ban Breathnach, *Simple Abundance: A Daybook of Comfort and Joy* (New York: Warner Books, 1995), July 14.
7. In Mary Pipher, *The Shelter of Each Other: Rebuilding Our Families* (New York: Ballantine Books, 1996), 246.
8. "Where to Eat," *Consumer Reports*, 13.
9. Eades, *The Protein Power LifePlan*, 353–54.
10. "Where to Eat," *Consumer Reports*, 12.
11. Ibid.
12. Marjorie Tall, from personal letter in author's possession, February 2000.
13. Michelle Beran, in "My Mom's Best Meal," *1998 Taste of Home Annual Recipes* (Greendale, Wis.: Reiman Publications, 1997), 201.
14. See Janet Peterson, "It's Your Night to Cook," *Ensign*, January 1987, 64.
15. Emma Lou Thayne, *As for Me and My House* (Salt Lake City: Bookcraft, 1989), 80, 81.
16. Sharon Martin, from personal letter in author's possession, 5 April 2000.
17. Mendelson, *Home Comforts*, 38.
18. Mary Engelbreit, *Mary Engelbreit's Queen of the Kitchen Cookbook* (Kansas City, Mo.: Andrews McMeel, 1998), 7.
19. Beran, in "My Mom's Best Meal," 201.
20. Mendelson, *Home Comforts*, 37–38.
21. Rachel Naomi Remen, *Kitchen Table Wisdom* (audiotape) San Bruno, Calif.: Audio Literature, 1996.
22. Shauna Frandsen, from personal letter in author's possession, 15 January 2000.
23. Liz Doxey, from personal letter in author's possession, 27 June 2000.
24. Janette C. Hales [Beckham], Young Women President's Message, April 1993 Open House, 6.
25. Jaroldeen Asplund Edwards, *Celebration! Ten Principles of More Joyous Living* (Salt Lake City: Deseret Book, 1995), 114–15.

COOKING TERMS

A new recipe for Shrimp Linguine or Frosty Pumpkin Pie sounds delicious, and you have all the ingredients in your pantry and refrigerator. You're just not sure what the directions to *sauté* or to *fold* mean. This helpful list defines basic cooking terms so that you can master any recipe in this book.

al dente: means "to the tooth" in Italian. Pasta that is cooked *al dente* is tender but still retains some firmness.

beat: to make a mixture lighter or frothy by stirring rapidly either by hand or with an electric mixer, as to beat eggs.

blanch: to partially cook fruits or vegetables in boiling water. This is also done to loosen the skins on tomatoes and peaches.

blend: to combine ingredients until they are uniformly mixed, as to blend oil, vinegar, and seasonings for a salad dressing.

boil: to cook food in liquid or to bring a liquid itself to the boiling point. When a liquid is boiling, bubbles which cannot be stirred down appear on the surface and throughout the liquid. When cooking pasta, for example, water is brought to a boil before pasta is added.

braise: to cook meat slowly over medium or low heat in a small amount of liquid in a covered pan. A pot roast is braised, often along with potatoes and other vegetables.

broil: to cook under direct, dry heat in an oven (with gauge on broil). Fish and meat are often broiled, as broiling is a quick method of cooking and requires no fats.

brown: to cook meat (or some vegetables) in a skillet, broiler, or oven until the outside of the ingredient has turned brown in color, as to brown pork chops, steak, or ground beef. Browning is often the first step in meat preparation.

chop: to cut in small pieces, as to chop nuts. Chopping can be done with a knife or a food processor.

cool: to reduce temperature of food by letting it stand at room temperature, refrigerating it, or immersing it in ice water, as to cool cooked potatoes before combining with other ingredients for potato salad.

Cooking Terms

cream: to soften butter, margarine, or shortening by beating it with a spoon or electric mixer until it reaches a light, fluffy consistency. Butter and sugar are often creamed together in making cookies to form a smooth, soft dough.

crisp-tender: a term to describe vegetables that have been cooked until they are softened but still crisp, as in cooking asparagus or broccoli.

cube: to dice or cut into uniform cubelike shapes, usually about ½ inch in size, as to cube potatoes or steak.

dice: to cut into small pieces, uniform in size, usually about ⅛ to ¼ inch in size, as to dice carrots or chicken.

dissolve: to combine a liquid and a solid food until they are one mixture and the solid is liquefied, as in dissolving gelatin in water.

fold: to gently add ingredients to a mixture by using a spatula or spoon to stir the bottom of the mixture up to the top. A lighter ingredient, such as whipped cream, would be folded into a heavier mixture, such as softened cream cheese.

fry: to cook in hot fat until food has reached desired doneness, as to fry chicken or eggs.

grate: to reduce food to fine pieces or shreds by rubbing it over a grating surface, as to grate cheese or fresh nutmeg.

grease: to coat an item, such as a pan or cookie sheet, with a small amount of fat or oil. Before baking bread, for example, the pan must be greased to prevent the bread from sticking once it is finished and ready to remove.

grill: to cook or barbecue over hot coals outdoors. Gas grills, with controlled heat, have gained in popularity over charcoal grills or campfires.

knead: to work dough with your hands or in a bread mixer in a pressing, stretching, and folding motion until it becomes smooth and elastic. Bread must be kneaded in order to release the gluten in the yeast and produce a well-textured end product.

marinate: to put meats or vegetables into a marinade (usually made of oil, vinegar or lemon juice, and seasonings) to flavor and tenderize them. Meats to be grilled are frequently marinated.

mince: to chop food into pieces that are very small and irregular in shape.

Garlic, cilantro, and other fresh seasonings are minced so that their flavor is distributed evenly in the prepared dish.

mix: to combine or put together ingredients, as to mix ingredients for a sauce or batter.

parboil: to boil briefly as a preliminary or incomplete cooking procedure, as to parboil lasagne noodles and continue the cooking process while the lasagne bakes in the oven.

pare: to cut away or remove the outer skin of a fruit or vegetable, as to pare potatoes. Synonymous with **peel.**

peel: to cut away or remove the outer skin of a fruit or vegetable, as to peel the skin off apples or carrots.

puree: to change a solid food into a thick pulp by liquefying it in a blender or food processor. Tomatoes are often pureed before adding to sauces.

roast: to cook meat or vegetables in an oven using dry heat, usually without liquid, as to roast chicken, turkey, and beef.

sauté: to cook until ingredient is softened or browned in a small amount of fat, usually butter, margarine, or oil. Onions, garlic, and mushrooms are often sautéed before combining with other ingredients.

shred: to separate into small, thin, and irregular pieces, as in shredding cabbage or cooked chicken or roast beef. Food processors typically have shredding discs; cooked meat can be shredded by pulling apart with two forks.

sift: to process dry ingredients through a sieve or sifter, thus incorporating air and eliminating lumps. In making cakes, flour is often sifted to make it finer.

simmer: to cook food in liquid just below the boiling point (from 185° to 210° F. or 85° to 99° C.). The surface of the liquid will move slightly due to slowly rising bubbles. Simmering soups and stews over low heat for a period of time enhances flavor.

steam: to cook over, not in, boiling water. Steaming vegetables in a steamer basket (a collapsible basket placed in a pot and covered) or a special steamer pot enhances flavor and preserves nutrients.

stir: to mix ingredients together with a spoon or spatula, as to stir chopped nuts into cookie dough.

Cooking Terms

stir-fry: to quickly cook chopped and diced vegetables and meats in a small amount of oil over high heat, while stirring constantly. Stir-frying is a fast cooking method that combines several ingredients and often a sauce.

toss: to combine ingredients with a repeated, gentle, lifting motion, as in tossing green salads.

whip: to beat an ingredient rapidly with a whisk or electric mixer in order to incorporate air and increase volume, as to whip egg whites or cream until stiff.

BASIC PANTRY SUPPLIES AND SHOPPING CHECKLIST

A well-stocked pantry and refrigerator simplify and speed meal preparation. Having essential ingredients on hand eliminates frustration and time-consuming trips to the store.

Use this list to keep your supplies up to date. Make photocopies and use as a shopping list by checking or highlighting the items you need. Add other ingredients required for specific recipes and for breakfasts, lunches, and snacks.

BAKING

- ☐ almond extract
- ☐ baking powder
- ☐ baking soda
- ☐ biscuit mix
- ☐ cake mixes
- ☐ chocolate chips
- ☐ cocoa
- ☐ cornbread mix
- ☐ cornmeal
- ☐ cornstarch
- ☐ flour: all-purpose, cake, and whole wheat
- ☐ food coloring
- ☐ lemon extract
- ☐ mint extract
- ☐ nuts: almonds, walnuts, and pecans
- ☐ oatmeal
- ☐ salt
- ☐ sugar: brown, powdered, and white
- ☐ unsweetened baking chocolate
- ☐ vanilla
- ☐ yeast: regular and rapid-rise

CANNED GOODS

- ☐ applesauce
- ☐ chicken
- ☐ clams
- ☐ corn
- ☐ evaporated milk
- ☐ garbanzo beans
- ☐ green beans
- ☐ green chilies
- ☐ kidney beans
- ☐ mandarin oranges
- ☐ mushrooms
- ☐ peaches
- ☐ pears
- ☐ pineapple
- ☐ shrimp
- ☐ sliced olives
- ☐ sweetened condensed milk
- ☐ tomatoes: diced and stewed
- ☐ tomato juice
- ☐ tomato paste
- ☐ tomato sauce
- ☐ tuna fish

Basic Pantry Supplies and Shopping Checklist

DAIRY
- [ ] butter and margarine
- [ ] buttermilk
- [ ] cheddar cheese
- [ ] cottage cheese
- [ ] cream cheese
- [ ] half-and-half
- [ ] milk
- [ ] Monterey Jack cheese
- [ ] mozzarella cheese
- [ ] Parmesan cheese
- [ ] ricotta cheese
- [ ] sour cream
- [ ] Swiss cheese
- [ ] whipping cream
- [ ] yogurt

FISH
- [ ] halibut
- [ ] orange roughy
- [ ] salmon
- [ ] shrimp
- [ ] swordfish
- [ ] white fish: cod, haddock, or sole

FRESH FRUITS
- [ ] apples
- [ ] apricots (in season)
- [ ] avocados
- [ ] bananas
- [ ] berries (in season)
- [ ] cherries (in season)
- [ ] citrus: lemons, limes, oranges, tangerines
- [ ] grapes
- [ ] kiwifruit
- [ ] mangos
- [ ] melons (in season)
- [ ] nectarines (in season)
- [ ] papaya
- [ ] peaches (in season)
- [ ] pears (in season)
- [ ] pineapple
- [ ] plums

FRESH VEGETABLES
- [ ] asparagus
- [ ] beans: green, wax, yellow
- [ ] beets
- [ ] broccoli
- [ ] cabbage
- [ ] carrots
- [ ] cauliflower
- [ ] celery
- [ ] cucumbers
- [ ] lettuces: iceberg, red leaf, Romaine
- [ ] mushrooms
- [ ] onions: green, red, and yellow
- [ ] peas: snap and snow
- [ ] peppers: green, red, and yellow
- [ ] potatoes
- [ ] spinach
- [ ] squash
- [ ] sweet potatoes
- [ ] tomatoes
- [ ] zucchini

Basic Pantry Supplies and Shopping Checklist

FROZEN VEGETABLES
- ☐ broccoli
- ☐ corn
- ☐ mixed
- ☐ peas
- ☐ stir-fry mix

HERBS AND SPICES
- ☐ allspice
- ☐ basil
- ☐ bay leaves
- ☐ cayenne pepper
- ☐ chili powder
- ☐ chives
- ☐ cilantro
- ☐ cinnamon
- ☐ cloves
- ☐ cumin
- ☐ curry
- ☐ dill weed
- ☐ dry mustard
- ☐ garlic cloves
- ☐ garlic powder
- ☐ garlic salt
- ☐ minced garlic
- ☐ ground ginger
- ☐ minced ginger
- ☐ Italian seasoning
- ☐ lemon pepper
- ☐ marjoram
- ☐ mint
- ☐ nutmeg
- ☐ onion flakes
- ☐ onion powder
- ☐ onion salt
- ☐ oregano
- ☐ parsley
- ☐ pepper
- ☐ peppercorns
- ☐ poppy seeds
- ☐ poultry seasoning
- ☐ red pepper flakes
- ☐ rosemary
- ☐ sage
- ☐ tarragon
- ☐ thyme

MEATS
- ☐ bacon
- ☐ ground beef
- ☐ chicken: boneless, skinless breasts; bone-in breasts; tenders; whole
- ☐ ham
- ☐ pork chops
- ☐ pork roast
- ☐ pork tenderloin
- ☐ roast beef
- ☐ sausage
- ☐ steak (variety of)

OILS
- ☐ canola oil
- ☐ nonstick cooking spray
- ☐ olive oil
- ☐ peanut oil
- ☐ sesame oil

Basic Pantry Supplies and Shopping Checklist

- ☐ shortening
- ☐ vegetable oil

PASTAS
- ☐ egg noodles
- ☐ lasagna
- ☐ linguine
- ☐ macaroni
- ☐ manicotti
- ☐ spaghetti
- ☐ other varieties

RICE
- ☐ brown
- ☐ quick-cooking
- ☐ long-grain
- ☐ wild

SOUPS
- ☐ beef broth (or bouillon)
- ☐ chicken broth (or bouillon)
- ☐ cream of chicken
- ☐ cream of mushroom
- ☐ dry onion
- ☐ tomato

VINEGARS
- ☐ balsamic
- ☐ cider
- ☐ flavored (i.e., raspberry)
- ☐ red wine
- ☐ rice
- ☐ white

OTHER
- ☐ bottled lemon juice
- ☐ bread
- ☐ bread crumbs
- ☐ catsup
- ☐ Cool Whip®
- ☐ corn syrup
- ☐ croutons
- ☐ eggs
- ☐ graham crackers
- ☐ honey
- ☐ instant puddings
- ☐ Jell-O®
- ☐ mayonnaise
- ☐ Miracle Whip®
- ☐ molasses
- ☐ mustard: Dijon and yellow
- ☐ peanut butter
- ☐ pie crusts (crumb, pastry)
- ☐ raisins
- ☐ refrigerated biscuits
- ☐ salad dressings
- ☐ salsa
- ☐ soy sauce
- ☐ spaghetti sauce
- ☐ stuffing mix
- ☐ taco seasoning mix
- ☐ Tabasco sauce
- ☐ tortillas
- ☐ Worcestershire sauce

RECIPES

KEY

Throughout the recipes in this book are a variety of tips, quotes from expert cooks, and great ideas that will make meal planning easier and more effective as you work to bring your family together for dinnertime. Following is a key to the icons and symbols you will see on the following pages.

 TIMESAVING TIPS: great tips for those who want to save time and effort in the kitchen without sacrificing taste.

 MONEYSAVING TIPS: smart tips for the cost-conscious cook who is willing to spend a little more time in the kitchen if it means spending less money at the grocery store.

 IDEAS FOR MAKING DINNERTIME ENJOYABLE: innovative and fun ideas to make dinnertime memorable for every member of your family.

 IDEAS FOR GATHERING THE FAMILY FOR DINNER: simple ideas that will draw family members to the table for nightly meals.

 HOW TO'S: instructions for many basic recipe ingredients, such as cooked rice, boiled eggs, and creamy white sauce.

 RECIPE REMEDIES: quick fixes for those days when a recipe doesn't turn out just right.

 LEFTOVER DISGUISES: meal makeovers for those leftovers you can never get your family to eat.

 Recipes with this icon can be easily expanded to accommodate larger families or additional guests at the dinner table.

 Recipes with this icon are super easy to prepare.

SOUPS

Soups are "souper" meals almost by themselves. Soups are easy to prepare, economical, nutritious, and flexible in the amount of cooking time required. Soup can be made ahead and kept in the refrigerator or frozen for a night when there's no time for cooking.

The aroma of soup simmering on the stove draws family members to the kitchen, eagerly waiting for the call of "soup's on." Served with hearty rolls or breads or a green salad, soup is warming and satisfying.

Hearty Cream of Chicken Soup/25

Old-Fashioned Chicken Noodle Soup/26

Vegetable Beef Soup/28

Easy "Homemade" Soup/29

Taco Soup/30

Sopa de Tortilla con Naranja (Tortilla Soup with Orange)/31

Cheesy Vegetable Soup/32

Vegetable Cheese Soup/33

Clam Chowder/34

Quick and Easy Chili/35

Chili/36

White Chili/37

Oven Stew/38

Bean and Salsa Soup/39

Easy Minestrone Soup/40

Chunky Baked Potato Soup/41

Tomato Basil Soup/42

SOUPS

Hearty Cream of Chicken Soup
KRISTINE WESTERLIND

The flavor of this soup comes from its many herbs and seasonings, which take only a minute to add.

- 3 boneless, skinless chicken breasts
- 3 celery stalks, chopped
- 4 carrots, sliced
- 1 small onion, chopped
- 1 bay leaf
- 1 teaspoon marjoram
- 1 to 1½ teaspoons garlic powder
- 1 teaspoon basil
- 1½ to 2 teaspoons pepper
- ½ teaspoon thyme
- 1 teaspoon sage
- 1 teaspoon rosemary
- 1 to 2 tablespoons chopped fresh parsley
- 1 teaspoon salt
- 2 (10¾-ounce) cans cream of mushroom soup
- 2 cups cooked noodles (optional)

Place chicken breasts, celery, carrots, onion, herbs, and seasonings in a slow cooker or large soup pot. Cover with about 2 quarts water. Bring to a boil, reduce heat, and cook over medium-low heat until chicken is tender (1 to 2 hours, depending on heat).

Remove chicken breasts and dice. Return chicken to pot. Add cream of mushroom soup. Stir until smooth. Add noodles, if desired. Milk may be added to thin soup to desired consistency.

Serves 10 to 12.

It breathes reassurance, it offers consolation, after a weary day it promotes sociability. . . . There is nothing like a bowl of soup. —LOUIS DEGOUY

Old-Fashioned Chicken Noodle Soup
SUSAN MORGAN

Homemade noodles might sound complicated, but they actually aren't, and they taste so-o-o good.

1 whole chicken or 4 to 5 bone-in chicken breasts

2 to 3 quarts water

1 large onion, quartered

3 celery stalks, quartered

⅓ cup chopped fresh parsley

2 to 3 tablespoons chicken bouillon granules

1 bay leaf

1 teaspoon salt

½ teaspoon pepper

¼ teaspoon thyme

2 carrots, thinly sliced or diced

1 celery stalk, sliced

Frozen peas (optional)

Chopped broccoli (optional)

Frozen corn (optional)

Homemade noodles or 1 (8-ounce) package noodles

In a large soup pot or Dutch oven, put chicken, water, onion, celery, parsley, bouillon, bay leaf, salt, pepper, and thyme. Bring to a boil; reduce heat and simmer 2½ to 3 hours. Remove chicken from broth. Strain broth and skim fat. Return broth to pot.

Remove chicken from bones and add to broth. Add carrots, celery, and other vegetables as desired. Bring to a boil again; reduce heat. Add packaged or homemade noodles. Cook 10 to 15 minutes, until vegetables are tender and noodles are cooked.

HOW TO MAKE CHICKEN BROTH

PLACE A WHOLE CHICKEN OR 4 TO 5 BONE-IN CHICKEN BREASTS IN A LARGE POT OR DUTCH OVEN. COVER WITH ABOUT 6 TO 8 CUPS WATER. ADD 1 ONION, QUARTERED OR SLICED; 3 TO 4 CELERY STALKS WITH LEAVES, CUT IN SECTIONS; AND 1 TO 2 CARROTS, SLICED OR CUT IN SECTIONS. ADD 1½ TEASPOONS SALT, ½ TO 1 TEASPOON PEPPER, 1 TEASPOON POULTRY SEASONING OR BASIL OR THYME, 1 TO 2 SPRIGS PARSLEY, AND 1 TO 2 BAY LEAVES. FOR A MORE INTENSE FLAVOR, ADD 2 TO 3 TABLESPOONS OF CHICKEN BOUILLON GRANULES OR 2 TO 3 CUBES.

BRING WATER TO A BOIL, THEN REDUCE HEAT AND SIMMER FOR 1½ TO 2 HOURS. WHILE BROTH IS COOKING, SKIM OFF FOAM THAT RISES TO THE SURFACE. AFTER THE BROTH IS COOKED, REMOVE THE

(Continued on pg. 27)

SOUPS

Noodles

    1 cup flour
    ½ teaspoon salt
    2 tablespoons milk
    1 egg, beaten

Mix flour and salt in a medium bowl, making a well in the center. Mix together milk and egg in a small bowl. Pour into flour well. Stir until mixture forms a dough. Knead on a floured board 8 to 10 times. Roll very thin. Let stand 20 minutes. (Can let dry 2 hours before cooking.) Cut into 1-inch strips, as wide as desired. Drop into boiling broth.

Serves 8 to 10.

(Continued from pg. 26)

CHICKEN AND VEGETABLES FROM THE POT. SET CHICKEN ASIDE TO BE USED FOR SOUP OR OTHER DISH. STRAIN THE BROTH THROUGH A STRAINER. SKIM OFF FAT. FAT IS MORE EASILY REMOVED FROM REFRIGERATED STOCK BECAUSE IT COAGULATES ON THE TOP OF THE BROTH.

YIELDS ABOUT 6 CUPS OF BROTH. CHICKEN BROTH CAN BE FROZEN FOR LATER USE.

A QUICKER METHOD IS TO COMBINE IN A LARGE SAUCEPAN OR SOUP POT 2 (14½-OUNCE) CANS CHICKEN BROTH WITH 1 ONION, CHOPPED; 1 CELERY STALK WITH LEAVES, CUT IN SECTIONS; 1 CARROT, SLICED; 2 SPRIGS PARSLEY; AND ½ TEASPOON BASIL OR THYME. SIMMER FOR 30 MINUTES. STRAIN BROTH. YIELDS ABOUT 3 TO 3½ CUPS OF BROTH.

Vegetable Beef Soup ★ ◡

JANET PETERSON

M-m-m-m—this soup looks and tastes good!

1 pound round steak, cut in ½-inch cubes
1 to 2 tablespoons oil
1 (14½-ounce) can diced tomatoes, undrained
3 cups water
2 potatoes, peeled and cubed
2 medium onions, chopped
3 celery stalks, sliced
2 carrots, sliced or diced
3 teaspoons beef bouillon granules or 3 bouillon cubes
½ teaspoon basil
½ teaspoon oregano
½ teaspoon salt
¼ teaspoon pepper
½ cup frozen corn
½ cup frozen peas

Brown steak in hot oil in a soup pot or Dutch oven. Add tomatoes, water, potatoes, onions, celery, carrots, bouillon, basil, oregano, salt, and pepper. Bring to a boil, then simmer 2 to 3 hours on low heat. Ten minutes before serving add corn and peas. This soup can also be prepared in a slow cooker on high for 5 to 6 hours. Thirty minutes before serving, add corn and peas and cook until vegetables are tender.

Serves 6 to 8.

ONCE A WEEK ASSIGN DIFFERENT FAMILY MEMBERS VARIOUS PARTS OF DINNER TO PREPARE. ONE PERSON COULD PREPARE THE SALAD, ANOTHER THE VEGETABLES, ANOTHER THE MAIN COURSE, AND ANOTHER DESSERT. ALLOW FAMILY MEMBERS TO COLLABORATE ON THE MENU OR TO MAKE IT POTLUCK.

Easy "Homemade" Soup ★

KRISTINE WESTERLIND

This soup is not exactly homemade, but it is easy and feels healthier than just a can of soup.

- ½ to 1 cup chopped vegetables, such as carrots, broccoli, cauliflower, or green pepper
- 1 to 2 tablespoons butter or margarine
- ¼ to ½ cup chopped leftover cooked meat, such as chicken, beef, pork, or ham
- 1 (10¾-ounce) can soup, such as minestrone or cream of chicken
- 1 soup can water

Sauté any variety of vegetables in butter in a medium saucepan; add any leftover cooked meat. Add a can of soup to vegetables and meat. Add a can of water. Heat.

Serves 2 to 3.

WHEN YOU DON'T HAVE TIME TO MAKE YOUR OWN STOCK, USE BOUILLON GRANULES OR CUBES, OR CANNED CHICKEN OR BEEF BROTH.

Taco Soup ★ ⬯
ELAINE JACK

"I like taco soup served with a dollop of sour cream and hot garlic bread."

1 pound ground beef
½ cup chopped onions
1 (28-ounce) can diced tomatoes
1 (12-ounce) can corn, undrained
1 (15-ounce) can kidney beans, undrained
1 (4-ounce) can diced green chilies
1 (1½-ounce) envelope taco seasoning mix
Tomato juice (optional)
Grated cheddar cheese
Sour cream

Brown ground beef and onions in a Dutch oven or soup pot. Add tomatoes, corn, kidney beans, chilies, and taco mix. Simmer 15 to 20 minutes. Add a little tomato juice if soup seems too thick. Top with cheddar cheese and sour cream.

Serves 4 to 6.

Although it may take extra planning with juggling school activities, work schedules and social activities, [mealtime] is definitely worth saving. Mealtimes play an important role in the social as well as nutritional well-being of families. Regular mealtimes bring consistency and stability to family members. —MARY MATTHEWS

Sopa de Tortilla con Naranja (Tortilla Soup with Orange)
CAMMY FULLER

"This soup recipe was given to me by a wonderful cook, Kathleen Stout, from Upper Saddle River, New Jersey. It is one of our favorites, and the secret ingredient is definitely the orange juice!"

- ¼ cup oil
- 8 small or 4 large corn tortillas cut in ½-inch strips or 2 cups corn chips
- 1 medium onion, chopped
- 1 clove garlic, minced
- 4 celery stalks, thinly sliced
- 2½ cups chicken broth (canned or homemade)
- 1½ cups orange juice
- 1½ cups tomato sauce
- 1 (4-ounce) can chopped green chilies
- 1 tablespoon chopped fresh cilantro (no substitutions)
- 3 carrots, sliced
- 1 pound boneless, skinless chicken breasts, cut into pieces
- Grated Monterey Jack cheese

In a large soup pot or Dutch oven, heat oil and fry tortillas over medium heat until lightly brown and crisp. Remove to a paper towel and drain. (Corn chips may be substituted.)

In the same pot, sauté onion, garlic, and celery. Stir in broth, orange juice, tomato sauce, chilies, cilantro, and carrots. Reduce heat, cover, and simmer until carrots are tender. Add uncooked chicken pieces and simmer, uncovered, about 8 minutes, stirring occasionally, just until chicken is done. Do not boil.

To serve, placed toasted tortillas (or chips) in soup bowls. Ladle soup over tortillas. Sprinkle with cheese.

Serves 4.

Cheesy Vegetable Soup
MARIE GALBRAITH

Put hot soup in a pretty or fun soup tureen and set it on the table. Family members can ladle the amount of soup they would like.

B<small>UY PACKAGES OF ALREADY SHREDDED CHEESE.</small>

2 tablespoons chopped onion
1 tablespoon butter or margarine
1 cup frozen corn
½ cup chopped broccoli
¼ cup grated carrot
1 medium potato, diced
¾ to 1 cup water (enough to barely cover vegetables)
1 (10¾-ounce) can cream of potato soup
1 cup milk
¼ cup grated cheddar cheese
1 ounce provolone cheese, cut up
Dash of pepper

In a medium saucepan, cook onion in butter until tender but not brown. Add corn, broccoli, carrots, potato, and water. Bring to boiling and reduce heat. Cover and simmer 10 minutes or until vegetables are tender. Stir in soup, milk, cheeses, and pepper. Cook and stir over medium heat until cheese is melted and mixture is heated through.

Serves 4.

SOUPS

Vegetable Cheese Soup
DEBBIE NELSON

During the school year, have a once-a-week Soup Night. Your family will enjoy sampling a variety of soups.

- 2 cups diced potatoes
- 1 large onion, sliced
- 1 cup diced carrots
- 1 cup sliced celery
- ¼ cup butter or margarine
- 2 (10¾-ounce) cans chicken broth
- 2 teaspoons chicken bouillon or 2 bouillon cubes
- 2 cups milk
- ½ cup flour
- 3 cups grated cheddar cheese
- 1 teaspoon dry mustard
- ⅛ teaspoon cayenne pepper

In a large saucepan, sauté potatoes, onion, carrots, and celery in butter. Add broth and bouillon. Simmer 30 minutes, or until vegetables are tender. In a medium bowl, mix milk with flour. Blend until smooth. Gradually add milk mixture to vegetables, stirring constantly. Add grated cheese, mustard, and cayenne pepper. Simmer and stir until cheese melts.

Serves 4 to 6.

PUT SEVERAL DIFFERENT KINDS OF LEFTOVER VEGETABLES AND THEIR COOKING WATER IN A FREEZER CONTAINER. MAKE VEGETABLE SOUP BY THAWING THEN ADDING TOMATO JUICE AND SEASONINGS.

Clam Chowder

CHRISTINE NEILSON

Clam chowder, a green salad, and sourdough rolls or bread make a filling meal.

1 cup finely chopped onions
1 cup diced celery
2 cups finely diced potatoes
2 (6½-ounce) cans minced clams, drained (reserve juice)
¾ cup butter or margarine
¾ cup flour
1 quart half-and-half or part milk
1½ teaspoons salt
Dash of pepper

Soup, stews, gravy, batter, or sauces that are too thick can be remedied by adding water, milk, broth, or juices in small quantities until desired adjustment is made.

Put onions, celery, and potatoes in a large saucepan. Drain juice from clams and pour over vegetables. Add enough water to barely cover vegetables; cook over medium heat until soft. Melt butter in a separate large saucepan or pot. Stir in flour. Using a whisk, slowly add half-and-half, stirring constantly. Add salt and pepper. Cook until thickened. Add clams and cooked vegetables, and heat through.

Serves 8 to 10.

Quick and Easy Chili ★ ◡

CHRISTINE NEILSON

Hot cornbread is a great companion to chili.

- 1½ to 2 pounds ground beef
- 1 large onion, chopped
- 1 (28-ounce) can tomatoes
- 2 cups beef bouillon (2 cubes or 2 teaspoons beef granules with 2 cups water)
- 1 teaspoon sugar
- ½ teaspoon pepper
- 3 (14½-ounce) cans spicy chili beans (or mild chili beans, depending on taste)
- Grated cheese

Brown ground beef and onions in a large soup pot. Drain grease. Add tomatoes, bouillon, sugar, pepper, and chili beans. Simmer on low at least one hour. (Simmering longer will enhance flavor.) Serve with grated cheese.

Serves 12.

My earliest memories revolve around holidays when grandparents, cousins, uncles, and aunts gathered for wonderful dinners of roast chicken, served with mountains of mashed potatoes and three or four different vegetables. . . . When you opened the door you were immediately welcomed by the steamy, warm aroma of roasting meats and simmering sauces. . . .

When I was grown, I learned recipes for more exotic dishes, but I never lost my love for the meals we ate when I was a child. . . . Some people's roots may be traced through family trees; mine can be found in the food we ate. —SARA PITZER

Chili

KAYLENE REDD

The aroma of chili cooking in the kitchen is very inviting.

1 to 2 cups dry red beans, rinsed
1 small onion, chopped
1½ teaspoons salt
Dash of pepper
1 quart tomato juice
1 (10¾-ounce) can tomato soup
½ cup catsup
¼ teaspoon garlic powder
2 teaspoons cumin
1½ to 2 teaspoons chili powder
1 bay leaf
1 pound ground beef, browned and drained

Soak beans in several inches of water overnight in a large soup pot. The next morning, add more water to cover beans. Add onion. Simmer 3 hours. Add salt, pepper, tomato juice, tomato soup, catsup, garlic powder, cumin, chili powder, bay leaf, and ground beef. Simmer 1 hour.

Serves 6 to 8.

MAKE CHILI BURGERS FROM LEFTOVER CHILI AND JUST-COOKED HAMBURGER PATTIES. SERVE WITH A DOLLOP OF SOUR CREAM AND A SPRINKLING OF GRATED CHEESE.

White Chili

LINDA RAY

Your family will want second bowls of this unusual chili. This makes a large pot of soup, which can be frozen for later use, enjoyed another night, shared with a neighbor, or cut in half.

 1 pound white beans, soaked overnight in water or 3 (15½-ounce) cans great northern beans
 2 cups chicken broth
 1 to 2 cloves garlic, minced
 2 medium onions, chopped
 1 tablespoon oil
 2 (4-ounce) cans diced green chilies
 2 teaspoons cumin
 1½ teaspoons oregano
 ¼ teaspoon cloves
 ¼ teaspoon cayenne pepper
 4 cups cooked, diced chicken breasts
 2 to 3 cups grated Monterey Jack cheese

Garnish
 Chopped green onions
 Chopped parsley
 Chopped tomatoes
 Crushed corn chips
 Guacamole
 Salsa
 Sliced olives
 Sour cream

COMBINE LEFTOVER CHILI WITH MACARONI AND CHEESE TO MAKE A CASSEROLE. SPRINKLE WITH GRATED CHEESE AND BAKE.

Drain beans. Put in a large soup pot or Dutch oven with broth, garlic, and half of the onions. Bring to a boil; reduce heat and simmer 3 hours. Sauté remaining onions in oil. Add to beans. Add chilies, cumin, oregano, cloves, cayenne pepper, and chicken. Simmer 1 hour. Ladle into bowls. Sprinkle with cheese and choice of garnish.

Serves 10 to 12.

Oven Stew ★

MARJORIE TALL

Prepare this stew early in the day, put it in the oven, then enjoy the day and a delicious dinner later.

- 1 to 2 pounds lean beef cubes
- 4 to 5 celery stalks, sliced
- 4 to 5 carrots, sliced
- 1 large onion, chopped
- 3 to 5 potatoes, cubed (leave skins on)
- 2 (10¾-ounce) cans cream of tomato soup
- 2 soup cans water
- Salt and pepper to taste
- Basil to taste

Heat oven to 325° F.

Combine beef cubes, celery, carrots, onion, potatoes, soup, water, salt, pepper, and basil in a 3-quart casserole dish. Bake, covered, 5 to 6 hours.

Serves 4 to 6.

USE INSTANT POTATOES TO THICKEN SOUPS AND STEWS.

Bean and Salsa Soup ★ ⬇

DEBBIE NELSON

Be adventurous and try new soup recipes.

- 1 (15-ounce) can black beans
- 2 (15½-ounce) cans great northern beans
- 1 (12-ounce) can corn
- 1 (16-ounce) jar salsa
- 1 (14½-ounce) can diced carrots or 1 cup diced carrots, cooked
- 1 (28-ounce) can diced tomatoes
- 1 (14½-ounce) can chicken broth

Mix black beans, great northern beans, corn, salsa, carrots, tomatoes, and chicken broth in a large soup pot. Bring to a boil and simmer 10 minutes.

Serves 8 to 10.

ADD SOUR CREAM AND GRATED CHEDDAR CHEESE TO LEFTOVER CHILI FOR A CHIP DIP.

Easy Minestrone Soup ★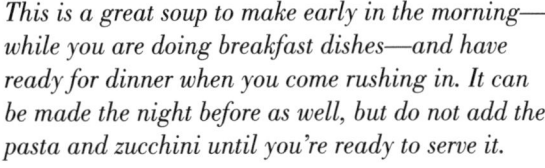

JULIE MARSHALL

This is a great soup to make early in the morning—while you are doing breakfast dishes—and have ready for dinner when you come rushing in. It can be made the night before as well, but do not add the pasta and zucchini until you're ready to serve it.

- 1 pound ground beef
- 1 medium onion, chopped
- 1 (28-ounce) can Italian-styled tomatoes
- 1 (15-ounce) can kidney beans, drained
- 1 (12-ounce) can corn, drained, or 1 cup frozen corn
- 1 (15-ounce) can garbanzo beans, drained
- 1 (14½-ounce) can green beans, drained
- 3 to 4 cups water or tomato juice
- 1 teaspoon salt
- ¼ to ½ teaspoon pepper
- 1 clove garlic, minced
- 2 to 3 teaspoons Italian seasoning (or substitute ½ to 1 teaspoon oregano, ½ to 1 teaspoon basil, ½ to 1 teaspoon thyme, ½ teaspoon rosemary, ½ teaspoon sage)
- 1 cup pasta, any variety
- 1 small zucchini, thinly sliced

BUY ITEMS YOU USE FREQUENTLY IN LARGE QUANTITIES; THIS MAKES THE COST PER UNIT LESS.

Brown ground beef with onion in a large soup pot or Dutch oven. Drain grease. Add tomatoes, kidney beans, corn, garbanzo beans, and green beans. Add water or tomato juice. Add salt, pepper, garlic, and Italian seasoning. Bring to a boil and simmer a few minutes. Remove from heat, and refrigerate if eating later. Or add pasta and zucchini and cook 8 to 10 minutes, until pasta is cooked.

Serves 6 to 8.

Chunky Baked Potato Soup

CHRISTI JENSEN

Collect interesting soup mugs in your travels and serve soup to your family in them.

- 5½ cups chicken broth (homemade or canned)
- 3 pounds potatoes, peeled and cut into 1-inch cubes
- 4 slices bacon, chopped
- 1 tablespoon butter or margarine
- 1 medium onion, chopped
- 1 clove garlic, minced
- 2 tablespoons flour
- Salt and pepper to taste
- ½ cup half-and-half or milk
- Grated cheese
- Chopped green onions or chives

USE POWDERED MILK TO COOK WITH; IT IS MORE ECONOMICAL AND LOWER IN FAT.

Combine stock or broth and potatoes in a large saucepan. Boil until potatoes are almost tender and still hold their shape, about 10 minutes. Remove from heat. Reserve liquid.

Cook bacon in a large soup pot until crisp. Remove from pot and crumble. Drain all but 1 tablespoon of bacon drippings. Melt butter in same pot. Add onion and garlic and sauté. Add flour; stir 2 minutes until thickened. Gradually stir in 1 cup cooking liquid from potatoes. Season with salt and pepper. Gently stir onion mixture into potato mixture, being careful not to break up potatoes. Add half-and-half and simmer until soup is slightly thickened, about 10 minutes. Sprinkle individual servings with bacon, cheese, and green onions or chives.

Serves 6.

Tomato Basil Soup ★

NANCY LUMBRA

Only slightly more work than opening a can of tomato soup.

> 4 cups canned tomatoes, pureed
> 4 cups tomato juice
> 12 to 14 fresh basil leaves, minced
> 1 cup cream
> ¼ cup butter or margarine
> ¼ to ½ teaspoon ground black pepper
> Salt to taste

Combine tomatoes, tomato juice, and basil leaves in a large saucepan or soup pot. Bring to a boil. Reduce heat and simmer 30 minutes. Add cream and butter, stirring to blend. Add pepper and salt. Heat through, but do not boil.

Serves 8.

WHEN SHORT OF TIME TO MAKE TOMATO SOUP, DOCTOR CANNED TOMATO OR VEGETABLE SOUP BY SUBSTITUTING V-8 JUICE FOR THE WATER.

SALADS

Salads are quite versatile on the dinner table. They can act as the main dish, be served as a first or second course, or be an accompaniment to the main course. While green salads are the most common, they need not be ordinary. Vegetable, fruit, and pasta salads offer new and diverse combinations, interest, and taste.

Summer Fruit Salad/45

Fresh Fruit with Raspberry Dip/46

Strawberry and Melon Salad
with Lime Dressing/47

Cherry Pie Salad/48

Cinnamon Pears/49

Cranberry Salad/50

Raspberry Tapioca Salad/51

Tomato Salad/52

Corn Salad/53

Carrot Apple Salad/54

Bacon, Cauliflower, and
Lettuce Salad/55

Santa Fe Potato Salad/56

Red Potato and
Green Bean Salad/57

Potato Salad/58

California Salad/59

Iceberg Salad with Cashews/60

Caesar Salad/61

Apple Avocado Salad/62

Spinach Salad/63

Bacon and Tomato Salad/64

Spring Salad with
Orange Dressing/65

Coleslaw/66

Chicken Salad Supreme/67

Chinese Chicken Salad/68

Garden Chicken Salad/70

Cilantro, Chicken, and
Black Bean Salad/71

Taco Salad/72

Mexican Chow Mein/73

Pasta-Vegetable Salad/74

Bow-Tie Pasta and
Chicken Salad/75

Poppy Seed Dressing/76

Basic Vinaigrette/76

Raspberry Vinaigrette/77

Lemon Vinaigrette/77

Citrus Dressing for Fresh Fruits/78

Summer Fruit Salad ★

GERTRUDE MUECKE

A lovely medley of summer fruits. Try various combinations of fruits, such as raspberries, blackberries, blueberries, watermelon, grapes, nectarines, and kiwis.

- ½ cantaloupe, balled or cubed
- 1 (8-ounce) can pineapple chunks, including juice
- 2 peaches, sliced
- 2 apples, diced
- 2 bananas, sliced
- 1 pint strawberries, sliced
- 1 (6-ounce) can frozen orange juice, thawed
- Mint leaves (optional)

Layer cantaloupe, pineapple, peaches, apples, bananas, and strawberries in a glass bowl. Pour juice over fruit; cover and refrigerate 1 hour before serving. Garnish with mint, if desired.

Variation:

Instead of using orange juice, mix ½ cup lime juice, ½ cup water, and ½ cup sugar in a small bowl. Pour over fruit and refrigerate 1 hour before serving.

Serves 8 to 10.

Forgo as many convenience foods as you can; for example, sweetened cereals, precut and washed salad greens, frozen vegetables with sauces, precut fruits such as watermelon and cantaloupe, baking mixes, and spaghetti sauce.

Fresh Fruit with Raspberry Dip ★ ⬯
PAULA HEATH

A summer delight, especially during winter months. Recipe can be easily halved.

- 1 (16-ounce) container Cool Whip®, thawed
- 1 (16-ounce) carton vanilla yogurt
- 1 (10-ounce) package frozen raspberries, thawed
- Fresh fruits, as desired: strawberries, cantaloupe, honeydew melon, pineapple, watermelon

In a medium bowl, stir Cool Whip®, yogurt, and raspberries together. Place in a serving dish. Arrange fresh fruits on a platter.

Serves 20 to 25 people.

MAKE LAUGHTER YOUR FAVORITE DINNER RECIPE. TELL LEGENDARY FAMILY STORIES OR RECOUNT THE DAY'S MORE HUMOROUS EXPERIENCES (EVEN EXPERIENCES THAT WERE NOT HUMOROUS EARLIER IN THE DAY CAN BRING ON LOADS OF LAUGHTER A FEW HOURS LATER).

Strawberry and Melon Salad with Lime Dressing ★ ⌣

DIANNA HALL

Year-round, this salad is appealing. "In our family, it is a Christmas tradition."

- ⅔ cup chopped pecans
- 12 cups fresh spinach or red leaf, green leaf, or romaine lettuce, torn (or combination)
- 2 cups sliced strawberries
- 2 cups balled or cubed honeydew melon

Heat oven to 350° F.

Place pecans on a small cookie sheet or cake pan. Bake 8 to 10 minutes to toast. Cool. Or place pecans on a glass plate or dish and microwave 2 minutes on high. Stir and microwave 1 more minute.

In a large salad bowl, combine spinach, strawberries, melon, and pecans. Toss with dressing.

Dressing

- ¼ cup lime juice
- ¼ cup honey
- ¼ teaspoon ginger
- 2 tablespoons oil

Blend lime juice, honey, ginger, and oil in a small bowl.

Serves 12 to 15.

USE A MELON BALLER TO CORE A PEAR. SLICE THE PEAR IN HALF LENGTHWISE. REMOVE THE CORE WITH THE MELON BALLER, THEN DRAW THE MELON BALLER TO THE TOP OF THE PEAR TO REMOVE THE INTERIOR STEM.

Cherry Pie Salad ★ ⬇

SANDY GUNDERSEN

A rich salad that takes 5 minutes or less to prepare.

1 (14-ounce) can sweetened condensed milk
1 (8-ounce) container Cool Whip®
1 (20-ounce) can crushed pineapple, drained
1 (16-ounce) can cherry pie filling
1 cup chopped pecans
2 cups miniature marshmallows

Mix condensed milk, Cool Whip®, pineapple, pie filling, pecans, and marshmallows in a large bowl. Chill several hours before serving.

Serves 8 to 10.

Precede family dinners with family prayer by having everyone kneel around the table in a circle. Bless the food in a separate prayer after everyone is seated.

SALADS

Cinnamon Pears ★
MARJORIE TALL

The colors are beautiful for Christmas (or Valentine's Day), and this recipe is so easy and fun.

- ¼ to ½ cup red cinnamon candies
- 2 (29-ounce) cans pear halves

Place cinnamon candies in a large saucepan on stove and add enough water to cover. Heat candies until melted. Add pears. Simmer about 15 to 20 minutes, being careful not to let pears get too soft. Remove pan from heat and let pears stew in the hot juice until they become bright red. Remove from juice and chill in refrigerator. Serve pears on a lettuce bed with a little softened cream cheese (or cream cheese mixed with nuts) on top. Or do not remove pears from juice and serve with juice in small bowls.

Serves 6 to 8.

The heart of the home has always been the kitchen—the delicious smell of cooking food, the hustle and bustle of the preparation, and the informal gathering of family and friends. —SUSAN BRANCH

Cranberry Salad

MARDY EREKSON

"We enjoy this salad for Thanksgiving and Christmas."

- 4 cups cranberries
- 2 cups sugar
- 2 cups seedless red grapes, halved
- 1 (8-ounce) can pineapple tidbits, drained
- 1 cup cream, whipped
- 1 cup pecans, chopped

Freeze cranberries. Grind or coarsely chop cranberries in a food processor. Put cranberries in a bowl, add sugar, and let sit several hours to allow cranberries to absorb sugar. Transfer cranberries to a strainer or colander and place over a bowl to drain for 1 hour. Combine cranberries with grapes, pineapple, whipped cream, and pecans. Chill until served.

Serves 8.

TYPE YOUR BASIC SHOPPING LIST ON THE COMPUTER. KEEP A COPY IN THE KITCHEN TO ADD TO DURING THE WEEK. ADD SPECIALTY ITEMS FOR PARTICULAR RECIPES.

SALADS

Raspberry Tapioca Salad
JANET PETERSON

Refreshing! Try various combinations, such as strawberry Jell-O® and frozen strawberries or orange Jell-O® and mandarin oranges.

> 3 cups water
> 1 (3-ounce) package raspberry Jell-O®
> 1 (3.4-ounce) package instant vanilla pudding
> 1 (3-ounce) package tapioca pudding
> 1 (10-ounce) package frozen raspberries, thawed
> 1 (8-ounce) can crushed pineapple, drained
> 1 (8-ounce) container Cool Whip®, thawed

In a large saucepan, bring water to a boil. Stir in Jell-O® and puddings with a whisk. Bring to a boil again, stirring constantly. Boil 1 minute. Remove from heat and cool. Fold in raspberries, pineapple, and Cool Whip. Put mixture into a large serving bowl or individual bowls. Chill in refrigerator 2 hours or more.

Serves 12.

The hectic world in which we live has pressed in on all sides, making us feel that eating on the run, while unpleasant, is a necessity of modern life. However, it is possible for us to change this trend. With some determination and planning, we can maintain the "Thanksgiving atmosphere" through the year. The most important ingredient is not what's on the table; we can serve a home-cooked meal or a pizza. What does make a difference is that we regularly set aside time to eat together. —SHIRLEY DOBSON

Tomato Salad ★

JAN MARTIN

Use just-picked homegrown tomatoes and basil for optimum taste.

½ cup olive oil
3 tablespoons red wine vinegar
1 teaspoon Worcestershire sauce
¾ teaspoon salt
1 tablespoon sugar
⅛ teaspoon pepper
½ clove garlic, minced
2 tablespoons chopped green onions
1 teaspoon dried basil or 1 tablespoon chopped fresh basil
Pinch of thyme
2 to 3 tomatoes, sliced
⅓ cup feta or cottage cheese (optional)

BUY FRUITS AND VEGETABLES IN SEASON AT A PRODUCE MARKET, WHERE PRICES ARE GENERALLY LOWER THAN IN GROCERY STORES.

In a small bowl, mix together oil, vinegar, Worcestershire sauce, salt, sugar, pepper, garlic, onions, basil, and thyme. Place sliced tomatoes in a flat glass dish (9-inch square or 7x11-inch or larger). Pour oil mixture over tomatoes and marinate several hours. Remove tomatoes from marinade and arrange on a platter. Sprinkle feta or cottage cheese over tomatoes, if desired.

Serves 4 to 6.

Corn Salad ★
JANET PETERSON

A nice change from green salads.

- 2 cups fresh or frozen corn, uncooked
- ¾ cup chopped tomatoes
- ½ cup chopped green pepper
- ½ cup chopped celery
- 2 to 3 slices bacon, cooked and crumbled
- ¼ cup chopped green onions
- ¼ cup ranch dressing or favorite vinaigrette

Combine corn, tomatoes, green pepper, celery, bacon, and green onions in a salad bowl. Pour dressing over corn mixture and toss gently to coat. Cover and chill at least 30 minutes to blend flavors.

Serves 8.

Have a weekly planning meeting that includes putting dinner on the schedule.

Carrot Apple Salad ★
JULIE TULLIS

Carrots with a citrus taste.

2 medium carrots, grated
2 small apples, finely chopped
2 tablespoons lemon juice
2 tablespoons orange juice
2 to 3 tablespoons sugar
½ cup raisins or dried cranberries
Romaine or red leaf lettuce

Mix carrots and apples in a medium bowl. Add lemon juice, orange juice, sugar (to taste), and raisins. Stir to combine. Chill 20 minutes. Serve on a lettuce leaf.

Serves 4.

At our house, when the boys were growing up, we were both working from early in the morning until at least eight o'clock in the evening. The kids were all involved in sports, in school plays and clubs, in scouting, in fund-raisers, and all the other activities that kids want to participate in. Yet it was a rare night that we didn't all five sit down for a family dinner of real food, usually cooked at home. It may have been late—often, as is the European fashion, dinner didn't begin until 9 P.M.—but at no other point in the day could we really visit with each other. Dinnertime was family time, when we could each share the victories and frustrations of our day and tell stories and jokes. —MICHAEL R. EADES AND MARY DAN EADES

Bacon, Cauliflower, and Lettuce Salad
SHAUNA FRANDSEN

Make this salad the night before; add the lettuce just before serving. Great for a family picnic.

- ¾ to 1 cup mayonnaise
- ⅓ cup sugar
- 1 small cauliflower, cut or broken into small florets
- 4 green onions, chopped
- ½ pound bacon, cooked and crumbled
- ⅓ cup grated Parmesan cheese
- 1 head lettuce, torn into small pieces

Mix mayonnaise and sugar in a small bowl, stirring until sugar is dissolved. In a large salad bowl, combine cauliflower, onions, bacon, and cheese. Add dressing and stir. Refrigerate overnight. Just before serving, add lettuce.

Serves 6 to 8.

ALWAYS READ YOUR RECIPES BEFORE YOU BEGIN COOKING SO THAT YOU CAN GATHER EQUIPMENT AND INGREDIENTS, UNDERSTAND DIRECTIONS, AND ALLOW FOR THE TIME NEEDED TO PREPARE THE DISH.

Santa Fe Potato Salad
LORRAINE DAY

A Southwest version of potato salad and a zesty addition to a summer barbecue.

- 1 to 2 pounds small red potatoes, quartered, cooked, and cooled
- 1 large tomato, chopped
- ½ cup sliced black olives
- ¼ cup chopped green onions
- ¼ cup minced cilantro
- 1 (15-ounce) can black beans (optional)

Put potatoes, tomato, olives, green onions, cilantro, and beans in a large bowl.

Dressing
- ¼ cup salsa or picante sauce
- 1 to 2 tablespoons lime juice
- 1 tablespoon olive oil
- ¼ teaspoon salt
- ⅛ teaspoon pepper

Blend salsa, lime juice, oil, salt, and pepper in a small bowl. Add dressing to salad and stir to coat vegetables.

Serves 10 to 12.

The table is where we mark milestones, divulge dreams, bury hatchets, make deals, give thanks, plan vacations, and tell jokes. It's also where children learn the lessons that families teach: manners, cooperation, communication, self-control, values. —DORIS CHRISTOPHER

Red Potato and Green Bean Salad
LISA HUNTSMAN

This recipe is easy to make, looks "gourmet-ish," and tastes great.

- ¾ pound fresh green beans, cut into 3- to 4-inch pieces
- 1½ pounds small red potatoes, quartered, cooked, and cooled
- 1 small red onion, chopped
- ¼ cup minced fresh basil or 2 teaspoons dried basil
- Salt and pepper to taste

Cook green beans in a pot of salted, boiling water until crisp-tender, about 5 minutes. Drain and put into a bowl of ice water to cool. Drain. Combine beans, potatoes, onions, and basil in a large bowl.

Dressing
- ¼ cup balsamic vinegar
- 2 tablespoons Dijon mustard
- 2 tablespoons fresh lemon juice
- 1 clove garlic, minced
- Dash of Worcestershire sauce
- ½ cup extra-virgin olive oil

Blend vinegar, mustard, lemon juice, garlic, Worcestershire sauce, and oil in a small bowl. Add dressing to salad; toss to coat. Season with salt and pepper.

Serves 8 to 10.

PURCHASE PLASTIC WRAP IN LARGE ROLLS AT DISCOUNT STORES. COVER LEFTOVERS IN REFRIGERATOR TO USE FOR ANOTHER MEAL.

Potato Salad
RHODA PETERSON

HOW TO HARD BOIL EGGS

FIRST METHOD: PLACE DESIRED NUMBER OF EGGS TO BE COOKED IN A SAUCEPAN. COVER WITH COLD WATER. BRING TO A BOIL OVER HIGH HEAT. IMMEDIATELY REMOVE FROM HEAT AND LET STAND 18 MINUTES. DRAIN HOT WATER, THEN RUN COLD WATER OVER EGGS TO STOP COOKING PROCESS.

SECOND METHOD: PLACE DESIRED NUMBER OF EGGS TO BE COOKED IN A SAUCEPAN. COVER WITH COLD WATER. BRING TO A BOIL OVER HIGH HEAT. REDUCE HEAT BUT MAINTAIN A GENTLE BOIL. COOK 9 TO 10 MINUTES. DRAIN HOT WATER, THEN RUN COLD WATER OVER EGGS TO STOP COOKING PROCESS.

This recipe can be adjusted for any number of people—plan on 1 potato per serving.

12 large potatoes
1 heaping teaspoon salt (adjust to taste)
½ large onion, chopped
2 dill pickles, chopped
6 hard-boiled eggs, sliced
1 cup Kraft Miracle Whip®
1 tablespoon milk
1 tablespoon prepared mustard
Paprika

Boil potatoes in unsalted water with skins on. Drain, cool, and peel. Cut into bite-size pieces. Put potatoes in layers in a large bowl, sprinkling each layer with salt. Add onions and gently mix. Add pickles and most of the egg slices, reserving some for garnish.

Mix Miracle Whip® with milk and mustard. Pour over potatoes. Toss gently. Arrange egg slices on top of salad. Sprinkle with paprika.

Serves 12.

California Salad

SHERI CALDWELL

Amounts of ingredients are variable according to preference. This salad is delicious with any combination. Makes a great salad without berries, too.

- 2 tablespoons sugar
- ⅓ to ½ cup sliced almonds
- 2 to 3 heads various lettuce leaves or spinach, torn
- 1 (11-ounce) can mandarin oranges, drained
- 1 avocado, diced
- 2 to 3 green onions, chopped or ¼ cup chopped red onion
- 2 kiwis, sliced
- ½ cup raspberries and/or sliced strawberries (optional)
- ⅓ cup blueberries (optional)
- Raspberry vinaigrette* or poppy seed dressing*

Don't make dinner a time to solve family problems or differences. Strive to make meals enjoyable experiences.

Put sugar in a small skillet. Add almonds and melt sugar over medium high heat, stirring constantly. Watch carefully, as sugar burns easily. Put sugared almonds onto a plate to cool.

In a large salad bowl, put lettuces and/or spinach and any combination of mandarin oranges, avocado, onions, kiwis, and berries, as desired. Add sugared almonds. Toss with raspberry vinaigrette or poppy seed dressing just before serving.

Serves 10 to 12.

*See page 76 for poppy seed dressing recipe.

*See page 77 for raspberry vinaigrette recipe.

Iceberg Salad with Cashews
PAMELA MARTINEZ

Always a hit at family get-togethers.

1 medium head iceberg lettuce, torn
⅓ cup thinly sliced green onions
½ cup chopped cashews
2 tablespoons minced parsley
3 tablespoons roasted sunflower seeds
3 slices bacon, cooked and crumbled
Olive oil
¼ cup white wine vinegar
2 teaspoons sugar
Salt and pepper to taste
¼ cup Parmesan cheese

Use a salad spinner to dry salad greens.

In a salad bowl, mix together lettuce, onions, cashews, parsley, and sunflower seeds. In a medium skillet, cook bacon until crisp. Reserve drippings. Crumble bacon and add to lettuce mixture.

Pour bacon drippings into a measuring cup and add enough oil to make ⅓ cup total. Pour into a saucepan and add vinegar and sugar. Heat, stirring until sugar is dissolved. Cool. Pour over lettuce and toss well. Season to taste with salt and pepper. Garnish with Parmesan cheese.

Serves 6.

Caesar Salad

KATHY CRAWFORD

You'll savor every mouthful of this excellent rendition of Caesar salad.

- 1 head romaine lettuce, torn
- Freshly ground pepper
- 3 to 4 tablespoons freshly grated Parmesan cheese
- Croutons
- Anchovies (optional)

Put lettuce in a large salad bowl. Grind a generous amount of black pepper over the salad and add Parmesan cheese in stages, tossing the salad gently in between. Add croutons and anchovies, if desired, and then dressing. Toss salad thoroughly but gently and serve immediately.

Dressing

- ½ teaspoon Dijon mustard
- ¼ cup rice vinegar
- ¼ cup lemon juice
- 1 to 1¼ cups olive oil (according to taste)
- 2 tablespoons mayonnaise
- ¼ to ½ teaspoon salt (to taste)
- ¾ teaspoon Italian seasoning
- 1 to 2 cloves garlic, minced

Combine mustard, vinegar, lemon juice, oil, and mayonnaise in a small, deep bowl. Beat vigorously with a whisk until dressing holds together. Add salt, Italian seasoning, and garlic and whisk some more.

Serves 4 to 6.

WHEN YOU BRING HOME YOUR GROCERIES FROM THE STORE, IMMEDIATELY SEPARATE AND WASH ALL LETTUCE LEAVES. DRAIN LETTUCE IN A COLANDER PLACED IN THE KITCHEN SINK. WHEN LETTUCE IS THOROUGHLY DRAINED, STORE IT, ALONG WITH A PAPER TOWEL TO ABSORB MOISTURE, IN A RESEALABLE PLASTIC BAG IN THE REFRIGERATOR. LETTUCE WILL THEN BE CRISP AND READY FOR SALADS.

Apple Avocado Salad
BEVERLY BLUNCK

Try a different variety of apple when making this salad for a unique taste each time.

- 3 cups torn romaine lettuce leaves
- 3 cups torn spinach leaves
- 4 slices bacon, cooked and crumbled
- 1 large avocado, diced
- 1 medium red apple, diced

Mix lettuce, spinach, bacon, avocado, and apple in a salad bowl.

Dressing
- 3 tablespoons red wine vinegar
- 1 teaspoon Dijon mustard
- 1 teaspoon sugar
- Salt and pepper to taste
- 1 tablespoon minced fresh parsley
- ½ cup olive or canola oil

In a small, deep bowl whisk together vinegar, mustard, sugar, salt, pepper, and parsley. Slowly add oil while whisking rapidly until well blended. Toss salad with dressing just before serving.

Serves 6 to 8.

Since we are forced to nourish ourselves, why not do it with all possible skill . . . and ever-increasing enjoyment? —M. F. K. FISHER

Spinach Salad
CAROL PARRIS

A super salad for a family reunion. Red onion slices need to be marinated in the dressing the night before.

Dressing
- 1½ tablespoons poppy seeds
- ¾ cup white vinegar
- 1½ cups vegetable or olive oil
- ¾ cup sugar
- 1½ tablespoons chopped onion
- 1½ teaspoons salt
- ¾ teaspoon dry mustard
- 1 large red onion, thinly sliced

Blend poppy seeds, vinegar, oil, sugar, onion, salt, and mustard in a blender. Place red onion slices in a small bowl. Pour dressing over onions, cover bowl, and marinate overnight.

- 2 (10-ounce) packages or 2 bunches of spinach, torn
- 2 heads lettuce, torn
- ½ pound bacon, cooked and crumbled
- ¾ pound Swiss cheese, grated
- 1 cup cottage cheese
- 1 cup sliced fresh mushrooms
- 2 to 3 tomatoes, diced or 1 cup grape or cherry tomatoes (optional)

In a large salad bowl, mix spinach, lettuce, bacon, Swiss cheese, cottage cheese, and mushrooms. Add tomatoes, if desired. Add dressing with onions. Toss gently.

Serves 18 to 20.

Bacon and Tomato Salad

JUDITH NIELSON

When the whole clan gets together, serve them this scrumptious salad.

- 1 head iceberg lettuce, torn
- 1 head romaine lettuce, torn
- 1 head green leaf lettuce, torn
- 1½ pounds thick-sliced pepper bacon, cooked and crumbled
- 1 pound Swiss cheese, cut into thin strips
- 2 cups chopped tomatoes
- 1 bunch green onions, thinly sliced

In a very large salad bowl, mix lettuces, bacon, cheese, tomatoes, and green onions. Just before serving, toss with salad dressing.

Dressing

- 1½ cups mayonnaise
- ¾ cup sugar
- 1 teaspoon freshly ground pepper
- 1 teaspoon salt

In a small bowl, mix together mayonnaise, sugar, pepper, and salt. Stir until sugar is dissolved.

Serves 20 to 25.

ADD LEFTOVER COOKED GREEN BEANS OR PEAS TO SALADS.

Spring Salad with Orange Dressing ★

KALLIE DENT

Rice vinegar is essential to this dressing.

- 2 to 3 tablespoons butter or margarine
- ½ cup sugar
- ¼ to ⅓ cup sliced almonds
- 1 head red or green leaf lettuce, torn
- 3 to 4 cups spring mix (loose or in package in produce section)
- 1 jicama, cut in thin strips
- 6 kiwis, sliced
- 1 bunch red or purple grapes, cut in halves
- 2 cups sliced strawberries

Melt butter in a small skillet. Add sugar and almonds. Stir until sugar is dissolved and almonds coated. Cool.

Combine lettuces, spring mix, jicama, kiwis, grapes, and strawberries in a large salad bowl. Add sugared almonds.

Dressing

- ½ cup sugar
- ⅓ cup rice vinegar
- ⅓ cup orange juice
- 1 cup olive oil
- 1 (0.7-ounce) envelope Good Seasons® Italian dressing mix

Mix sugar, rice vinegar, orange juice, olive oil, and Italian dressing mix. Stir until sugar is dissolved. Serve with salad.

Serves 8 to 10.

TOAST NUTS SUCH AS ALMONDS AND PECANS IN THE MICROWAVE. PLACE NUTS IN A GLASS BOWL AND MICROWAVE, UNCOVERED, ON HIGH 2 MINUTES. STIR AND MICROWAVE 1 MORE MINUTE.

Coleslaw ★
DEE KREIDER

This salad should be made the day before serving. It keeps well in the refrigerator for a week.

- 1 head cabbage, shredded
- 1 green pepper, chopped
- 1 onion (red or white), chopped
- ¾ cup oil
- 1 cup white vinegar
- 1 teaspoon salt
- 1 cup sugar
- 1 tablespoon celery seed

Buy packages of already cut and mixed coleslaw and salad greens.

Put cabbage, green pepper, and onion in a glass salad bowl. Mix oil, vinegar, salt, sugar, and celery seed in a small bowl. Pour over slaw mixture. Refrigerate overnight.

Serves 4 to 6.

Chicken Salad Supreme
MARJORIE TALL

This main-dish salad is lovely and luscious!

2½ cups cooked, diced chicken
1 cup finely chopped celery
1 cup green grapes, halved
½ cup sliced almonds, toasted or plain
2 tablespoons fresh minced parsley
1 teaspoon salt
1 cup mayonnaise
½ cup whipping cream, whipped

Garnishes

Lettuce leaves
Cantaloupe slices
Strawberries
1 (11-ounce) can mandarin oranges
Stuffed green olives

Dice leftover cooked chicken for salads, sandwiches, pastas, and other chicken dishes.

Combine chicken, celery, grapes, almonds, parsley, salt, mayonnaise, and whipped cream. Serve on lettuce leaves. Garnish with cantaloupe slices, strawberries, mandarin oranges, and/or stuffed green olives.

Serves 8.

Chinese Chicken Salad
KATHY CRAWFORD

The dressing for this salad is also good on an iceberg lettuce salad with shredded fresh vegetables.

- 2 cups cooked and diced chicken breasts
- 3 cups shredded iceberg lettuce or 1½ cups shredded iceberg lettuce and 1½ cups shredded cabbage
- ¼ cup chopped onion
- ½ cup celery, thinly sliced on the diagonal
- ½ cup shredded carrots
- 2 to 3 green onions, shredded*
- ½ cup thinly sliced red pepper (optional)
- 1 cup chow mein noodles
- 2 tablespoons chopped roasted peanuts
- 1 tablespoon sesame seeds, toasted**
- 3 to 4 tablespoons minced cilantro

* To shred green onion, slice onion lengthwise down the middle, then chop at an angle.

** To toast sesame seeds, place them in a baking pan and bake 5 to 7 minutes at 350° F., watching so they don't burn.

In a large salad bowl, mix together chicken, lettuce and/or cabbage, onion, celery, carrots, green onions, and red pepper, if desired. Before serving, put chow mein noodles over top, sprinkle with peanuts and sesame seeds, and garnish with minced cilantro.

Oriental Dressing

- ¼ cup cider vinegar
- ¼ cup soy sauce
- 2 tablespoons sesame oil
- ½ to 1 teaspoon hot chili oil
- ½ teaspoon salt

SALADS

- 2 teaspoons sugar
- 1 to 2 cloves garlic, crushed
- 1 to 2 teaspoons finely grated ginger or 1 to 1½ tablespoons bottled minced ginger

Whisk together vinegar, soy sauce, sesame oil, chili oil, salt, sugar, garlic, and ginger in a small, deep bowl. Add dressing to salad and toss lightly. Serve immediately.

Serves 8 to 10.

HOW TO CUT AND SEED PEPPERS

THE SEEDS AND INNER MEMBRANES OF PEPPERS NEED TO BE REMOVED PRIOR TO USE. WEARING PLASTIC OR RUBBER GLOVES WHEN CUTTING HOT PEPPERS, SUCH AS JALAPEÑOS OR SERRANOS, IS VITAL BECAUSE THE SEEDS AND MEMBRANES CONTAIN STRONG OILS AND ARE THE HOTTEST PARTS OF THE PEPPER. IT IS ALSO VERY IMPORTANT NOT TO TOUCH GLOVES OR HANDS TO YOUR FACE OR EYES DURING THE PROCESS.

CUT OFF THE ENDS OF THE PEPPER AND THEN CUT IT IN HALVES OR QUARTERS. WITH A PARING KNIFE, REMOVE THE INNER MEMBRANES AND SEEDS AND DISCARD. CHOP OR SLICE PEPPERS WITH KNIFE OR FOOD PROCESSOR.

Garden Chicken Salad
MARIE GALBRAITH

Serving a main dish salad, accompanied by fresh fruit and rolls or bread, is a lighter approach to dinner.

Dressing
- 2 tablespoons vegetable or olive oil
- 2 tablespoons lemon juice
- 2 tablespoons sesame seeds, toasted*
- 1½ teaspoons soy sauce
- ½ teaspoon salt
- ¼ teaspoon pepper
- ¼ teaspoon dry mustard

*Place sesame seeds in a baking pan and bake 5 to 7 minutes at 350° F., watching so they don't burn.

Blend oil, lemon juice, sesame seeds, soy sauce, salt, pepper, and mustard in a small bowl. Cover and refrigerate to blend flavors.

- 2 pounds boneless, skinless chicken breasts, cooked and diced
- 2 cups shredded lettuce
- 1 cup carrots, sliced or cut in julienne strips
- 1 cup cucumbers, sliced or cut in julienne strips
- ⅔ cup green onions, cut in 2-inch strips
- 1 cup fresh bean sprouts

In a large salad bowl, combine chicken, lettuce, carrots, cucumbers, green onions, and bean sprouts. Cover and refrigerate several hours until ready to serve. Just before serving, pour dressing over salad and toss gently.

Serves 8.

Cilantro, Chicken, and Black Bean Salad ★ ▽
JANET PETERSON

"Very popular with our family the first time I prepared this salad."

- 1 (15-ounce) can black beans, rinsed and drained
- 1 (11-ounce) can Mexican-style corn, drained
- 1 medium red pepper, cut in thin strips
- ⅓ cup chopped green onions
- ¼ cup sliced black olives (jalapeño flavored, optional)
- 1½ cups cooked or grilled chicken, cut into strips
- 4 cups lettuce, torn (romaine, red leaf, green leaf, or iceberg)

In a large salad bowl, combine black beans, corn, red pepper, green onions, olives, and chicken.

Place lettuce on individual plates or a large serving platter. Put bean and chicken mixture on top of lettuce.

Dressing

- ⅓ cup olive oil
- 2 tablespoons lime juice
- 2 tablespoons chopped cilantro
- 1½ teaspoons sugar
- 1 clove garlic, minced
- ½ teaspoon chili powder
- ½ teaspoon salt
- ¼ teaspoon pepper

Combine oil, lime juice, cilantro, sugar, garlic, chili powder, salt, and pepper in a small bowl. Whisk or mix to blend. Pour dressing over bean mixture.

Serves 6.

IF A MEMBER OF YOUR FAMILY IS LIVING AWAY FROM HOME, ARRANGE TO HAVE DINNERTIME CONFERENCE CALLS ON OCCASION. THIS WILL ALLOW EVERYONE IN THE FAMILY TO TALK TO THE ABSENT FAMILY MEMBER, MAKING IT SEEM FOR A MOMENT AS IF HE OR SHE IS HOME FOR DINNER.

Taco Salad

STEPHANIE BYWATER

Most children like taco salad because they can add as many accessories as they wish—and that means lots of chips.

- 1½ to 2 pounds ground beef
- 1 cup chopped onions
- 1 (30-ounce) can refried beans
- 1 (15-ounce) can tomato sauce
- 1 (1¼-ounce) package taco seasoning
- ⅛ teaspoon Tabasco® sauce
- Salt and pepper to taste
- 1 head lettuce, shredded
- Zesty® Italian salad dressing
- 1 (16-ounce) package Fritos® or corn chips
- ½ pound cheddar cheese, grated
- 4 tomatoes, diced
- 1 bunch green onions, chopped
- 1 cup sour cream
- 1 cup guacamole or diced avocados

Brown ground beef in a skillet. Drain fat. Add onion and cook until tender. Add refried beans, tomato sauce, taco seasoning, Tabasco® sauce, salt, and pepper. Simmer 10 minutes, until flavors are blended. Pour desired amount of salad dressing over lettuce and toss to coat.

To serve salad:

Place a bed of shredded lettuce on each plate. Circle with chips. Spoon on ground beef mixture. Top with cheese, tomatoes, green onions, and a spoonful each of sour cream and guacamole or avocados.

Serves 12.

Mexican Chow Mein ★ ◡

NANCY HUGHES

An even simpler version of taco salad.

- 1 (15- or 30-ounce) can chili
- 1 head lettuce, shredded
- 1 cup grated cheese (a combination of cheddar and Monterey Jack is good)
- 1 (16-ounce) package Fritos®
- 2 to 3 tomatoes, chopped
- Sour cream or cottage cheese
- 3 to 4 chopped green onions (optional)
- 1 (2¼-ounce) can sliced olives (optional)

Heat chili. On individual plates, layer lettuce, chili, cheese, Fritos®, tomatoes, sour cream or cottage cheese, and green onions and olives, if desired.

Serves 4 to 6.

IF EATING DINNER TOGETHER IS HAPPENING INFREQUENTLY, HOLD A FAMILY COUNCIL TO EVALUATE THE KINDS AND NUMBER OF OUTSIDE ACTIVITIES THAT ARE OCCUPYING FAMILY MEMBERS AT DINNERTIME. ENLIST FAMILY MEMBERS' SUPPORT TO IMPROVE THE SITUATION.

Pasta-Vegetable Salad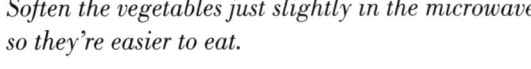
JILL SPENCER

Soften the vegetables just slightly in the microwave so they're easier to eat.

CREATE A PASTA SALAD WITH LEFTOVER COOKED SPAGHETTI NOODLES OR MACARONI. ADD CHOPPED RAW VEGETABLES SUCH AS CARROTS, BELL PEPPERS, BROCCOLI, CAULIFLOWER, TOMATOES, OR FROZEN PEAS OR CORN. COAT MIXTURE WITH BOTTLED ITALIAN SALAD DRESSING.

1 (16-ounce) package pasta (bow-tie, shell, elbow), cooked according to package directions and drained
1 green pepper, chopped
1 red pepper, chopped
1 small bunch broccoli, cut into florets
2 to 3 carrots, thinly sliced
1 medium red onion, thinly sliced
1 cup frozen peas, thawed
Grape tomatoes or diced tomatoes
1 small zucchini, thinly sliced (optional)
1 cup cubed mozzarella cheese
Pepperoni, thinly sliced (amount according to taste)
Fresh Parmesan cheese, grated
Bernstein's® Cheese and Garlic Italian dressing

Wash peppers, broccoli, and carrots, leaving a little water on vegetables. Place in a microwave dish and microwave on high 30 to 45 seconds to soften vegetables. Microwave red onion separately 20 seconds. Do not microwave peas, tomatoes, or zucchini.

Put cooked pasta in a large salad bowl. Add peppers, broccoli, carrots, onion, peas, tomatoes, zucchini, cheese, and pepperoni and mix. Stir in Parmesan cheese. Pour desired amount of dressing to coat pasta and vegetables. Store in refrigerator an hour or more to blend flavors.

Serves 12 to 16.

Bow-Tie Pasta and Chicken Salad
DELSIE BEKKER

Hearts of palm is the unusual ingredient in this salad—but easily found in most grocery stores.

- 3 to 4 boneless, skinless chicken breasts
- Juice of ½ lemon
- 1 to 2 tablespoons olive oil
- 1 cup sliced fresh mushrooms
- 2 to 3 tablespoons butter or margarine
- 1 (8- or 12-ounce) package bow-tie pasta, cooked according to package directions, drained, and cooled
- 1 (14.4-ounce) jar hearts of palm (slice or dice, if needed)
- 1 small red onion, chopped
- ½ cup pine nuts (optional)

Place chicken breasts on broiling pan. Squeeze lemon juice over breasts. Brush with olive oil. Broil chicken until done. Cool and dice. Place chicken in a large bowl. Sauté mushrooms in butter in a small skillet. Add to chicken mixture. Add pasta, hearts of palm, onion, and pine nuts, if desired.

Dressing

- ½ cup milk
- ½ cup mayonnaise
- 3 to 4 cloves garlic, minced
- 1 teaspoon salt
- 1 teaspoon white pepper
- 3 tablespoons Dijon mustard
- ½ tablespoon lemon juice

Mix milk, mayonnaise, garlic, salt, pepper, Dijon mustard, and lemon juice in a small bowl. Pour onto chicken and pasta mixture, stirring gently. If desired, add more salt and pepper.

Serves 12 to 14.

Poppy Seed Dressing ★
ELAINE JACK

Sweet and so good on fruit-lettuce combinations.

1 cup oil
⅓ cup sugar
⅓ cup red wine vinegar
½ teaspoon salt
½ medium onion, finely chopped
1 tablespoon dry mustard
2 tablespoons poppy seeds

Blend oil, sugar, vinegar, salt, onion, and mustard. Add poppy seeds.

Makes 1½ cups.

Basic Vinaigrette ★
KATHY CRAWFORD

It only takes a few minutes to make your own salad dressings. Bottled dressings just don't compare.

½ teaspoon Dijon mustard
⅓ cup wine vinegar or balsamic vinegar
⅔ to 1 cup olive oil (according to taste)
¼ teaspoon salt
½ teaspoon Italian seasoning
1 clove garlic, minced (optional)

MAKE YOUR OWN VINAIGRETTES FOR SALADS BY FLAVORING CIDER OR WINE VINEGAR WITH FRESH HERBS (BASIL, OREGANO, CHIVES, DILL, AND SO ON) AND ONE OR TWO CLOVES OF MINCED GARLIC.

Combine Dijon mustard and vinegar in a small, deep bowl. Blend thoroughly using a whisk. Gradually add olive oil, beating the mixture vigorously with whisk so that the dressing holds together without separating. Add salt, Italian seasoning, and garlic and whisk again. Store dressing in refrigerator and bring to room temperature before using. Whisk vigorously before serving to blend ingredients again.

Makes 1 to 1⅓ cups.

Raspberry Vinaigrette ★
BEVERLY BLUNCK

Flavored vinegars offer so much variety in making salad dressings.

- ¼ cup sugar
- ½ teaspoon salt
- ¼ teaspoon white pepper
- 1 clove garlic, minced
- ¼ cup raspberry vinegar
- 2 tablespoons olive oil

Combine sugar, salt, pepper, garlic, vinegar, and oil in a small, deep bowl or jar. Blend.

Makes ½ cup.

Lemon Vinaigrette ★
DIANNA HALL

Fresh lemon juice is the key to this vinaigrette.

- 2 tablespoons fresh lemon juice
- ¼ teaspoon salt
- ¼ teaspoon dry mustard
- ½ cup olive oil
- Freshly ground pepper

Whisk together lemon juice, salt, mustard, oil, and pepper in a small bowl. Serve on green salad.

Makes ½ cup.

EAT TOGETHER AROUND A TABLE SO THAT FAMILY MEMBERS CAN LOOK AT EACH OTHER.

Citrus Dressing for Fresh Fruits ★
JENNIFER DILL

Citrus juices keep fresh fruit from turning brown and add to its flavor.

- 6 ounces orange juice
- 2 tablespoons lemon juice
- 2 tablespoons lime juice
- ½ cup sugar

Combine orange, lemon, and lime juices, and sugar in a small bowl. Stir until sugar is dissolved. Marinate 4 to 6 cups fresh fruit at least 1 hour.

Makes 1¼ cups.

MAKE FRUIT SAUCE FROM LEFTOVER JUICES BY COMBINING AND COOKING UNTIL THICK: 1 TABLESPOON CORNSTARCH, ¼ CUP SUGAR, ⅛ TEASPOON CINNAMON, AND 1½ CUPS FRUIT JUICE. SERVE SAUCE OVER LEFTOVER VEGETABLES, FRUIT, PANCAKES, OR WAFFLES.

BREADS

Bread is often called the "staff of life." In one form or another—pumpernickel, challah, tortillas, or cornbread—it is basic to dinner in most cultures. Bread, freshly made, is one of the most enjoyed and satisfying offerings you can give your family. And many breads are easily mixed and quickly baked.

Cinnamon Pull-Aparts/81

Italian Pull-Aparts/82

Crispy Cheese Biscuits/83

Baking Powder Biscuits/84

Garlic Cheese Biscuits/85

Seasoned Rolls/86

Breadsticks/87

Ranch Bread/88

Frosted Half-Time Rolls/89

Orange Rolls/90

Two-Hour Rolls/91

White Bread/92

Flour Tortillas/93

Tennessee-Style Corn Bread/94

Banana Nut Bread or Muffins/95

Blueberry Muffins/96

Bran Muffins/97

Corn Muffins/98

Pumpkin Muffins/99

Cinnamon Pull-Aparts ★
DIANE WILSON

You'll get rave reviews and repeat requests for these.

- 1 teaspoon cinnamon
- ½ cup sugar
- ½ cup chopped nuts (optional)
- 2 to 3 (12-ounce) cans refrigerator biscuits, quartered
- ½ cup butter or margarine, melted
- 1 cup brown sugar

Heat oven to 350° F.

Put cinnamon, sugar, and nuts, if desired, in a resealable plastic bag. Add quartered biscuits to bag and shake to coat biscuits. Place biscuits in a greased 10-inch bundt pan.

Mix butter and brown sugar, stirring until sugar is dissolved. (Can also be put in saucepan and heated together.) Pour sauce over top of biscuits, distributing evenly. Bake 30 to 40 minutes. (Check at 30 minutes—3 cans of biscuits may take 40 minutes.) Turn pan upside down on serving plate to release the biscuit ring.

Serves 6 to 8.

BEGIN EARLY AS NEWLYWEDS AND THEN LATER WITH YOUNG CHILDREN TO HAVE REGULAR, WHOLESOME, AND PLEASANT MEALS.

Italian Pull-Aparts ★
SHELLEY SCHENCK

This savory biscuit ring will disappear in a hurry.

⅓ cup butter or margarine, melted
1 cup fresh, grated Parmesan cheese
2 teaspoons Italian seasoning
1 to 2 cloves garlic, minced
2 (12-ounce) cans refrigerated biscuits or 1(1 pound 1.3-ounce) can Pillsbury® Grands refrigerated biscuits

Heat oven to 375° F.

Put melted butter in a shallow bowl. In another shallow bowl combine Parmesan cheese, Italian seasoning, and garlic. Cut biscuits into quarters. Dip biscuits in butter mixture, then in cheese mixture. Spray or grease a 10-inch bundt pan. Drop or arrange biscuits in pan. Bake 28 to 30 minutes, until brown. Turn pan upside down on serving plate to release biscuits.

Serves 6 to 8.

One of the most important furnishings found in most homes is the kitchen table. Now, it may be small, it may be large, or in the form of a little counter with barely room to put the food and utensils. Its major function seems to be a place for the different members of the family to receive nourishment. . . .

My plea . . . is that each of us will look carefully at our homes and at the kitchen table and continually strive to bring heaven into our homes.
—LEGRAND R. CURTIS

Crispy Cheese Biscuits ★ ▽
TRACI COOK

These biscuits will accent a variety of main dishes.

- ⅔ cup crushed Rice Chex® cereal
- 3 tablespoons grated Parmesan cheese
- 2 tablespoons butter or margarine, melted
- 1 (1 pound 1.3-ounce) can Pillsbury® Grands refrigerated biscuits

Heat oven to 400° F.

Combine cereal, Parmesan cheese, and butter in a shallow dish. Separate biscuits and cut in half. Coat biscuits with crumb mixture. Place in a pie plate or on a cookie sheet. Bake 15 minutes.

Serves 4 to 6.

Round or square, mahogany or oak, the table is the heart of every home, the nucleus of domestic life. . . . When the chores are done and daylight is fading, the work table becomes the dinner table, and as we gather around it, we, too, are transformed. No longer separate and solitary, we regain our identities as part of a much greater whole: We become a family, sharing not just our suppers but also ourselves.

—DORIS CHRISTOPHER

Baking Powder Biscuits
SUSAN MORTENSEN

"The best!"

4 cups flour
1 teaspoon salt
1 tablespoon sugar
5 teaspoons baking powder
1 cup shortening
2 eggs, beaten
1½ cups milk

Heat oven to 425° F.

Combine flour, salt, sugar, and baking powder in a large bowl. Cut shortening into dry ingredients. Mix eggs and milk together in a small bowl, then add to flour mixture. Dough will be sticky. Knead lightly on a floured breadboard or counter about 20 times. Roll out and cut with a round cutter or drinking glass. Bake 10 minutes, until light brown.

Makes 2 dozen biscuits.

IF YOUR OLDER CHILDREN LIVE THROUGHOUT THE WORLD OR ARE AWAY AT COLLEGE, SHARE RECIPES VIA PHONE, E-MAIL, OR A FAMILY WEB SITE.

Garlic Cheese Biscuits
AMY GREENE

"These biscuits are heavenly. They taste just like those yummy biscuits Red Lobster serves."

2 cups Bisquick® mix
⅔ cup milk
½ cup grated cheddar cheese
¼ cup butter or margarine, melted
¼ teaspoon garlic powder

Heat oven to 450° F.

In a medium bowl, mix Bisquick®, milk, and cheese until soft dough forms. Beat vigorously 30 seconds. Drop dough by spoonfuls onto a greased cookie sheet. Bake 8 to 10 minutes, or until golden brown. Mix butter and garlic powder in a small bowl. Brush over warm biscuits before removing from cookie sheet. Serve warm.

Makes 10 to 12 biscuits.

PLAYING VERBAL GAMES AT THE DINNER TABLE. WILL HELP YOUNG CHILDREN THINK CREATIVELY AND ARE ALSO A LOT OF FUN. ASK KIDS TO NAME ALL THE VEGETABLES THAT BEGIN WITH THE LETTER B OR TO THINK OF ALL THE FOODS THEY LIKE THAT ARE RED. YOU COULD ALSO TELL THE BEGINNING OF A STORY AND LET EACH FAMILY MEMBER ADD TO THE STORY.

Seasoned Rolls ★ ☻
TRINA WEATHERSTON

The seasonings really perk up plain rolls.

Rhodes® frozen dinner rolls (use number desired)
⅓ cup butter or margarine, melted
⅛ cup chopped fresh parsley or 2 teaspoons dried parsley
¾ cup Parmesan cheese
¾ teaspoon garlic powder
1 teaspoon Salad Supreme®

Dip frozen rolls in butter in a shallow bowl. In another shallow bowl, mix parsley, Parmesan cheese, garlic powder, and Salad Supreme®. Coat rolls in cheese mixture. Place rolls on an ungreased cookie sheet. Cover and let rise 4 to 5 hours, until double in size.

Heat oven to 375° F. Bake 15 minutes.

Variable servings.

Food is so pleasurable and powerful that it plays an essential role in creating a home that works. For your home to feel solid, meaningful, dignified, and warm, you must have the means and skills to produce good, nutritious food, to dream up pleasant menus, and to set the table and serve the food in an attractive manner that is familiar and comfortable to guests. —CHERYL MENDELSON

Breadsticks

CHRISTINE NEILSON

Pair these breadsticks with a hearty soup or chili.

- 1 tablespoon yeast
- 1½ cups warm water
- 2 tablespoons sugar
- ½ teaspoon salt
- 3½ to 4 cups flour

Soften yeast in warm water. Mix sugar, salt, and 3½ cups flour together. Add yeast. Blend well, adding enough remaining flour to form soft dough. Knead 3 minutes. Cover and let rise 10 minutes.

Breadstick Spread

- ¼ cup butter or margarine, softened
- ¼ cup Parmesan cheese
- ¼ cup mayonnaise
- ¼ teaspoon parsley flakes
- ¼ teaspoon garlic salt

Blend butter, Parmesan cheese, mayonnaise, parsley, and garlic salt together in a small bowl.

Spray or grease a cookie sheet. Put dough in middle of pan and press to outer edges. (Coat hands with cooking spray if needed to prevent dough from sticking to hands.) Brush Breadstick Spread over dough. Cut dough down the middle and across to make sticks. (A pizza cutter works well.) Let rise until almost doubled in size.

Heat oven to 350° F.

Bake 20 to 25 minutes. Cool in pan.

Makes 40 breadsticks.

Ranch Bread ★
JOANNA JOHNSON

If only one loaf is needed for a meal, refrigerate remaining spread for future use.

2 loaves French bread
1 (0.4-ounce) envelope ranch dressing mix
½ cup butter or margarine, softened

Heat oven to 350° F.

Cut loaves in half lengthwise. Blend ranch dressing mix with butter. Spread mixture on bread. Wrap in aluminum foil. Heat 5 to 7 minutes, or until butter is melted and bread is hot.

Variable servings.

Breakfast prepares; dinner restores. Just as the purpose of breakfast is to send you out to your school or work fortified in mind and body, the purpose of dinner is to reclaim you for private life, pleasure, intimacy. Dinner is the most substantial meal of the day and the central daily event in the life of the home. It is the longest, largest, most elaborate meal, and it serves a variety of functions. Nutritionally, emotionally, and socially, dinner carries more of the burden than other meals of providing the benefits that derive from eating meals cooked at home.
—CHERYL MENDELSON

Frosted Half-Time Rolls
PAT MENLOVE

These rolls are finished in half the time of most roll recipes.

- ¾ cup milk
- ¾ cup water
- ⅓ cup sugar
- ⅓ cup shortening or oil
- 1 teaspoon salt
- 2 tablespoons yeast
- 1 large or 2 small eggs
- 3¼ cups flour

Heat milk to lukewarm. Transfer to a large bowl. Add water, sugar, shortening or oil, salt, yeast, egg, and flour. Whip with spoon. Let rise until double in volume. Spoon into well-greased muffin cups. Let rise again. (They rise quickly.)

Heat oven to 425° F.

Bake 12 to 15 minutes, until golden brown. Spread with frosting.

Frosting
- Juice of 1 orange
- Grated orange rind
- ¾ to 1 cup powdered sugar
- 3 to 4 tablespoons butter or margarine, melted

Mix orange juice, orange rind, powdered sugar, and butter to a thin consistency.

Makes 18 rolls.

MAKE DINNER INTERESTING BY COOKING THE SAME FOODS YOU LOVED AS A CHILD AND TELLING YOUR OWN CHILDREN ABOUT YOUR FAVORITE CHILDHOOD MEMORIES.

Orange Rolls
VANESSA QUIGLEY

"My Aunt Linda brought these yummy and super easy rolls to Christmas dinner in 1978, and we've been having them ever since."

- ½ cup butter or margarine, melted
- 1 cup sugar
- 3 tablespoons grated orange peel
- Favorite dinner roll recipe prepared according to directions or frozen white bread dough, thawed

Mix butter, sugar, and orange peel in a small bowl to make orange butter.

Divide dough and roll into rectangles about 8x12 inches on a floured board. Spread with orange butter. Roll up into a long log and slice into 1-inch rounds. Place on a sprayed or greased baking sheet, sides touching. Drizzle on any remaining orange butter. Let rise until double in size. Bake according to recipe or frozen dough directions.

Variable servings.

I have always thought of the kitchen as a gathering place. A kitchen worthy of its name speaks togetherness, warmth, sharing, and often clutter. The smell of peaches being bottled in the fall, chili sauce simmering on the stove, the sweet aroma of cinnamon rolls, vanilla added to a cake, or meat loaf conjure such nostalgic memories! —ELAINE L. JACK

Two-Hour Rolls

JEN EYRING

From start to finish, these rolls take just 2 hours, and actual preparation time just a few minutes.

- 4 to 5 cups flour
- 1 tablespoon instant yeast
- ¼ cup sugar
- 3 tablespoons oil
- 1 egg
- 1 teaspoon salt
- 1½ cups lukewarm water
- ¼ cup butter or margarine, melted

In a large bowl or the bowl of a bread mixer, mix half the flour with yeast. Add sugar, oil, egg, salt, and water. Blend well with mixer or dough hook. Add enough flour to make a soft dough that leaves the sides of the bowl. Let rise 15 minutes. Punch down and let rise another 15 minutes. Knead 1 to 2 minutes on a lightly floured board. Roll out into a large circle. Cut into wedges (a pizza cutter works well) and roll into crescent shapes. Place on an ungreased cookie sheet and cover with plastic wrap sprayed with cooking spray. Let rise 1 hour.

Heat oven to 350° F.

Bake 15 minutes, until lightly browned. Brush with melted butter while still hot.

Makes 3½ to 4 dozen rolls.

Mom taught us that good eating starts with good cooking. —LUCILE PROCTOR

White Bread
KATHLEEN MCGUIRE

With a bread mixer, which eliminates kneading by hand, making bread is quick and easy. There are few things as welcomed by family members as homemade bread.

- 4 tablespoons yeast
- 1 cup warm water
- 1 teaspoon sugar
- 1 quart warm water
- 1 cup sugar
- ½ cup butter or margarine, softened
- 1 tablespoon salt
- 7 to 9 cups flour

Dissolve yeast in 1 cup water in bowl or a large measuring cup. Sprinkle 1 teaspoon sugar over top and let yeast activate a few minutes. Put yeast mixture into bread mixer (or use the dough hook of a stand mixer). Add 1 quart water, sugar, butter, salt, and 2 cups flour. Mix until thoroughly blended. Add 2 to 3 more cups flour; mix. Add more flour, a half cup at a time, until dough pulls away from side of bowl. Mix 10 minutes.

Form bread into 3 to 4 loaves and put into greased 5x9-inch loaf pans. Cover and let rise until doubled in size. (Rising times vary depending on room temperature, yeast, and flour.)

Heat oven to 400° F.

Bake 10 minutes at 400° F. Turn heat down to 350° F. and bake 30 minutes. Remove bread from pans and cool on racks.

Makes 3 to 4 loaves.

Flour Tortillas
CHRISTINE NEILSON

Homemade tortillas are quick and easy and so good. Children love them hot and buttered.

- 3 cups flour
- 1½ teaspoons baking powder
- 1 teaspoon salt
- 1½ cups warm water
- 1 tablespoon shortening or oil

Stir flour, baking powder, and salt in a large mixing bowl. Add water a little at a time, mixing with dry ingredients until dough is very soft but not sticky. If after kneading a few minutes it feels too wet, add a little flour. Add oil or shortening and knead until dough is soft and satin-like. Cover and let rest while griddle heats over medium-high heat.

Make 12 dough balls a little larger than a golf ball. Use a heavy, weighted rolling pin for easier rolling. Tortillas should be about 5 to 6 inches round. Roll tortilla very thin, less than ⅛-inch thick. Spray a griddle or skillet with cooking spray or grease with oil. Cook tortillas until bubbles come through to top. Turn tortilla over and cook until done.

Makes 12 tortillas.

COMPARE PRICES PER UNIT (OUNCE AND POUND) OF VARIOUS BRANDS AS YOU GROCERY SHOP.

Tennessee-Style Corn Bread
JULIE ANNE CLAYTON

Corn bread with a little zip.

2 (8½-ounce) packages Jiffy® corn muffin mix
2 eggs
⅔ cup milk
1 cup grated jalapeño cheese (or less spicy cheese, if preferred)
1 (8½-ounce) can cream-style corn

Heat oven to 400° F.

Combine muffin mixes, eggs, and milk in a medium bowl. Stir until just blended. Spread half the batter in a sprayed or greased 7x11-inch baking pan. Sprinkle cheese over batter. Mix corn into remaining batter. Pour on top of cheese. Bake 30 to 35 minutes, until corn bread is browned and set in the center.

Serves 6 to 8.

HOLD FAMILY REUNIONS, WHETHER FOR AN AFTERNOON OR A WEEKEND, TO GATHER EXTENDED FAMILY MEMBERS. MAKE IT POTLUCK SO THAT PREPARING FOOD FOR A CROWD IS EASY. ENCOURAGE MINGLING THROUGH GAMES, SPORTS, CONVERSATION, SHARING MEMORIES OF ANCESTORS, AND SERVICE PROJECTS. HAVE MIXED SEATING AT DINNER TABLES (SO THAT INDIVIDUAL FAMILIES DO NOT ALL BUNCH TOGETHER).

BREADS

Banana Nut Bread or Muffins
CAROL PARRIS

Muffins are much quicker to make than rolls. Serve a basket of muffins with dinner, and if you're lucky, you may have a few left over for breakfast.

 1 cup sugar
 ½ cup butter or margarine
 2 eggs
 2 cups flour
 1 teaspoon baking soda
 ½ teaspoon salt
 3 bananas, mashed
 1 teaspoon vanilla
 ½ cup chopped nuts

Heat oven to 350° F.

Cream sugar and butter. Add eggs and beat well. Sift or mix flour, baking soda, and salt. Add bananas, vanilla, and nuts.

For muffins, spray or grease muffin cups or use cupcake papers in muffin pans. Fill muffin cups ⅔ full. Bake 20 to 25 minutes.

For bread, put batter in a paper-lined or well-greased and floured 5x9-inch loaf pan or two 4½x8½-inch pans. Bake 1 hour.

Makes 18 muffins or 1 large or 2 small loaves.

As a family, prepare a meal to share—with a neighbor, someone who is ill, or anyone who would benefit from a thoughtful gesture.

Blueberry Muffins
KASSIE WARNER

Buy fresh blueberries when they're at a good price, then put them in your freezer. You'll have large, luscious berries to add to many a recipe—salads, desserts, or these better-than-bakery muffins.

½ cup butter or margarine, softened
1 cup sugar
2 eggs
¾ cup sour cream
1 teaspoon vanilla
1⅓ cups flour
½ teaspoon salt
2 teaspoons baking powder
1 to 1½ cups frozen blueberries (leave frozen)

Heat oven to 375° F.

Cream butter and sugar in a large bowl. Add eggs, sour cream, and vanilla. Mix well. Add flour, salt, and baking powder. Stir only until mixed. Gently fold in blueberries. Spray or grease muffin cups or use cupcake papers in muffin pans. Fill muffin cups ⅔ full.

Topping

¼ cup butter or margarine, softened
3 to 4 tablespoons flour
3 tablespoons brown sugar
3 tablespoons sugar
¼ cup chopped pecans

Mix butter, flour, brown sugar, sugar, and pecans in a small bowl. Sprinkle over muffin batter. Bake 30 minutes.

Makes 12 muffins.

Bran Muffins ★

CHRISTINE NEILSON

This batter will keep in the refrigerator for 6 weeks. You can have freshly made muffins in just minutes.

- 2 cups boiling water
- 2 cups 100% bran cereal
- 1 cup plus 2 tablespoons shortening
- 2 cups sugar
- 4 eggs
- 1 quart buttermilk
- 4 cups All-Bran® cereal
- 5 cups flour
- 1 teaspoon salt
- 5 teaspoons baking soda
- 1 (15-ounce) package raisins

Heat oven to 400° F.

Pour boiling water over 100% bran cereal in a medium bowl. Let stand while creaming together shortening and sugar in a very large bowl. Add eggs, buttermilk, and both bran cereals. Mix together flour, salt, and baking soda. Add dry ingredients to bran mixture. Fold in raisins.

Spray or grease muffin cups or use cupcake papers in muffin pans. Fill muffin cups ⅔ full. Bake 15 to 18 minutes.

Put remainder of muffin mix in a large, covered container and keep in refrigerator. It may be stored up to 6 weeks. Nuts or other dried fruits, such as cranberries, may also be added.

Makes 6 to 7 dozen muffins.

TO GET TO KNOW EACH OTHER BETTER, PLAY FAMILY TRIVIA GAMES AT THE DINNER TABLE. PREPARE QUESTIONS AHEAD OF TIME OR MAKE THEM UP AS YOU GO. ASK QUESTIONS LIKE: HOW LONG HAVE MOM AND DAD BEEN MARRIED? WHAT IS (FILL IN THE BLANK)'S FAVORITE DESSERT? WHERE WOULD (FILL IN THE BLANK) LIKE TO GO ON A DREAM VACATION?

Corn Muffins
JANET PETERSON

Cake flour, which is finer than all-purpose flour, makes these muffins lighter.

½ cup butter or margarine, melted
1 egg
¼ cup oil
1 cup milk
1 cup cake flour or all-purpose flour
¾ cup cornmeal
1 tablespoon baking powder
¾ teaspoon salt
2 tablespoons sugar

Heat oven to 400° F.

In a medium bowl, mix together butter, egg, oil, and milk. In a large bowl, mix together flour, cornmeal, baking powder, salt, and sugar. Blend the butter mixture into the flour mixture, stirring until just moistened. Spray or grease muffin cups or use cupcake papers in muffin pans. Fill muffin cups ⅔ full with batter. Bake 15 to 18 minutes, until golden brown.

Makes 1 dozen muffins.

Of course there are also times when a meal out is the most fun, most delicious, and easiest thing to do, and times when it would be absurd not to order a pizza. Home and health are at risk only when home cooking and eating are not routine and ordinary pleasures in life. —CHERYL MENDELSON

Pumpkin Muffins
SANDY HUISH

Delicious with any meal.

- ½ teaspoon cloves
- ½ teaspoon nutmeg
- ½ teaspoon cinnamon
- 1½ cups sugar
- ¾ teaspoon salt
- 1 teaspoon baking soda
- 1½ cups flour
- ½ cup oil
- 2 eggs
- 1 cup canned pumpkin
- ⅓ cup water
- Raisins (optional)
- Nuts (optional)

Heat oven to 350° F.

In a large bowl, mix together cloves, nutmeg, cinnamon, sugar, salt, baking soda, and flour. Add oil, eggs, pumpkin, and water. Stir until moistened. Add raisins and nuts, if desired. Spray or grease muffin cups or use cupcake papers in muffin pans. Fill muffin cups ⅔ full with batter. Bake 20 minutes.

Makes 18 muffins.

SPECIAL OCCASIONS ARE WONDERFUL OPPORTUNITIES TO BRING FAMILIES TOGETHER. BLESSINGS OF NEW BABIES, BAPTISMS, MISSIONARY FAREWELLS AND HOMECOMINGS, ENGAGEMENTS, WEDDINGS, OR GRADUATIONS ARE EVENTS OF CELEBRATION AND CAN QUITE EASILY BE ACCOMPANIED BY FOOD.

BEEF

Beef has been a staple of the American dinner table for ages. In the past few years, however, it has fallen out of favor with many. But that need not be the case. Beef is a marvelous meat! It is high in protein, rich in taste, and offers great versatility in preparation. Selecting cuts with lower percentages of fat, mixing ground beef with ground turkey, and using low-fat ingredients can reduce calories and fat grams and bring beef back to your dinner table.

Beef Stroganoff/*103*

Beef Taco Bake/*104*

Scout Dinners/*105*

Classic Meatloaf/*106*

Beans and Beef/*107*

Sloppy Joes/*108*

Beef Noodle Casserole/*109*

Easy Meatballs/*110*

Pot Roast in Foil/*111*

Pot Roast with Vegetables/*112*

Cola Roast/*114*

Dilled Pot Roast/*115*

Fajita Stir-Fry/*116*

Chop Suey/*117*

Salsa Beef/*118*

Stir-Fry Steak Sandwiches/*119*

Roast Beef Sandwiches/*120*

Beef Stroganoff
KAYLENE REDD

Rich, beefy taste—without sour cream or mushroom soup.

- 6 slices bacon
- 2 pounds stew meat
- ½ teaspoon garlic powder
- 1 (4-ounce) can sliced mushrooms
- 2 (10½-ounce) cans beef consommé
- 1 teaspoon thyme
- 1 tablespoon parsley
- Dash of pepper
- 1 bay leaf
- ½ green pepper, chopped (optional)
- ⅓ cup butter or margarine, melted
- ⅓ cup flour
- 3 to 4 cups cooked rice

Use less expensive cuts of beef, such as round steak or chuck blade roast. Cook them for several hours with low, moist heat or marinate to tenderize the meat.

In a slow cooker, large skillet, or Dutch oven, brown bacon slices. Crumble and set aside. Brown stew meat in bacon drippings. Add garlic powder, mushrooms, consommé, thyme, parsley, pepper, bay leaf, and green pepper, if desired. Simmer 2 to 3 hours.

Just before serving, mix melted butter and flour in a small bowl until smooth. Remove bay leaf from beef sauce and add flour-butter mixture. Cook until slightly thickened. Add bacon pieces. Serve over rice.

Serves 6.

Beef Taco Bake ★
ERIN REID

Your family will love this simple dish.

- 1 pound ground beef
- 1 (10¾-ounce) can tomato soup
- 1 (16-ounce) jar medium or mild salsa
- ½ cup milk
- 6 to 8 flour or corn tortillas, cut into 1-inch pieces
- 1 cup grated cheddar cheese

Heat oven to 400° F.

In a large skillet, brown ground beef. Drain grease. Add soup, salsa, milk, tortillas, and half the cheese. Put mixture into a 9-inch square or 7x11-inch baking dish. Bake, covered, 30 minutes. Sprinkle with remaining cheese.

Serves 4.

SUNDAY DINNER CONVERSATION TOPICS FOR MANY FAMILIES OFTEN BEGIN WITH "WHAT DID YOU LEARN IN PRIMARY, SUNDAY SCHOOL, RELIEF SOCIETY, OR PRIESTHOOD QUORUM TODAY?" TRY ELABORATING ON THIS BY QUIZZING EACH OTHER ON WHAT THE SPEAKERS IN SACRAMENT MEETING SAID. CHILDREN CAN ASK QUESTIONS OF THEIR PARENTS, TOO. SUCH QUESTIONS CAN LEAD TO GOOD GOSPEL DISCUSSIONS AROUND THE DINNER TABLE.

Scout Dinners ★ ⏺

JANET PETERSON

You'll think you're on a Scout campout. Boneless, skinless chicken breasts can be used in place of beef patties. Add cream of chicken soup, choice of vegetables, and/or stuffing mix.

- 1½ to 2 pounds ground beef
- 1 (0.9-ounce) envelope onion soup mix or 1 medium onion, sliced
- 4 to 5 carrots, sliced
- 4 to 5 medium potatoes, peeled and sliced
- Salt and pepper to taste

Optional additions

- Cream of mushroom or golden mushroom soup
- Diced green pepper
- Frozen corn
- Frozen peas
- Sliced mushrooms
- Sliced zucchini

Heat oven to 375° F.

Mix ground beef with onion soup and form into 6 patties. Place each patty on an 18-inch-square piece of heavy-duty aluminum foil. Put carrots, potatoes, and onion (if not using soup) and other desired ingredients on top of patties. Secure foil by bringing sides up and folding over several times. Fold over the ends. Place packets on a cookie sheet and bake 45 to 50 minutes, until meat is cooked and vegetables are tender. Open packets carefully to let steam escape.

Serves 6.

BUILD TRADITIONS AROUND SOME OF THE LESS-CELEBRATED HOLIDAYS. (ANY OCCASION CAN BECOME A TRADITION OR A CELEBRATION.) FOR EXAMPLE, HAVE AN IRISH DINNER ON ST. PATRICK'S DAY. EAT CORNED BEEF, BOILED CABBAGE, AND IRISH SODA BREAD; OR, FOR A TWIST, EAT ONLY ITEMS THAT ARE GREEN.

Classic Meatloaf ★
JANET PETERSON

Pure comfort food, reminiscent of the past.

3 pieces bread
½ cup milk
1 egg, beaten
¼ to ½ cup chopped onion
¼ cup chopped celery
2 teaspoons Worcestershire sauce
1 teaspoon salt
½ teaspoon poultry seasoning
1½ pounds ground beef
⅓ cup brown sugar
⅓ cup catsup
1 teaspoon dry mustard

Heat oven to 350° F.

Tear bread into pieces and put in mixing bowl. Add milk, egg, onion, celery, Worcestershire sauce, salt, and poultry seasoning. Stir until well mixed. Add ground beef and mix. Put meat mixture into a 5x9-inch loaf pan or a 2-quart casserole dish. In a small bowl, mix brown sugar, catsup, and mustard. Spread over meat. Bake, uncovered, 1 hour.

Serves 6.

Save stale bread by placing it in a brown paper bag. Use for bread puddings and dressings or put in a food processor or blender to make dry bread crumbs.

Beans and Beef ★ 🥣
JANET PETERSON

"This has been our family's favorite ground beef dish for at least 20 years."

- 1½ pounds ground beef
- 1 medium onion, chopped
- 1 teaspoon mustard
- ½ teaspoon salt
- ¼ teaspoon pepper
- ½ cup catsup
- 1 tablespoon Worcestershire sauce
- 1 (31-ounce) can pork and beans

Brown ground beef with onion in a large skillet. Add mustard, salt, pepper, catsup, Worcestershire sauce, and beans. Mix, taking care not to mash the beans. Cook over low heat 20 to 25 minutes.

Serves 6 to 8.

HAVE PICNICS. EATING TOGETHER IN A MORE CASUAL SETTING IS A LOT OF FUN AND CREATES MEMORIES, WHETHER IT'S AT THE BEACH, IN THE CANYON, IN THE BACKYARD, OR IN THE FAMILY ROOM BY THE FIREPLACE IN THE WINTER.

Sloppy Joes ★ ⬇
PAT MENLOVE

Leftover vegetables, especially grated carrots, may be added to Sloppy Joes.

- 1 pound ground beef
- ½ teaspoon minced garlic
- 1 tablespoon dried onion flakes
- ½ cup catsup
- 2 tablespoons mustard
- 1 (10¾-ounce) can chicken gumbo soup
- 1 (8-ounce) can tomato sauce
- Salt and pepper to taste
- Hamburger buns or sandwich rolls

In a medium skillet, brown ground beef with garlic and onion flakes. Add catsup, mustard, soup, and tomato sauce. Stir to blend. If sauce is too thick, add water. Simmer, covered, for 30 minutes. Season with salt and pepper to taste. Serve on buns or rolls.

Serves 4 to 6.

GRIND LEFTOVER ROAST BEEF AND MIX WITH UNCOOKED GROUND BEEF TO EXTEND AND IMPROVE MEAT LOAF OR SLOPPY JOES.

Beef Noodle Casserole
PAT MENLOVE

Delicious! Serve with tossed green salad, French bread or breadsticks, and bottled peaches or pears.

- 1 pound ground beef
- 2 (8-ounce) cans tomato sauce
- ½ to 1 teaspoon garlic salt
- Freshly ground black pepper
- 1 (8- or 12-ounce) package egg noodles, cooked according to package directions and drained
- 1 (8-ounce) carton sour cream
- 2 to 3 green onions, chopped
- Sliced mushrooms (optional)
- ½ to 1 cup grated cheddar cheese

Heat oven to 350° F.

Brown ground beef in a large skillet. Add tomato sauce, garlic salt, and pepper. In a large saucepan or pot, cook noodles *al dente*. Drain and place in an ungreased 3-quart casserole dish.

Mix sour cream, onions (including most of the green tops), mushrooms (if desired), and a shake or two of pepper. Stir into noodles. Top with meat mixture. Sprinkle cheese over top. Bake, uncovered, 20 minutes, or until cheese is bubbly.

Serves 6.

MAKE DOUBLE AMOUNTS OF RECIPES; STORE IN REFRIGERATOR OR FREEZER TO REHEAT FOR A QUICK MEAL.

Easy Meatballs ★
KAYLENE REDD

These meatballs can also be cooked in a slow cooker.

- 1 (12-ounce) bottle chili sauce
- 1 (16-ounce) can jellied cranberry sauce
- 2 tablespoons lemon juice
- 1 tablespoon brown sugar
- 1 (24-ounce) bag precooked, seasoned Italian frozen meatballs
- Cooked rice, noodles, or potatoes

Heat oven to 300° F.

Mix chili sauce, cranberry sauce, lemon juice, and brown sugar in a small bowl. Pour sauce over frozen meatballs in a baking pan. Bake, uncovered, 1½ hours. Serve with rice, noodles, or potatoes.

Serves 4 to 6.

INSTEAD OF COOKING MEATBALLS IN A SKILLET ON TOP OF THE STOVE, THUS NECESSITATING THAT YOU TURN THEM ONE AT A TIME, PLACE THEM ON A GREASED BROILER PAN AND BAKE AT 350° F. FOR 20 TO 25 MINUTES. RATHER THAN ROLLING MEATBALLS, JUST CUT GROUND BEEF INTO 1-INCH CUBES.

Pot Roast in Foil ★
JUDITH NIELSON

Great Sunday pot roast recipe—perfectly timed for three-hour-church. Add frozen peas when it comes out of the oven, and by the time the prayer is over, they will be cooked, too!

- 1 (3- to 4-pound) roast (cross-rib, blade, rump, tip, chuck, or eye of round)
- 1 (10¾-ounce) can cream of mushroom soup
- 1 (0.9-ounce) envelope onion soup mix
- 4 large potatoes, peeled and quartered
- 8 medium carrots, cut in halves
- 2 tablespoons water
- 1 to 1½ cups frozen peas

Heat oven to 300° F.

Place a piece of foil, 18x30 inches, in an ungreased 9x13-inch pan. Place roast on foil. Mix mushroom and onion soups together and spread over beef. Add carrots and potatoes. Sprinkle with water. Fold foil over and seal. Bake 3 hours. For the last few minutes of cooking, undo foil and add frozen peas.

Serves 6 to 10.

Too much fat or grease in a meat dish or soup can be remedied by placing a slightly toasted piece of bread on top of the dish. Discard the toast when it has soaked up the fat. Grease or fat can also be removed from a skillet or pan in which ground beef, sausage, or bacon is cooked by tilting the pan so the grease accumulates in one side, then soaking it up with paper towels or removing with a spoon or turkey baster. More grease can be removed by placing cooked meat on a paper towel-lined plate.

Pot Roast with Vegetables
PAT MENLOVE

Put the roast in the oven before your three-hour Church block. Add the veggies when you get home and have dinner 1 hour later.

1 (3- to 4-pound or more) pot roast
2 to 3 tablespoons oil
2 to 3 garlic cloves, sliced, or 1 to 2 teaspoons garlic salt
Salt and pepper to taste
1 medium onion, sliced
½ green pepper, sliced
1 cup water
Potatoes, peeled and quartered
Sliced carrots
Celery stalks, quartered
Frozen peas
Sliced mushrooms
Dried or minced fresh parsley

FIX LUMPY GRAVY BY WHISKING WHILE IT IS COOKING OR REMOVING FROM HEAT AND POURING IT THROUGH A STRAINER.

Heat oven to 300° F.

In a big pot, sear (brown on high heat) roast in oil on all sides until brown and crusty. Remove from heat.

Put garlic cloves into seams of the meat (for best flavor) or shake on garlic salt. Sprinkle roast with salt and pepper. Place onion and green pepper on top surface of meat. Add a cup or so of water and cover with lid. Roast in oven 4 to 5 hours. Or simmer on stovetop and check frequently to make sure roast is in liquid and not dried out.

An hour before serving time, add potatoes, carrots, and celery all around roast. Add another cup or so of water. Do not cover roast with water—add just enough to keep 1 or 2 inches of liquid in the pot. Sprinkle vegetables with salt and pepper. Put lid back on and cook until vegetables are tender. Frozen peas and sliced mushrooms can be added 15 minutes before serving or cooked separately.

Remove vegetables from pot and put in a serving bowl. Cover with aluminum foil to keep moist. Put roast on a platter and cover to keep moist.

Gravy

½ cup flour
1½ to 2 cups cold water
Meat drippings
Salt and pepper to taste
Garlic to taste

Put flour and cold water in a blender. Blend on high speed until smooth. Stir up meat drippings with a metal or wooden spoon. It is fine to leave in any leftover onion or vegetable pieces. If there is no water in the pot, add a cup or so of water and stir up meat drippings. If there is lots of water (pot is half full), let liquid boil down to one quarter full. Put pot on stove on medium heat. Heat drippings until they are hot and bubbly, then stir in thickening and keep stirring to avoid lumps. If gravy is too thick, add a little cold water. Gravy thickens as it cools. Add salt, pepper, and garlic to taste.

Serves 6 to 10

USE A PRESSURE COOKER TO REDUCE THE COOKING TIME OF MEATS AND STEWS BY TWO-THIRDS.

Cola Roast ★ ⌣
JUNE HERNANDEZ

The cola sauce is also suitable for pork chops—brown, then bake 45 minutes.

1 (4- to 5-pound) beef roast or brisket
1 (12-ounce) bottle chili sauce
1 (0.9-ounce) envelope onion soup mix
1 (12-ounce) can cola drink (not diet)

Heat oven to 325° F.

Place roast or brisket in a roasting pan. Combine chili sauce, soup mix, and cola. Pour over roast or brisket. Bake 3 to 4 hours or put in a slow cooker and cook on medium-low heat 5 to 6 hours or more.

Serves 8 to 10.

SLICE LEFTOVER ROAST BEEF AND REHEAT WITH LEFTOVER GRAVY. SERVE OVER POTATOES, RICE, OR BREAD FOR A HOT ROAST BEEF SANDWICH.

Dilled Pot Roast ★
LINDA VANCE

Dill gives beef a new taste.

- 1 (3- to 3½-pound) pot roast
- 1 teaspoon salt
- ¼ teaspoon pepper
- 1 teaspoon dried dill weed or 3 to 4 sprigs fresh dill weed
- ¼ cup water
- 1 tablespoon vinegar
- 2 tablespoons flour
- 1 cup sour cream
- Cooked rice or noodles

Salt and pepper roast. Place in a slow cooker and sprinkle with dill weed. Add water and vinegar. Cook on low 5 to 6 hours. Remove from pot; turn control to high.

Dissolve flour in a small amount of cold water and stir into meat drippings. Cook on high about 10 minutes, or until slightly thick. Stir in sour cream. Serve meat with sauce over cooked rice or noodles.

Serves 6 to 8.

MAKE SUNDAY DINNER SPECIAL BY SERVING IT IN THE DINING ROOM WITH A PRETTY TABLECLOTH AND YOUR BEST DISHES AND SILVERWARE.

Fajita Stir-Fry
DEMETRIA DAVIS

"I am from Arizona and am one-fourth Mexican and Indian. You can cut out the cumin if you prefer a more American taste."

- 1 pound lean steak (or chicken), cut into thin strips
- 4 tablespoons oil
- 2 cloves garlic, minced
- 1 large onion, thinly sliced
- 1 to 2 jalapeño chilies, stemmed, seeded, and minced or 2 to 4 tablespoons canned diced green chilies
- 1 large red bell pepper, cut into thin slices
- 1 to 2 teaspoons cumin
- 3 tablespoons lime juice
- 1 teaspoon cornstarch
- 2 medium tomatoes, diced
- Lime wedges
- Flour tortillas, warmed
- Sour cream
- 1 large avocado, diced
- Salt and pepper

USING A FOOD PROCESSOR CAN SAVE CONSIDERABLE TIME. USE IT TO CHOP ONIONS; SLICE OR SHRED CARROTS, CABBAGE, CELERY, GREEN PEPPERS, CHEESE; OR TO MAKE BREAD CRUMBS.

Brown steak (or chicken) in oil. Add garlic, onion, chilies, and bell pepper. Stir-fry until crisp-tender (1 to 2 minutes). Mix together cumin, lime juice, and cornstarch in a small bowl. Add to pan; then add tomatoes. Put steak mixture in a serving dish. Garnish with lime wedges. Spoon steak mixture into tortillas. Add sour cream, avocado, squeeze of lime juice, and salt and pepper to taste. Roll up and eat with your hands.

Serves 4 to 6.

Chop Suey

LINDA LOSCHER

Tastes best if made the day before so the flavors can blend.

- 2 pounds round steak or stew meat, cut in small pieces
- 1 to 2 tablespoons oil
- 4 cups water
- 2 onions, chopped
- 4 cups diced or sliced celery
- 5 tablespoons soy sauce
- ¼ cup molasses
- 2 beef bouillon cubes or 2 teaspoons beef bouillon granules
- 2 (14-ounce) cans chop suey vegetables
- 1 (14-ounce) can bean sprouts
- 1 (4-ounce) can mushrooms (optional)
- 3 to 4 tablespoons cornstarch
- ½ cup water
- 6 cups cooked rice
- Chow mein noodles

CUBE LEFTOVER ROAST BEEF FOR USE IN SOUPS AND STEWS.

Brown steak or stew meat in oil. Add 4 cups water and simmer 20 minutes on medium heat. Add onions, celery, and soy sauce and simmer on low heat about 30 minutes, until meat is tender. Add molasses, bouillon, vegetables, sprouts, and mushrooms, if desired. Bring to a boil. Mix cornstarch in ½ cup water. Add to chop suey and continue to cook until thickened. Serve over rice and top with chow mein noodles. Have soy sauce on table so individuals can use as desired.

Serves 8 to 10.

Salsa Beef ★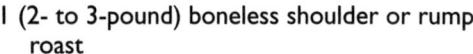
JANET PETERSON

Salsa and cilantro add excitement to roast beef.

- 1 (2- to 3-pound) boneless shoulder or rump roast
- 1 tablespoon oil
- 1 cup medium salsa
- 2 tablespoons brown sugar
- 1 tablespoon soy sauce
- 1 teaspoon minced garlic
- 3 tablespoons chopped cilantro
- 1 tablespoon lime juice
- 3 cups cooked rice

GRIND LEFTOVER ROAST BEEF AND MIX WITH MAYONNAISE, MUSTARD, AND PICKLE RELISH FOR SANDWICHES.

Trim fat from roast and cut into 2-inch cubes. Heat oil in a large covered pot or Dutch oven and brown meat. Pour off drippings. Add salsa, brown sugar, soy sauce, and garlic. Bring to a boil, then reduce heat to low. Cover and simmer 1 hour or longer. Remove lid and continue cooking an additional 30 minutes. Remove beef from heat and add cilantro and lime juice. Stir. Serve over cooked rice.

Serves 4 to 6.

Stir-Fry Steak Sandwiches
JANET PETERSON

Partially frozen steak can easily be cut into thin strips.

- 1 pound sirloin steak
- 2 tablespoons oil
- 1 teaspoon instant beef bouillon granules
- ¼ teaspoon dry mustard
- ⅛ teaspoon ginger
- ⅛ teaspoon pepper
- 1 small onion, sliced
- ½ green pepper, chopped
- 1 medium tomato, chopped
- Hard rolls

Cut steak in very thin strips. Stir-fry steak in hot oil in a large skillet until browned.

Remove steak from skillet to medium bowl. Combine bouillon, mustard, ginger, and pepper in a small bowl. Sprinkle over steak. Stir-fry onion and green pepper in skillet, about 2 minutes. Add to steak mixture. Stir-fry tomato, about 2 minutes. Return steak mixture to skillet to heat through. Serve on hard rolls.

Serves 4 to 6.

Soups, stews, gravies, batters, or sauces that are too thin can be remedied by adding a tablespoon or two of cornstarch or flour mixed with enough water to make a smooth paste and cooking until desired consistency is reached.

Roast Beef Sandwiches ★ ⌣
DIANE WILSON

Fully flavored and super-tender hot beef sandwiches.

1 (3- to 4-pound) rump roast
1 (1¼-ounce) package sloppy joe mix
1 (0.87-ounce) package brown gravy mix
2 cups water
Buns or kaiser rolls
Sliced cheese (optional)

Heat oven to 425° F.

Put roast in a Dutch oven or roasting pan. Blend sloppy joe mix, gravy mix, and water. Pour over roast and cover. Bake at 425° F. for 15 minutes. Turn oven down to 350° F. and bake 4 to 5 hours. Take roast out of oven and shred with 2 forks. Serve on buns. Add sliced cheese, if desired.

Serves 8 to 10.

KEEP A JAR OF AN EQUAL MIXTURE OF FLOUR AND CORNSTARCH. PLACE THREE OR FOUR TABLESPOONS OF THIS MIXTURE IN ANOTHER JAR AND ADD SOME WATER. SHAKE WELL TO FORM A SMOOTH PASTE THAT WILL THICKEN GRAVY.

CHICKEN

Chicken is probably the most versatile food around. It is inexpensive, low in fat, and can be used in a multitude of ways—in soups, salads, pastas, and main dishes; served hot or cold; grilled, broiled, baked, stewed, roasted, boiled, microwaved, fried, or braised.

Chicken Provence/*123*

Mandarin Chicken/*124*

Mexican Fiesta Biscuit Bake/*125*

Swiss Chicken/*126*

Cranberry Chicken/*127*

Chicken Enchiladas/*128*

Salsa Chicken Enchiladas/*129*

Haystacks/*130*

Chicken Dumplings/*131*

Poppy Seed Chicken/*132*

Peanut Chicken/*133*

Chicken Waikiki/*134*

Parmesan Chicken/*135*

Crispy Herb Chicken/*136*

Chicken Pot Pies/*137*

Tex-Mex Chicken and Rice Casserole/*138*

Imperial Baked Chicken/*139*

Italian-Seasoned Chicken with Noodles/*140*

Lemon Chicken/*141*

Ranch Chicken/*142*

Orange Chicken/*143*

Barbecue Chicken Breasts/*144*

Chicken Tacos/*145*

Quick Chicken a la King/*146*

Chicken Cashew Stir-Fry/*147*

Chicken Provence

ANNA PETERSON

French cuisine simplified.

- 1 (3- to 4-pound) whole chicken
- 1 clove garlic
- 2 sprigs fresh rosemary
- 1 sprig fresh sage
- 1 sprig fresh thyme
- Juice of 1 lemon
- Olive oil
- ¼ teaspoon basil
- ¼ teaspoon rosemary
- ¼ teaspoon savory
- ¼ teaspoon thyme
- ¼ teaspoon marjoram
- 20 small red potatoes, washed

Heat oven to 450° F.

Wash and dry chicken and put in a roasting pan. Put garlic, sprigs of rosemary, sage, and thyme inside chicken cavity. Squeeze lemon juice over outside of chicken. Brush chicken with olive oil. Mix basil, rosemary, savory, thyme, and marjoram in a small dish. Sprinkle over chicken. Bake 30 minutes. Add potatoes. Bake another 30 minutes.

Serves 6.

Fashions and foods change along with the faces. Mother's pot roast morphs into my lighter, healthier tenderloin, her Southern fried chicken into my low-fat boneless chicken breasts. But other things don't change with the generations. For instance, like my mother and grandmother, I still come to the table to connect with the people I love. —DORIS CHRISTOPHER

Mandarin Chicken ★
SUSAN MORGAN

Chicken is so versatile. Here is just one of the myriad ways to prepare it.

¼ cup soy sauce
¼ cup honey
¼ cup lemon juice
½ cup catsup
4 boneless, skinless chicken breasts
2 to 3 cups cooked rice

Heat oven to 350° F.

In a small bowl, mix soy sauce, honey, lemon juice, and catsup. Place chicken breasts in an 8-inch square glass pan or similar dish. Pour sauce over chicken breasts. Cover and marinate 24 hours in refrigerator. Bake, covered, 45 minutes and an additional 10 to 15 minutes, uncovered. Serve with rice. May also be grilled on medium heat 20 to 25 minutes.

Serves 4.

ESTABLISH THE TRADITION OF READING THE BOOK OF MORMON TOGETHER AT DINNERTIME BY KEEPING A COPY OF THE BOOK OF MORMON ON THE KITCHEN TABLE. TO START OUT WITH, HAVE EACH PERSON (CHILDREN INCLUDED) READ ONLY ONE VERSE EACH EVENING; GRADUALLY ADD MORE VERSES OR TAKE TIME FOR FURTHER DISCUSSION AS THE TRADITION BECOMES MORE PERMANENT.

Mexican Fiesta Biscuit Bake ★

REBECCA ANDERSON

"When I got this recipe, we ate it weekly for the next six months, it was so good. Great for those missionary dinners."

- 1 (1 pound 1.3-ounce) can Pillsbury® Grand Biscuits, cut into quarters
- 1 (16-ounce) jar thick and chunky salsa
- 12 ounces Monterey Jack cheese, grated
- ½ cup chopped green pepper
- ½ cup chopped onion
- 2 tablespoons chopped cilantro (or amount to taste)
- 1 to 2 cloves garlic, minced
- 4 chicken breasts, cooked and diced
- Sour cream for topping

Heat oven to 375° F.

Place quartered biscuits in a large bowl. Add salsa, cheese, green pepper, onion, cilantro, garlic, and chicken. Mix. Place mixture in a greased 8-inch square pan. Bake, uncovered, 35 to 40 minutes. Serve with a dollop of sour cream.

Serves 5 to 6.

MAKE SURE DINNERTIME BELONGS ONLY TO YOU. LET THE ANSWERING MACHINE RESPOND TO PHONE CALLS, TURN OFF THE TELEVISION, AND PUT AWAY THE NEWSPAPER.

Swiss Chicken ★
CINDY ANDERSON

HOW TO COOK CHICKEN

- **HOW TO BOIL CHICKEN PIECES OR BREASTS**

PUT CUT CHICKEN PIECES IN A LARGE SAUCEPAN OR POT. COVER WITH SEVERAL INCHES OF WATER. ADD 1 TEASPOON OR SO OF SALT. BRING WATER TO A BOIL. REDUCE HEAT AND SIMMER ABOUT 20 MINUTES. OTHER SEASONINGS MAY BE ADDED, SUCH AS PEPPER, GARLIC, BAY LEAF, ONION, CELERY, OR POULTRY SEASONING.

- **HOW TO BROIL CHICKEN PIECES OR BREASTS**

BRUSH CHICKEN WITH OLIVE OIL, SALT, AND PEPPER OR SPRINKLE WITH OTHER SEASONINGS. PUT CHICKEN PIECES ON A BROILER PAN AND PLACE PAN 4 TO 5 INCHES FROM BROILING UNIT. BROIL ABOUT 20 MINUTES, TURNING ONCE, UNTIL CHICKEN IS LIGHTLY BROWNED AND COOKED THROUGH.

- **HOW TO FRY CHICKEN PIECES OR BREASTS**

FRIED CHICKEN USUALLY HAS A COATING OF BREAD CRUMBS OR FLOUR AND SEASONINGS. PRIOR TO FRYING CHICKEN, DIP IN MILK OR A BEATEN EGG AND PUT PIECES IN A PLASTIC OR PAPER BAG FILLED WITH BREAD CRUMBS OR FLOUR AND DESIRED SEASONINGS. SHAKE TO COAT CHICKEN PIECES. HEAT A SMALL AMOUNT OF OIL IN A LARGE SKILLET. COOK, UNCOVERED, OVER MEDIUM HEAT 15 MINUTES, TURNING TO

(Continued on pg. 127)

This can also be cooked outdoors in a Dutch oven.

8 boneless, skinless chicken breasts
Salt and pepper
6 ounces Swiss or Monterey Jack cheese, grated
2 (10¾-ounce) cans cream of mushroom soup
1 pint sour cream
⅓ cup butter or margarine
3 cups Pepperidge Farm® seasoned stuffing

Heat oven to 325° F.

Sprinkle chicken on both sides with salt and pepper. Arrange chicken in a 9x13-inch baking dish or 3-quart casserole dish. Sprinkle cheese over chicken. Combine soup and sour cream and pour over chicken. Melt butter and mix with stuffing. Spread over the top of the cream mixture. Bake, covered, 1½ hours.

Serves 8.

CHICKEN

Cranberry Chicken ★ ⊽
MARIANNE LLOYD

Whenever you serve this chicken, people will ask you for the recipe and will be amazed at how easy it is.

- 1 (16-ounce) can whole berry cranberry sauce
- 1 (8-ounce) bottle French dressing
- 1 (0.9-ounce) envelope onion soup mix
- 8 boneless, skinless chicken breasts (or number desired)

Heat oven to 350° F.

Combine cranberry sauce, dressing, and soup mix. Put chicken breasts in a sprayed or greased 3-quart casserole dish or 9x13-inch baking dish. Pour mixture over chicken breasts. Bake, uncovered, 45 to 60 minutes.

Serves 8.

(Continued from pg. 126)

BROWN PIECES ON BOTH SIDES. REDUCE HEAT AND COVER SKILLET. COOK 25 MINUTES. UNCOVER SKILLET AND COOK AN ADDITIONAL 5 TO 10 MINUTES, UNCOVERED, TO CRISP THE OUTSIDE OF CHICKEN.

- **HOW TO GRILL CHICKEN PIECES OR BREASTS**

GRILLING CHICKEN OFTEN INVOLVES MARINATING CHICKEN PIECES FOR SEVERAL HOURS TO DEEPLY FLAVOR IT. AFTER MARINATING, PLACE CHICKEN PIECES ON AN OILED BARBECUE GRILL 4 TO 6 INCHES FROM THE COALS. GRILL CHICKEN ON MEDIUM HIGH HEAT 20 TO 25 MINUTES, TURNING SEVERAL TIMES AND BASTING WITH RESERVED MARINADE, IF BEING USED. COOK CHICKEN UNTIL MEAT IS NO LONGER PINK, BUT DO NOT OVERCOOK AS IT WILL BE DRY.

- **HOW TO MICROWAVE CHICKEN PIECES OR BREASTS**

PUT CHICKEN PIECES IN A MICROWAVE OR GLASS BAKING DISH. SPRINKLE WITH SALT AND PEPPER AND OTHER DESIRED SEASONINGS. COVER DISH WITH A LID, WAX PAPER, OR VENTED PLASTIC WRAP. MICROWAVE ON HIGH 10 TO 15 MINUTES, UNTIL CHICKEN IS COOKED THROUGH.

- **HOW TO ROAST CHICKEN**

ROASTING WORKS BEST WITH A WHOLE CHICKEN RATHER THAN PIECES. REMOVE THE NECK AND GIBLETS FROM THE CHICKEN CAVITY. RINSE THE CAVITY AND PAT DRY. SEASON THE OUTSIDE OF THE CHICKEN WITH SALT, PEPPER, AND DESIRED HERBS. PUT THE CHICKEN, BREAST SIDE UP, IN A ROASTING PAN. POTATOES, CARROTS, AND CELERY CAN BE PLACED AROUND THE CHICKEN IN THE ROASTING PAN, IF DESIRED. ROAST THE CHICKEN, UNCOVERED, 1 HOUR, UNTIL THE MEAT IS NO LONGER PINK AND THE JUICES RUN CLEAR. A MEAT THERMOMETER INSERTED IN THE BREAST BEFORE ROASTING SHOULD READ 170° TO 180° F. WHEN CHICKEN IS DONE.

Chicken Enchiladas
TERE WEIR

Nearly everyone enjoys these enchiladas.

- 2 (10¾-ounce) cans cream of chicken or mushroom soup or 1 can of each
- 1 pint sour cream
- 1 medium onion, chopped
- 1 (2¼-ounce) can chopped or sliced olives
- 1 (4-ounce) can diced green chilies
- 4 to 6 boneless, skinless chicken breasts, cooked and cubed
- 8 to 10 flour tortillas, cut into bite-size pieces
- ¾ pound cheese, grated (cheddar and Monterey Jack make a good combination)

Heat oven to 350° F.

Mix soups, sour cream, onion, olives, and green chilies in a large bowl. Add cooked chicken and stir. Place half of tortilla pieces in bottom of a greased 9x13-inch pan. Spread half of chicken mixture over tortillas. Mix cheeses if using more than one kind. Sprinkle half of cheese over mixture. Repeat layers. Bake, uncovered, 45 to 60 minutes.

Serves 8 to 10.

I know that young children will wander away from the table, and that family life is never smooth, and that life itself is full, . . . not only of charm and warmth and comfort but of sorrow and tears. But whether we are happy or sad, we must be fed. —LAURIE COLWIN

Salsa Chicken Enchiladas
LISA BOYCE

"This recipe came to me from my good friend Jen Thomas. It's delicious!"

- 4 boneless, skinless chicken breasts
- 3 cups chicken broth
- ⅓ cup flour
- 1 (12-ounce) jar thick and chunky salsa
- 1 (4-ounce) can diced green chilies (optional)
- 1 cup chopped onion
- 1 teaspoon sugar
- ½ to 1 teaspoon cumin
- ½ teaspoon basil
- ½ teaspoon oregano
- Dash of garlic salt or garlic powder
- Salt and pepper to taste
- 10 large flour tortillas
- ¾ cup sour cream
- 2 cups (or more) grated Monterey Jack cheese

Boil chicken breasts in salted water in a large saucepan until cooked. (Reserve broth or use canned broth.) Cool chicken and cut into small pieces.

In a large saucepan, cook chicken broth and flour over medium heat, stirring until broth thickens. Reduce heat and add salsa, chilies, onion, sugar, cumin, basil, oregano, garlic, salt, and pepper. Mix well and heat through.

Heat oven to 400° F.

Dip tortillas in the salsa mixture to soften. Place a small amount of chicken and cheese in each tortilla (don't overstuff). Roll tortilla up and place in a greased 9x13-inch baking dish. Add sour cream to salsa mixture and mix well. Pour over tortillas. Top with grated cheese. Bake 15 minutes.

Serves 4 to 6.

Haystacks
TERRI AVERY

A DIY (Do-It-Yourself) dinner.

4 to 6 bone-in or boneless, skinless chicken breasts
1 large onion, sliced
2 (10¾-ounce) cans cream of chicken soup
½ cup sour cream
¼ to ½ teaspoon garlic powder
Salt and pepper to taste
6 cups cooked rice

Any or all of the following:
Almonds
Celery, thinly sliced
Cheddar or Monterey Jack cheese, grated
Chinese noodles
Coconut
Green onions, chopped
Green pepper, chopped
Mushrooms
Olives, sliced
Peas
Pineapple chunks or tidbits, drained
Soy sauce
Tomatoes, diced

Boil chicken in salted water with onion in a large saucepan or pot. Remove onion. Dice chicken. Save broth.

In a large saucepan, mix soups, thinned with a little water or chicken broth. Add sour cream. Heat thoroughly, then add chicken and garlic powder. Add salt and pepper to taste.

To serve haystacks, put rice on individual plates, then chicken mixture, and add toppings as desired.

Serves 5 to 6.

To grate cheese more easily, place it in the freezer for 15 to 20 minutes before grating.

Chicken Dumplings
MARILYN LINN

Also known as Chicken Squares or Chicken Pillows, these are popular by any name.

- 2 (3-ounce) packages cream cheese, softened
- 2 tablespoons butter or margarine, softened
- 2 cups cooked and diced chicken breasts
- ¼ teaspoon salt
- ⅛ teaspoon pepper
- 1 to 2 tablespoons chopped green onions (optional)
- 1 celery stalk, thinly sliced (optional)
- ⅓ cup sliced mushrooms (optional)
- 2 (8-ounce) cans crescent rolls
- Crushed croutons or bread crumbs mixed with chopped nuts

Heat oven to 350° F.

Mix softened cream cheese with butter. Add chicken, salt, and pepper and mix. Add green onions, celery, and mushrooms, if desired. Place a heaping tablespoon of mixture in the center of a crescent roll. Fold corners toward middle and seal. (By pressing 2 crescent rolls together, a larger dumpling can be made.)

Place dumplings on a greased cookie sheet. Bake 20 to 25 minutes. Serve with heated gravy.

(For a fancier version, dip dumplings in melted butter, then roll in crushed croutons or bread crumbs mixed with chopped nuts.)

Gravy
- 1 (10 ¾-ounce) can cream of chicken soup
- ½ soup can of milk

Stir soup and milk together in a small saucepan. Heat thoroughly but do not boil.

Serves 6 to 8.

SOFTEN CREAM CHEESE QUICKLY IN THE MICROWAVE. UNWRAP CHEESE, PUT ON A MICROWAVE-SAFE PLATE, AND HEAT ONE MINUTE AT 50 PERCENT POWER.

Poppy Seed Chicken
PAULA HEATH

You'll never have leftovers of this chicken dish.

1 (10¾-ounce) can cream of chicken soup
1½ cups sour cream
2 cups cooked and cubed chicken
1 (8-ounce) box Ritz® crackers, crushed
½ cup butter or margarine, melted
1 tablespoon poppy seeds

Heat oven to 350° F.

Mix soup and sour cream. Add chicken. Mix crackers with butter and poppy seeds. Divide cracker mixture in half and mix one half with the chicken mixture. Spread half of the remaining cracker mixture in a greased 9x13-inch pan. Spread chicken mixture over cracker crumbs. Put remaining crackers on top. Bake, uncovered, 30 minutes.

Serves 8.

USE KITCHEN SHEARS FOR QUICKLY CUTTING MANY FOODS, SUCH AS MEATS AND BREADS, INTO CUBES.

Peanut Chicken
SHAUNA FRANDSEN

An authentic Japanese recipe.

2 eggs
½ teaspoon salt
3 to 4 tablespoons cornstarch
8 boneless, skinless chicken breasts
2 to 3 tablespoons oil
½ to ¾ cup chopped peanuts
3 to 4 green onions, finely chopped

Break eggs into a shallow bowl. Add salt and enough cornstarch to make a sticky dough (not too thick). Add chicken, coating breasts with cornstarch mixture. In a large skillet, cook chicken in hot oil until done in the middle and golden brown on both sides. Slice chicken pieces diagonally. Arrange on a platter and cover with sweet and sour sauce. Garnish with peanuts and green onions.

Sweet and Sour Sauce

1 clove garlic, minced
1 teaspoon oil
½ teaspoon salt
2 cups water
2 to 3 tablespoons cider vinegar
1 cup sugar
¾ cup catsup
1 to 2 tablespoons cornstarch
¼ cup cold water

Sauté garlic in oil. Add salt, 2 cups water, vinegar, sugar, and catsup. Bring to a boil. Thicken to desired consistency with paste made of cornstarch and cold water.

Serves 6 to 8.

FREEZE NUTS, BOTH SHELLED AND UNSHELLED, TO KEEP THEM LONGER. CRACKING SHELLED NUTS IS EASIER WHEN THEY ARE FROZEN.

Chicken Waikiki ★
BARBARA TOWNSEND

Has anyone ever been to Hawaii and not brought back macadamia nuts?

¼ cup apple juice
½ cup lemon juice
¼ cup Worcestershire sauce
6 boneless, skinless chicken breasts
⅓ cup butter or margarine
¾ cup finely chopped macadamia nuts
¾ cup plain dry bread crumbs

Mix apple juice, lemon juice, and Worcestershire sauce in a small bowl. Marinate chicken breasts in mixture in a resealable plastic bag or glass baking dish about 1 hour.

Heat oven to 325° F.

Melt butter in a 9x13-inch baking dish in oven. Blend nuts and bread crumbs together in a shallow bowl. Dip drained chicken breasts in melted butter, then coat completely with crumb mixture. Arrange chicken in baking dish atop any remaining melted butter. Bake, uncovered, 30 to 40 minutes.

Serves 6.

HOW TO MAKE WHITE SAUCE

WHITE SAUCE IS VERSATILE AS A THICKENER FOR SOUPS, A SAUCE FOR VEGETABLES, OR A BINDER FOR MEAT OR FISH DISHES.

PROPORTIONS OF FLOUR AND BUTTER TO MILK AND SALT VARY ACCORDING TO THICKNESS DESIRED IN SAUCE. WHITE SAUCE IS A BASIC SAUCE TO WHICH MANY OTHER INGREDIENTS, SUCH AS CHEESE OR MUSTARD, CAN BE ADDED.

MIX FLOUR WITH 2 TO 3 TABLESPOONS OF WATER IN A SMALL BOWL AND WHISK UNTIL SMOOTH, OR PUT FLOUR AND WATER IN A SMALL JAR WITH A LID AND SHAKE UNTIL BLENDED, OR BLEND IN A BLENDER. MELT BUTTER IN A MEDIUM SAUCEPAN OVER LOW HEAT; ADD FLOUR MIXTURE. STIR UNTIL A SMOOTH PASTE IS FORMED. SLOWLY ADD MILK,

(Continued on pg. 135)

Parmesan Chicken ★

JANICE CARROLL

Light and easy.

- ¼ cup butter or margarine, melted
- 1 cup plain dry bread crumbs
- ½ to 1 teaspoon sage or poultry seasoning
- 4 to 6 boneless, skinless or bone-in chicken breasts or chicken pieces
- Parmesan cheese, grated

Heat oven to 350° F.

Put melted butter in a shallow bowl. In another shallow bowl, mix bread crumbs with sage or poultry seasoning. Dip chicken first in butter then in bread crumbs. Place chicken on a sprayed or greased cookie sheet or baking dish. Sprinkle with Parmesan cheese. Bake 30 to 40 minutes.

Serves 4 to 6.

(Continued from pg. 134)

STIRRING CONSTANTLY UNTIL SAUCE IS THICKENED. ADD SALT AND ANY OTHER SEASONINGS DESIRED.

THIN SAUCE:
1 TABLESPOON BUTTER
1 TABLESPOON FLOUR
2 TO 3 TABLESPOONS WATER
1 CUP MILK
¼ TEASPOON SALT

MEDIUM SAUCE:
2 TABLESPOONS BUTTER
2 TABLESPOONS FLOUR
2 TO 3 TABLESPOONS WATER
1 CUP MILK
¼ TEASPOON SALT

THICK SAUCE:
3 TABLESPOONS BUTTER
3 TABLESPOONS FLOUR
2 TO 3 TABLESPOONS WATER
1 CUP MILK
¼ TEASPOON SALT

Crispy Herb Chicken ★ 🥣
KATHY CRAWFORD

Amazingly easy. May be refrigerated up to 24 hours before cooking.

1½ cups Rice Krispies® cereal
1 (0.7-ounce) envelope Good Seasons® Italian salad dressing mix
4 to 6 boneless, skinless chicken breasts or chicken pieces
⅓ cup butter or margarine, melted

Heat oven to 350° F.

Crush Rice Krispies® in a blender or food processor. Combine crushed cereal with salad dressing mix in a shallow bowl. Dip chicken pieces in melted butter, then roll in cereal mixture to coat. Place in a 10-inch square or 9x13-inch baking dish. Sprinkle additional cereal mixture over chicken. Bake, uncovered, 30 to 45 minutes, until tender.

Serves 4 to 6.

I can still picture how my dear mother stood in front of the hot stove, humming to herself as she cooked. Maybe that was her way of staying on track with us rambunctious children running in and out of the kitchen.

And maybe that's why I have such a love of cooking—Mother always made it look like such fun! —HELEN VAIL

Chicken Pot Pies

JANET PETERSON

Chicken pot pies are reminiscent of dinner at Grandma's.

- ¼ cup butter or margarine
- ⅓ cup flour
- ¼ teaspoon pepper
- 1 (10½-ounce) can chicken broth
- ¾ cup milk
- 2 cups cooked, cubed chicken
- ¼ cup chopped onion
- 1 (4-ounce) can sliced mushrooms
- 1 cup frozen peas
- 1 cup sliced, cooked carrots
- 1 (1 pound 1.3-ounce) can Pillsbury® Grands refrigerated biscuits

Heat oven to 350° F.

Spray 8 (10-ounce) custard cups with cooking spray. Melt butter in a large skillet; stir in flour and pepper. Cook 1 to 2 minutes, until smooth and bubbly. Gradually stir in broth and milk. Cook until thickened, stirring constantly. Add chicken, onion, mushrooms, peas, and carrots. Heat through. Spoon mixture into custard cups. Separate dough into 8 biscuits. Stretch dough to fit custard cup. Place on top of mixture and make 2 or 3 slits in each biscuit. Bake 18 to 20 minutes, or until biscuits are golden brown.

Serves 8.

It seems to me that our three basic needs, for food and security and love, are so entwined that we cannot think of one without the other. —M.F.K. FISHER

Tex-Mex Chicken and Rice Casserole
ROCKY SONNENBERG

Sure to become one of your family favorites.

- 1 tablespoon oil
- 1 cup chopped onion
- 1 (7-ounce) package chicken flavor Rice-a-Roni®
- 1 cup rice
- 2 (14½-ounce) cans chicken broth
- 2½ cups water
- 4 cups diced, cooked chicken
- 4 medium tomatoes, chopped
- 1 (4-ounce) can green chilies
- 1 (15-ounce) can kidney beans, drained
- 2 tablespoons black olives, chopped
- 2 teaspoons basil
- 1 teaspoon chili powder
- ¼ teaspoon cumin
- ⅛ teaspoon pepper
- 1 cup grated cheddar cheese

DURING DINNER, ASK EACH FAMILY MEMBER TO SAY SOMETHING THEY APPRECIATE ABOUT THE PERSON SITTING NEXT TO THEM.

Heat oven to 425° F.

Heat oil in a large skillet. Sauté onion, rice from the Rice-a-Roni® package, and rice. Add the Rice-a-Roni® seasoning packet, chicken broth, and water. Bring to a boil; reduce heat, and cover. Simmer 20 minutes. Stir in chicken, tomatoes, chilies, beans, olives, basil, chili powder, cumin, and pepper. Put mixture in a 3-quart casserole dish and bake, uncovered, 20 minutes. Sprinkle cheese on during the last 5 minutes.

Serves 6 to 8.

Imperial Baked Chicken ★
BEVERLY BLUNCK

Your family will request this often.

- 2 cups dry fine bread crumbs
- ¼ cup fresh parsley, minced
- Salt and pepper to taste
- 1 cup (or less) butter or margarine, melted
- 1 clove garlic, minced
- 1 tablespoon Dijon mustard
- 1 teaspoon Worcestershire sauce
- 8 boneless, skinless chicken breast halves

Heat oven to 350° F.

Mix together bread crumbs, parsley, salt, and pepper in a shallow bowl. Mix together butter, garlic, mustard, and Worcestershire sauce in a separate dish. Dip chicken halves in butter mixture and then roll in crumb mixture. Place chicken in a foil-lined 9x13-inch baking pan. Drizzle with remaining butter. Bake, uncovered, 1 hour, or until done.

Serves 8.

If you have satisfying, well-designed meals at home, you are going to be less prone to overeating and nibbling, not only because of the kinds of foods you are likely to prepare but because the very emotional satisfactions offered by home-cooked meals help assuage the empty feelings that make some of us eat when we are not really hungry. —CHERYL MENDELSON

Italian-Seasoned Chicken with Noodles
KAYLENE REDD

"Our family eats this at least once a week—we like it that much."

3 tablespoons butter or margarine

6 boneless, skinless chicken breasts

Salt and pepper to taste

1 (0.7-ounce) envelope Good Seasons® Italian salad dressing mix

1 (10¾-ounce) can cream of mushroom soup

1 (8-ounce) package cream cheese, cubed or 1 (3-ounce) package cream cheese for less rich sauce

1 tablespoon dry onion flakes

1 (8-ounce) package egg noodles, cooked according to package directions and drained

Melt butter in a slow cooker. Coat chicken breasts with butter on both sides and place in a slow cooker. Sprinkle with salt and pepper, then dry salad dressing mix. (Don't add water.) Cover and cook on low heat 5 to 6 hours.

About 45 minutes before serving, mix soup, cream cheese, and onion flakes in a small bowl. Pour over chicken. Cover and cook on medium heat, stirring occasionally, until cream cheese is melted and sauce is heated thoroughly. Serve over cooked egg noodles.

Serves 6.

Coming to the dinner table is not only about the food. . . . It is about conversation and community. It is the place where arguments can be put aside, television and phone calls avoided. This is the one time when the entire family has a chance to share details of their days. —NANCY SNYDERMAN

Lemon Chicken ★

JENNIFER PULSIPHER

This is so easy; yet it can pass for gourmet. Great for those unexpected dinner guests.

> 4 to 6 boneless, skinless chicken breasts
> 1½ cups flour
> ¼ cup butter or margarine
> 2 tablespoons olive oil
> Salt and pepper to taste
> 4 to 5 cups cooked rice

Pound chicken breasts flat with a mallet. Put flour in a plastic bag, add chicken breasts, and shake to coat. Melt butter and oil in a large skillet. Cook chicken breasts on moderately high heat, approximately 4 minutes on each side or until cooked through. Sprinkle with salt and pepper. Place chicken in an ovenproof dish; keep warm in oven set at 250° F. Prepare lemon sauce.

Lemon Sauce

> 3 tablespoons butter or margarine
> 3 tablespoons minced fresh parsley
> Juice of 1 lemon

Add butter to skillet and melt, scraping up brown bits in pan. Remove from heat; add parsley and lemon juice. Pour hot sauce over chicken. Serve with rice.

Serves 4 to 6.

EXPAND YOUR FAMILY'S FOOD HORIZONS BY HOLDING COMPARATIVE TASTING CONTESTS. BUY SEVERAL VARIETIES OF APPLES OR PEACHES AND HAVE FAMILY MEMBERS TASTE AND COMPARE.

Ranch Chicken ★ ◡
JANET PETERSON

"Everyone in our family likes Ranch dressing. Putting it on chicken is another way to enjoy it."

⅔ cup crushed cornflakes
⅔ cup grated Parmesan cheese
1 (0.6-ounce) envelope ranch dressing mix
6 to 8 boneless, skinless chicken breasts
⅔ cup butter or margarine, melted

Heat oven to 350° F.

Mix cornflakes, Parmesan cheese, and salad dressing mix in a shallow bowl. Dip chicken in butter, then roll in ranch dressing mixture. Place chicken in a 9x13-inch pan. Bake, uncovered, 45 minutes.

Serves 6 to 8.

I never put stock in the old notion that a kitchen is the sole province of girls and women.

... The culinary arts have all the right ingredients for little boys. For starters, there's a wide array of fascinating gadgets to play with, not to mention the delicious alchemy of making a mess.

To earn his Cub Scouts' Family Member Badge last fall, Nate had to complete the following requirements as described in his official Webelo handbook: Help plan the meals for your family for at least one week. Help buy the food. Prepare at least three meals for the family. ...

"I don't know why you complain about cooking dinner, Mom—it's really fun," Nate said as he seized a spatula and swirled the contents of another saucepan. ...

Served by candlelight, Nate's pan-broiled steak was a remarkable success. ... I whispered an early prayer of Thanksgiving for the Boy Scouts of America, who were providing a terrific service for busy families of tomorrow. Though my Cub didn't quite realize it yet, he'd learned how to prepare the most nurturing gift anyone could offer—the gift of a homemade meal.

—CYNTHIA LA FERLE

Orange Chicken
PAULA HEATH

Orange-sweetened chicken—delectable.

- 4 to 6 boneless, skinless chicken breasts
- 2 tablespoons butter or margarine
- ½ teaspoon seasoned salt
- ⅛ teaspoon pepper
- 3 tablespoons brown sugar
- 1 tablespoon cornstarch
- ¼ teaspoon salt
- ⅛ teaspoon ground ginger
- ½ cup orange marmalade
- ½ cup orange juice
- 1 teaspoon lemon juice
- Orange slices or 1 (11-ounce) can mandarin oranges
- 4 to 5 cups cooked rice

Melt butter in a large skillet. Brown chicken, sprinkling each side with seasoned salt and pepper. In a small bowl, mix together brown sugar, cornstarch, salt, ginger, orange marmalade, orange juice, and lemon juice. Pour mixture over chicken. Bring to a boil. Reduce heat to medium-low, cover, and simmer 25 to 35 minutes. Add orange slices and cook 10 more minutes. Serve with rice.

Serves 4 to 6.

Buy chicken breasts with bones and remove them yourself—not a difficult and time-consuming process and much less expensive than buying boneless, skinless breasts.

Barbecue Chicken Breasts ★ ⌣

ARLENE HOBBS

Cooking the chicken breasts for a long time allows the barbecue sauce to accentuate their flavor.

- 10 to 12 boneless, skinless chicken breasts
- 2 tablespoons oil
- ¼ cup Worcestershire sauce
- 2 tablespoons dry onion flakes
- 2 tablespoons dry mustard
- 1 tablespoon chopped fresh parsley (or 1 teaspoon dried parsley)
- 1 teaspoon cider vinegar
- 1 cup catsup
- 1 cup brown sugar
- 2 teaspoons oil

In a large skillet or Dutch oven, brown chicken breasts on both sides in 2 tablespoons hot oil. In a medium bowl, mix Worcestershire sauce, onion flakes, mustard, parsley, vinegar, catsup, brown sugar, and 2 teaspoons oil. Place chicken in a slow cooker or Dutch oven and pour sauce over chicken. Cover and cook on medium-high heat 2 to 3 hours.

Serves 10 to 12.

Some of my best memories are those of family mealtimes. Growing up in a family of five children, it was natural and routine for all of us to sit down together for dinner every evening around 6 P.M. We seldom had to be called to dinner. When the aroma of Mother's cooking drifted from the kitchen, it was time for my usual task of setting the dinner table. Remembering those unhurried mealtimes that brought our family close together brings back good memories. —BEVERLY BLUNCK

Chicken Tacos ★ ⬇

DEBBIE NELSON

Why go to Taco Bell when you can make your own superior tacos?

>   Chicken tenders or boneless, skinless chicken breasts
>   Mild picante sauce
>   Flour tortillas

Optional toppings
>   Chopped green onions
>   Chopped tomatoes
>   Grated cheese
>   Shredded lettuce
>   Sliced olives
>   Sour cream

Place chicken tenders or breasts in a slow cooker or Dutch oven and cover with picante sauce. Cook 2 hours on medium-high heat or 8 hours on low heat. Put chicken mixture in center of warmed tortillas. Add desired toppings.

Servings variable.

If your children are grown or older, turn dinnertime into a forum for discussion of current issues and happenings in the area and around the world. It beats the doldrums of the evening news but serves to keep everyone informed of current events. Make sure that your conversations are lively and friendly.

Quick Chicken a la King ★
EVA WALLACE

Families have enjoyed chicken a la king for generations. Serve over toast, baking powder biscuits, rice, or puff pastries.

IF SEVERAL RECIPES YOU ARE PREPARING DURING THE WEEK CALL FOR CHOPPED ONION, GREEN PEPPER, OR COOKED AND DICED CHICKEN, PREPARE ENOUGH FOR ALL THE MEALS AT ONE TIME. KEEP IN CONTAINERS OR BAGS IN THE REFRIGERATOR.

¼ cup chopped onion
2 tablespoons butter or margarine
2 tablespoons flour
1 (10¾-ounce) can cream of mushroom soup
1 cup milk
1½ cups cooked diced chicken or turkey
1 (4-ounce) can sliced mushrooms or ½ cup sliced fresh mushrooms
2 tablespoons chopped pimiento
⅓ cup chopped green pepper
½ cup sour cream

In a large skillet, sauté onion in butter until limp but not brown. Add flour. In a small bowl, blend soup and milk. Add to onion mixture. Cook and stir until thickened. Add chicken or turkey, mushrooms, pimiento, and green pepper. Heat but do not boil. Add sour cream. Serve over toast, baking powder biscuits, rice, or puff pastries.

Serves 4 to 5.

Chicken Cashew Stir-Fry

JANET PETERSON

Stir-frying is a quick method of cooking. The slicing and chopping of chicken and vegetables does take some time but can be done ahead.

- 4 to 5 boneless, skinless chicken breasts, cut in thin strips
- 2 tablespoons soy sauce or chicken broth
- 1 tablespoon cornstarch
- 2 tablespoons oil
- ½ teaspoon salt
- 4 to 5 green onions, sliced
- ¾ cup sliced fresh mushrooms
- 2 tablespoons oil
- 2 cups shredded cabbage or bean sprouts
- ½ to ¾ pound snow peas
- 1 (6-ounce) package cashews, salt rinsed off
- 1 teaspoon cornstarch
- ¼ cup soy sauce or chicken broth
- 1 cup chow mein noodles (optional)
- 4 to 5 cups cooked rice

To THINLY SLICE MEAT FOR STIR-FRY DISHES, USE PARTIALLY FROZEN MEAT, WHICH SLICES MORE EASILY AND QUICKLY.

In a small bowl, combine chicken strips with 2 tablespoons soy sauce or chicken broth and 1 tablespoon cornstarch. Stir to evenly coat chicken. Let stand at room temperature 15 minutes. Heat 2 tablespoons oil with salt in a large skillet or wok. Stir-fry chicken until it is white and cooked through. Add onions and mushrooms. Stir-fry 2 to 3 minutes, until soft. Remove chicken, onion, and mushrooms from skillet and put in a bowl or on a plate.

Add remaining 2 tablespoons of oil to skillet or wok. Add cabbage or bean sprouts and snow peas. Stir-fry 3 to 4 minutes, until vegetables are crisp-tender. Add chicken mixture to skillet or wok. Add cashews. Mix 1 teaspoon cornstarch with ¼ cup soy sauce or chicken broth. Stir into chicken mixture. Cover and steam 1 minute. Uncover and stir until sauce is thickened. Sprinkle with chow mein noodles, if desired. Serve over rice.

Serves 4 to 6.

FISH

Fish has gained immense popularity due to its health appeal, wide availability, easy preparation, and delicate taste. It can also add diversity and excitement to dinner menus.

Shrimp Stroganoff/*151*

Shrimp Linguini/*152*

Angel Hair Pasta and Shrimp/*153*

Salmon with Papaya-Mango-Pineapple Salsa/*154*

Baked Salmon/*155*

Mediterranean-Style Salmon/*156*

Chili-Crusted Salmon and Roasted Scalloped Potatoes/*157*

Halibut with Mustard Sauce/*158*

Sautéed Halibut with Nectarine Salsa/*159*

Company Fish/*160*

Easy Baked Fish/*161*

Portuguese Fish/*162*

Orange Roughy in Salsa/*163*

Cheddar Tuna Pie/*164*

Shrimp Stroganoff
DONNA LINDSAY

An unusual and delicious approach to stroganoff.

- 1½ pounds medium or large shrimp, peeled and deveined
- ½ cup butter or margarine, divided
- ½ pound fresh mushrooms, sliced
- ⅔ cup chopped onion
- 1 clove garlic, minced
- 2 tablespoons flour
- 1 cup chicken broth
- 1 tablespoon tomato paste or catsup
- ¾ teaspoon Worcestershire sauce
- 1 tablespoon fresh dill weed or 1 teaspoon dried dill weed
- 1 cup sour cream
- 1 teaspoon salt (or to taste)
- 3 to 4 cups cooked rice

MAKE COOKING DINNER A SIGNIFICANT PART OF YOUR FAMILY VACATION PLANS. WHEN TRAVELING, RENT A PLACE WITH A KITCHEN SO YOU CAN COOK. TRIPS TO LOCAL FOOD MARKETS MAY BECOME YOUR TRIP'S HIGHLIGHT. WHEN STAYING ON A SEACOAST, YOU CAN EVEN CATCH YOUR OWN FISH FOR DINNER.

In a large skillet, sauté shrimp in 6 tablespoons butter 5 minutes. Remove shrimp and sauté mushrooms, onions, and garlic in remaining butter. Cook 5 minutes. Add flour and mix well. Add chicken broth, tomato paste or catsup, Worcestershire sauce, dill weed, and salt. Simmer 2 minutes. Add sour cream and mix well. Add shrimp. Heat mixture but do not boil. Serve over cooked rice.

Serves 4 to 6.

Shrimp Linguini
DEMETRIA DAVIS

Very colorful. The marinated shrimp are what make the dish.

1¼ pounds medium shrimp, peeled and deveined
2 to 3 garlic cloves, minced
Salt and freshly ground pepper to taste
6 tablespoons olive oil, divided
1 medium bunch broccoli, cut into florets
4 to 6 tablespoons butter, at room temperature
1 (8-ounce package) linguini or 10 ounces fresh linguini, cooked according to package directions
½ red bell pepper, cut in strips
½ yellow bell pepper, cut in strips

WHEN USING FROZEN SHRIMP IN RECIPES, SOAK THE SHRIMP IN SALTED, ICE-COLD WATER FOR 15 MINUTES. THIS MAKES THE SHRIMP TASTE FRESHER.

Combine shrimp, garlic, salt, pepper, and 4 tablespoons oil in a medium bowl. Cover and marinate 1 to 4 hours in refrigerator. Remove shrimp and reserve marinade. Steam broccoli in a steamer basket over boiling water or cook in boiling water in a saucepan about 8 minutes.

Heat 2 tablespoons oil and 2 tablespoons butter over medium heat in a large skillet. Add shrimp and sauté 1 to 2 minutes until shrimp turns pink, tossing often. Reserving fat in skillet, transfer shrimp to a bowl. Put 2 to 4 tablespoons butter in a large bowl. Add cooked linguini and toss. Add shrimp and broccoli and toss. Add shrimp marinade to skillet. Cook over medium heat, stirring about 1 minute. Pour part of marinade over pasta. Toss gently. Garnish with red and yellow peppers.

Serves 4.

FISH

Angel Hair Pasta and Shrimp
JENNIFER PULSIPHER

Perfect for an easy, romantic dinner for two.

- ¼ pound angel hair pasta, cooked according to package directions
- 1 clove garlic, minced
- 2 tablespoons olive oil
- 1 tablespoon minced fresh basil
- 1 cup chopped roma tomatoes
- Salt and freshly ground pepper to taste
- 8 to 10 large shrimp, peeled and deveined

Drain cooked pasta, rinse in cold water, and set aside. Cook garlic in 1 tablespoon oil in a medium skillet until light brown. Add basil, tomatoes, salt, and pepper. Cook over medium heat, stirring occasionally.

In another skillet, sauté shrimp in 1 tablespoon olive oil 5 to 7 minutes, being careful not to overcook. Add pasta to tomato mixture and heat through. Put pasta on serving plates and top with shrimp.

Serves 2.

A good cook is like a sorceress who dispenses happiness.
—ELSA SCHIAPARELLI

Salmon with Papaya-Mango-Pineapple Salsa
SHAUNA HAYCOCK

You may find the salmon only an excuse to make this tropical salsa. It would also be superb with halibut.

- 1 mango, diced
- 1 papaya, diced
- 1 cup diced fresh pineapple
- 3 green onions, chopped
- 3 tablespoons fresh lemon juice
- 3 to 4 tablespoons minced cilantro
- 2 tablespoons chopped jalapeño pepper or 2 tablespoons canned diced green chilies (more if desired)
- 1 teaspoon salt
- 4 to 6 salmon or halibut fillets

In a large bowl, combine mango, papaya, pineapple, onions, lemon juice, cilantro, and jalapeño pepper or chilies. Mix well. Set aside.

Put 1½ inches of water in a large skillet and stir in salt. Put salmon or halibut in skillet and bring water to a boil. Reduce heat and cover pan. Cook about 8 to 10 minutes, until fish flakes easily. Or brush fish with extra-virgin olive oil and grill 5 to 6 minutes per side until done. Serve with salsa.

Serves 4 to 6.

For as long as I could remember, a sign hung in my mother's kitchen that read, "No matter where I serve my guests, it seems they like my kitchen best." That was true of my mother's kitchen, especially for family members, and I know it is also true in my own home. —D. LOUISE BROWN

Baked Salmon ★
CHERYL ELMER

Fresh vegetables add color and flavor to the salmon.

- 4 skinless salmon fillets (have butcher skin salmon at time of purchase)
- 1 cup sliced fresh mushrooms
- 1 cup chopped tomatoes
- 2 teaspoons chopped fresh basil or ½ teaspoon dried basil
- 1 teaspoon lemon pepper
- ½ teaspoon garlic powder
- 4 lemon slices

Heat oven to 425° F.

Spray a 9x13-inch baking pan with cooking spray. Place salmon in pan. Evenly spread mushrooms and tomatoes over salmon. Sprinkle salmon with basil, lemon pepper, and garlic powder. Bake, covered, 15 to 20 minutes, until fish flakes easily in center. Serve with lemon slices.

Serves 4.

Food is often tied up with family metaphors. In our family it is pie. Everyone knows everyone else's favorite kinds, and the merits of these choices are hotly disputed. . . . Pie means that an event is special, that we are together and celebrating. In other families, Grandmother's noodles come to stand for Grandmother. The fresh-caught trout eaten in a mountain campground stands for a time when the family was young and happy. People speak with such longing of their mother's biscuits or their father's farm-raised chickens. It isn't just the food they are missing but the emotions that are connected to those meals and the people who served the food. —MARY PIPHER

Mediterranean-Style Salmon ★

SHARON MARTIN

You'll think you're eating dinner at a ristorante along the Mediterranean coast.

- 4 to 5 pounds salmon fillets or 1 whole fish, cleaned and boned
- ¼ cup extra-virgin olive oil
- Juice of 4 lemons
- 4 cloves garlic, minced
- ½ cup white grape juice
- 1 tablespoon chopped fresh Italian parsley
- Salt and pepper
- 12 small black or green olives, pitted and halved
- 2 bay leaves

Heat oven to 350° F.

Rinse and pat salmon dry. In a small bowl, stir together oil, lemon juice, garlic, grape juice, parsley, salt, and pepper. Spoon 2 tablespoons of mixture into a baking dish that is large enough to hold fillets. Place fish in pan. Cover with olives and bay leaves, and pour remaining oil mixture over. Cover with aluminum foil and bake about 30 minutes, until salmon is opaque in center.

Serves 8 to 10.

When my brothers, sisters and I were young, our friends frequently asked to stay for dinner. Mom never said no. She would always make extra in case there was an additional person or two around the table. These days, folks still stop by Mom's house just to see what's cooking (and to taste-test a dish or two, of course). They're never disappointed. —DEBRA FALKINER

Chili-Crusted Salmon and Roasted Scalloped Potatoes
ANNA PETERSON

Pleasantly spicy, and a novel way to serve potatoes.

- 1 tablespoon chili powder
- 1 tablespoon brown sugar
- 1 teaspoon salt
- 1½ pounds potatoes, peeled and thinly sliced
- 3 green onions, chopped
- 1 tablespoon olive oil
- ¼ teaspoon pepper
- 4 skinless salmon fillets

Heat oven to 450° F.

In a small bowl, combine chili powder, brown sugar, and salt. In a 9x13-inch glass baking dish, toss potatoes with chopped green onions, oil, pepper, and 1 tablespoon chili mixture. Cover with foil and bake 20 minutes.

While potatoes are cooking, rub remaining chili mixture on salmon. Place fillets over potatoes and bake, uncovered, 10 to 12 minutes longer, or until fish flakes easily and potatoes are tender. Garnish with additional chopped green onions.

Serves 4.

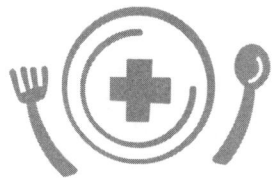

OVERCOOKED AND DRY FISH CAN BE REMEDIED BY SERVING A CITRUS SAUCE, CHEESE SAUCE, OR SALSA OVER IT. ANOTHER REMEDY WOULD BE TO MAKE FISH CAKES. SEE THE LEFTOVER DISGUISE ON PAGE 160.

Halibut with Mustard Sauce
MARILYN LINN

Imagine—your main course cooked in 5 to 10 minutes!

8 halibut fillets (or haddock, sole, or cod)
Salt and pepper to taste
1 to 2 small zucchini, unpeeled and sliced about ¼-inch thick
2 tomatoes, sliced (optional)
Nutmeg (freshly ground preferred)
¼ cup chopped chives

Sauce

2 garlic cloves
2 shallots or ½ small onion
½ cup oil
2½ tablespoons Dijon mustard
1 tablespoon lemon juice
2 teaspoons dried basil

GENERALLY, FILLETS COST MORE PER POUND THAN STEAKS. CUT YOUR OWN FILLETS FROM HALIBUT AND SALMON STEAKS WITH A SHARP, THIN-BLADED KNIFE.

Heat oven to 500° F.

Rinse halibut and pat dry. Sprinkle generously with salt and pepper. Place each fillet on a piece of heavy-duty foil large enough to wrap it tightly.

To make sauce, mince garlic and shallots or onion in a food processor. Add oil, mustard, lemon juice, and basil. Combine the mixture by turning the machine on and off. Spread sauce evenly over halibut. Place zucchini in overlapping rows on top of the sauce and halibut. Top with tomato slices, if desired. Sprinkle with nutmeg and chives.

Wrap each fillet with foil to make an airtight packet. Put packets on a baking sheet. Bake 5 to 10 minutes, depending on thickness of fillets, being careful not to overcook.

Serves 8.

Sautéed Halibut with Nectarine Salsa
KRISTEN HUBBS

Fresh peaches could be used in place of nectarines.

　　1½ pounds halibut fillets
　　1 nectarine, peeled and pureed
　　3 tablespoons flour
　　2 tablespoons peanut or olive oil

Place halibut in a shallow glass dish, cover with pureed nectarine, and marinate 1 hour. Remove halibut from the marinade and coat lightly with flour. Heat oil in a large skillet and sauté fillets about 3 to 5 minutes per side, until fish flakes easily. Arrange halibut on serving plates pooled with 4 to 5 tablespoons nectarine salsa.

Nectarine Salsa
　　4 nectarines, peeled and diced
　　½ red bell pepper, diced
　　1 cup finely chopped scallions or green onions
　　½ cup finely chopped fresh chives
　　1 tablespoon chopped cilantro
　　Juice of 2 limes

Combine nectarines, bell pepper, scallions or onions, chives, cilantro, and lime juice in a large bowl.

Serves 4.

Don't chop or mince cilantro—just pull the leaves off the stems and use a little more than the recipe calls for.

Company Fish ★
LYNDA COOPER

Ranch dressing and mayonnaise keep the fish very moist.

1 cup ranch dressing
4 to 6 white fish fillets (cod, sole, haddock, or halibut)
½ cup mayonnaise
Fresh Parmesan cheese, grated

Heat oven to 325° F.

Spread ranch dressing in the bottom of a 9x13-inch pan or smaller baking dish, depending on size of fillets. Place fillets on top of dressing. Cover with mayonnaise and cheese. Bake, uncovered, 30 minutes.

Serves 4 to 6.

MAKE FISH CAKES OUT OF LEFTOVER TROUT, SALMON, CRAB, OR HALIBUT. FOR EACH CUP OF FISH CUT OR BROKEN INTO SMALL PIECES, ADD ½ CUP LIGHTLY CRUSHED CRACKER CRUMBS, 1 BEATEN EGG, AND SALT AND PEPPER TO TASTE. A LITTLE MILK MAY BE ADDED TO MOISTEN THE MIXTURE. SEASONINGS MAY ALSO BE ADDED. FORM INTO SMALL, FLAT CAKES. SPRAY A LARGE SKILLET WITH COOKING SPRAY OR MELT 1 TO 2 TABLESPOONS BUTTER. COOK CAKES UNTIL LIGHTLY BROWNED AND COOKED THROUGH.

Easy Baked Fish ★
TERESA POWERS

Your basic fish—serve with a green salad and a colorful vegetable.

> 4 to 6 white fish fillets (cod, sole, haddock, or halibut)
> ¼ teaspoon garlic salt
> 1 tablespoon paprika
> 1 tablespoon parsley flakes
> Butter or margarine
> Juice of 1 lemon

Heat oven to 350° F.

Spray a 9x13-inch baking dish with cooking spray and place fish in dish. Sprinkle with garlic salt, paprika, and parsley flakes. Dot with butter. Squeeze lemon juice over fish. Bake about 20 minutes.

Serves 4 to 6.

ADD LEFTOVER FISH TO A WHITE SAUCE AND SERVE OVER RICE, TOAST, OR PASTA.

Portuguese Fish ★
KATHY VIRGIN

JUST FOR FUN, HAVE A "CRAZY" DINNER. USE UNUSUAL DINNERWARE AND UTENSILS AND START WITH DESSERT.

Blue-ribbon fish.

1 medium onion, sliced
1 pound white fish (cod, sole, haddock, or halibut), cut in serving pieces
1 green pepper, cut in strips
½ pound fresh mushrooms, sliced
2 to 4 tablespoons olive oil
½ teaspoon salt
⅛ teaspoon pepper
¼ teaspoon oregano
¼ teaspoon paprika

In a large skillet, sauté onion, green pepper, and mushrooms in oil. Add fish and cook until lightly browned. Sprinkle salt, pepper, oregano, and paprika over fillets. Cover skillet and steam 10 minutes on medium-low heat.

Serves 3 to 4.

FISH

Orange Roughy in Salsa ★
NANCY FLAMM

What could be easier than 2 ingredients ready in 10 minutes?

    4 to 6 orange roughy fillets
    1 (12- or 16-ounce) jar chunky salsa

Place orange roughy in a large skillet. Spread salsa over fillets. Bring to boil and reduce heat. Cover skillet and simmer fillets 10 to 12 minutes, until center of fish flakes easily.

Serves 4 to 6.

It is possible to reconcile today's hectic pace with our need to celebrate and connect with our families. What most of us need is a starting point, some means of taking that first, wobbly step toward the fridge and that vaguely familiar appliance, the stove. Let go of unrealistic expectations and impossible standards, and the side dish of guilt that goes with them. Times have changed; things are different. About the only things that haven't changed are our need to celebrate and to spend time with our families. And while it may no longer be realistic to expect the whole clan to march into the kitchen at five-thirty sharp every night, that isn't to say we can't get it together three nights a week, or even one. Don't view this tradition as a chore, but rather a celebration. —DORIS CHRISTOPHER

Cheddar Tuna Pie

ANNA PETERSON

A classy treatment of tuna fish.

2½ cups cooked rice
4 eggs
2 tablespoons butter or margarine, melted
2 tablespoons chopped fresh parsley
1½ cups grated cheddar cheese
1 (6-ounce) can tuna, drained
1½ cups milk
½ teaspoon salt
⅛ teaspoon pepper
¼ teaspoon dry mustard
6 tomato slices

A PASTRY BLENDER CAN DO MORE THAN CUT SHORTENING INTO FLOUR. USE IT TO CHOP CANNED TOMATOES, HARD-BOILED EGGS, OR AVOCADOS.

Heat oven to 375° F.

Combine rice, 1 slightly beaten egg, butter, and parsley. Spread in a 9-inch pie plate, pressing it into a piecrust. Sprinkle ¾ cup cheese over crust. Top with ½ of the tuna and sprinkle remaining cheese. Beat together milk, 3 remaining eggs, salt, pepper, and mustard. Pour over cheese and tuna. Sprinkle remaining tuna. Bake 20 minutes. Arrange tomato slices on top and return to oven 5 minutes.

Serves 6.

✚ PORK AND HAM ✚

Although pork and ham come from the same animal, they receive entirely different treatments when cooking. Ham comes to you from the market precooked, partially cooked, or smoked and needs very little attention. You simply need to bake it and add glazes or side dishes. Pork, on the other hand, benefits from longer cooking with other ingredients to flavor and tenderize it.

Red Pork Chops/*167*

Pork Chops with Brown Rice/*168*

Creole Pork Chops/*169*

Roast Pork with Cherry Sauce/*170*

Pork Tenderloin/*171*

New England Ribs/*172*

Crepes Ensenada/*173*

Glazed Ham/*174*

Red Pork Chops ★
LEIGH CHIPMAN

A flavorful red sauce colors the pork chops. This dish is accompanied well by baked potatoes or rice.

- 4 to 6 pork chops
- ½ cup water
- ½ cup catsup
- 1 tablespoon Worcestershire sauce
- ½ cup brown sugar
- 2 tablespoons lemon juice
- Dash of Tabasco® sauce

Heat oven to 350° F.

In a large skillet, brown pork chops well on both sides. Place chops in a 3-quart casserole dish or 9x13-inch baking dish. Mix water, catsup, Worcestershire sauce, brown sugar, lemon juice, and Tabasco sauce in a small bowl. Spread sauce evenly over chops. Bake, covered, 45 minutes to 1 hour.

Serves 4 to 6.

PUT ON A THEME DINNER. HAVE A HAWAIIAN LUAU OR A FALL HARVEST. OR PRETEND THAT DINNER IS REALLY A TRIP TO THE WINTER OLYMPICS, A FISHING EXCURSION AT THE LAKE, OR A NIGHT AT A LOCAL TEAM'S BASKETBALL GAME. PLAN FOOD, TABLE SETTING, AND DECORATIONS AROUND THE THEME.

Pork Chops with Brown Rice
MARLENE BACON

A splendid combination of flavors all cooked in one pan.

- 4 pork chops
- 1 tablespoon oil
- 2 (4.5-ounce) packages quick-cooking brown and wild rice with mushrooms
- 1½ cups water
- ½ cup sliced fresh mushrooms or 1 (4-ounce) can sliced mushrooms
- 1 celery stalk, sliced
- ½ cup sour cream

In a large skillet, brown pork chops in hot oil over medium heat. Remove chops from skillet and discard drippings. In the same skillet, combine rice mix, water, mushrooms, and celery. Place chops over rice mixture. Bring to a boil. Reduce heat and simmer, covered, 30 minutes. Remove chops from skillet; keep warm. Stir sour cream into rice mixture. Heat through but do not boil.

Serves 4.

There is nothing that smells better than the aroma of a well-used kitchen—hot rolls as they come from the oven, a pot roast cooking slowly, or a pot of chili or quick stew. —MARJORIE TALL

Creole Pork Chops ★
STEPHANIE BYWATER

A very easy version of Creole cooking.

- 2 tablespoons oil
- 2 green peppers, cut in strips
- 2 large onions, sliced
- 4 to 6 pork chops
- Salt and pepper
- 1 (0.7-ounce) envelope Good Seasons® Italian dressing mix
- 1 (28-ounce) can tomatoes
- 4 to 5 cups cooked rice

Heat oil in a large skillet and sauté green peppers and onion. Remove green peppers and onion from skillet. In same skillet, brown pork chops on both sides, sprinkling with salt and pepper. Remove from skillet and drain fat. In a small bowl, mix salad dressing and tomatoes. Add sautéed peppers and onions. Return pork chops to skillet and pour tomato sauce over. Cover and bring to a boil. Reduce heat and simmer 45 to 50 minutes. Or place chops and sauce in a casserole dish and bake, covered, 45 to 50 minutes at 350° F. Serve with rice.

Serves 4 to 6.

As a family, volunteer at a local soup kitchen or food bank. This will help family members to appreciate dinner at home even more and to gain satisfaction in serving others.

Roast Pork with Cherry Sauce
JANET PETERSON

Spiced cherry sauce makes pork roast an elegant Sunday dinner.

- 1 teaspoon salt
- 1 teaspoon pepper
- 1 teaspoon sage
- 1 (3- to 4-pound) boneless pork loin roast
- 1 (16-ounce) can pie cherries in water
- 1⅓ cups sugar
- ¼ cup vinegar
- 1 teaspoon cinnamon
- 1 teaspoon ground cloves
- 1 tablespoon lemon juice
- 3 tablespoons cornstarch
- 2 to 3 drops red food coloring

Heat oven to 325° F.

Combine salt, pepper, and sage in a small bowl. Rub roast with seasonings. Place roast in a roasting or baking pan. Bake, uncovered, 2 to 2½ hours.

Fifteen minutes before roast is done, drain cherries, reserving juice. Add enough water to the cherry juice to measure ¾ cup. Put ½ cup juice in saucepan with sugar, vinegar, cinnamon, cloves, and lemon juice. Bring to a boil. Mix cornstarch with remaining cherry juice. Add to saucepan. Cook until thickened. Add cherries and food coloring. Remove roast from oven and slice. Serve with cherry sauce.

Serves 8 to 10.

A friend once said: "When someone's feet are under your dinner table, they're your friend for life." I think that goes for family, too! —D. LOUISE BROWN

Pork Tenderloin ★
PAULA HEATH

The sweet and tangy marinade permeates the pork.

- 1 (10-ounce) jar currant jelly
- 1 jar white grape juice (fill empty jelly jar)
- 3 tablespoons Dijon mustard
- 2 to 3 small pork tenderloins

In a small saucepan, mix jelly, white grape juice, and mustard. Cook until jelly is dissolved. Cool. Put tenderloins and jelly mixture in a resealable plastic bag. Marinate tenderloins in refrigerator overnight or all day.

Heat oven to 350° F.

Remove tenderloins from marinade and place in a 9x13-inch or 10-inch square baking dish. Pour marinade over tenderloins. Bake, covered, 1 hour. Remove tenderloins from oven and slice into thin slices.

Serves 4 to 6.

The time spent at the dinner table is just a part of the wonderful potential of home cooking. Food preparation offers a time to share techniques, culinary secrets, and easy conversations of daily activities and thoughts. Some of my most joyful memories involve friends and family members helping and sharing with me in the kitchen. In addition, cleanup can also be a fun, golden opportunity of togetherness, while working in unison. My family formed an assembly line of clearing, washing, drying, and putting away the dishes while singing merrily as we worked.
—BETTY DRAPER

New England Ribs ★
JANET PETERSON

Pure maple syrup makes these ribs authentic New England.

5 to 6 pounds spareribs
1 teaspoon salt
1½ cups pure maple syrup
¾ cup applesauce
½ cup catsup
¼ cup lemon juice
½ teaspoon paprika
1 clove garlic, minced
½ teaspoon cinnamon

Put ribs in a Dutch oven or large pot and cover with salted water. Bring water to a boil. Reduce heat and simmer 30 minutes. While ribs are cooking, combine maple syrup, applesauce, catsup, lemon juice, paprika, garlic, and cinnamon in a medium bowl.

Heat oven to 325° F.

Remove ribs from pot and put in a 9x13-inch pan or large baking dish. Pour sauce over ribs. Bake, uncovered, 1½ hours.

Serves 6 to 8.

Whether we're single, married, with or without children, we all have to eat dinner. The evening meal should be the highlight of the day. If the day has been peaceful, pleasurable, and profitable, it's time to celebrate. If the day has been difficult and discouraging, it's time for comfort and consolation—blessings by themselves and reason to celebrate. Either way the celebrating table bids. —SARAH BAN BREATHNACH

Crepes Ensenada
NANCY SIMPSON

Using ready-made tortillas instead of home-cooked crepes keeps preparation to a minimum.

- 12 thin slices ham
- 12 (8-inch) flour tortillas
- 1 pound Monterey Jack cheese, cut lengthwise into 12 sticks
- 1 (4-ounce) can diced green chilies
- Paprika

Heat oven to 350° F.

Place 1 slice ham on each tortilla. Put 1 stick of cheese in center and top with a few chili pieces. Roll tortilla and secure with toothpick. Place tortillas slightly separated in a greased or sprayed 9x13-inch pan. Pour cheese sauce over tortillas. Sprinkle with paprika. Bake, uncovered, 45 minutes.

Cheese Sauce

- ½ cup butter or margarine
- ½ cup flour
- 4 cups milk
- ¾ pound cheddar cheese, grated
- 1 teaspoon dry mustard
- ½ teaspoon salt
- Dash of pepper

Melt butter and blend in flour to form a smooth paste. Add milk, grated cheese, mustard, salt, and pepper. Cook, stirring until cheese is melted and sauce is smooth.

Serves 6.

Glazed Ham ★
CHRISTI JENSEN

Bone-in hams have so much more flavor than water-added compressed hams. Enhance your ham with one of these glazes.

4- to 6-pound bone-in ham

Heat oven to 325° F.

Place ham fat side up in a shallow baking pan. Spread desired glaze on ham. Bake 20 minutes per pound, basting frequently.

Apricot Glaze

    1 (12-ounce) can apricot nectar
    1 cup brown sugar
    1 cinnamon stick
    6 whole cloves

Combine nectar and sugar in a small saucepan. Cook, stirring until sugar is dissolved. Add cinnamon sticks and cloves. Boil gently 10 minutes, until slightly thickened. Remove spices from nectar.

Honey Mustard Glaze

    ¾ cup brown sugar
    1½ tablespoons honey
    2 tablespoons Dijon mustard
    ¼ teaspoon salt
    1½ tablespoons water

In a small bowl, mix the brown sugar, honey, mustard, salt, and water.

Serves 12 to 18.

GRIND LEFTOVER HAM AND MIX WITH MAYONNAISE, MUSTARD, DICED GREEN PEPPER OR GREEN CHILIES, GRATED CHEESE, CHOPPED ONIONS, AND SLICED OLIVES. FILL SOURDOUGH OR HARD ROLLS WITH MIXTURE, WRAP IN FOIL, AND BAKE UNTIL HEATED THROUGH.

GRILLING

Barbecuing is a fun way to cook, whether it's midsummer or midwinter. Grilling meats and fish is an efficient, flavorful, and adventurous means of meal preparation. Many grilled recipes call for marinades or sauces that add a special flavor and signal a great backyard chef.

Sweet and Sour Chicken Kabobs/177

Italian Chicken Breasts or Steaks/178

Lime Chicken/179

Grilled Basil Chicken/180

Lemon-Dill Marinated Flank Steak or Chicken/181

Aloha Grilled Steak and Pineapple/182

Korean Barbecue Steak/183

New York Steak with Tomato Relish and Black-Eyed Peas/184

London Broil/186

Super Hamburgers/187

Chili Burgers/188

California Burgers/189

Salsa Fish/190

Grilled Shrimp/191

Dill Salmon/192

Teriyaki Salmon/193

Grilled Swordfish with Red Pepper Sauce/194

Grilled Swordfish or Halibut a la Orange/195

Grilled Orange Roughy with Salsa/196

Sea Bass or Haddock with Black Bean Relish/197

Barbecued Spareribs/198

Grilled Seasoned Ham/199

Grilled Pork Chops with Apples/200

Grilled Toast/201

Hot Bacon Potato Salad/202

Cheesy Potatoes/203

Parmesan Potato Packets/204

Sweet and Sour Chicken Kabobs
LISA BROWN

Soak bamboo skewers in water for 1 hour (while chicken is marinating) to prevent burning on the grill.

- 1 (20-ounce) can pineapple chunks
- ½ cup soy sauce
- ¼ cup oil
- 1 teaspoon dry mustard
- ¼ teaspoon pepper
- 3 to 4 boneless, skinless chicken breasts, cut in medium-size pieces
- 2 green peppers, cut into large pieces
- 1 (8-ounce) can water chestnuts
- Cherry tomatoes or grape tomatoes
- Whole fresh mushrooms

To CLEAN A BARBECUE GRILL RACK, SPRAY WITH OVEN CLEANER (OUTDOORS). PLACE RACK IN A CLEAN PLASTIC GARBAGE BAG AND CLOSE THE BAG. LET STAND OVERNIGHT. THE GRIME ON THE RACK WILL COME OFF EASILY.

Drain pineapple and set aside, reserving juice. In a small saucepan, combine juice with soy sauce, oil, mustard, and pepper. Bring to a boil. Simmer 5 minutes. Cool. Place chicken pieces in a glass baking dish or resealable plastic bag. Cover with marinade, reserving ¼ cup marinade. Marinate chicken 1 hour in refrigerator. Drain chicken. Thread chicken pieces, green peppers, pineapple, water chestnuts, cherry tomatoes, and mushrooms on skewers. Grill 20 minutes, turning and basting occasionally with reserved marinade.

Serves 6 to 8.

Italian Chicken Breasts or Steaks ★ ⬇

JANET PETERSON

Brush grill rack with oil or spray with cooking spray to prevent food from sticking.

- 1 (8-ounce) bottle Italian salad dressing
- ¼ cup white grape juice or apple juice
- 1 to 2 cloves garlic, minced
- 4 to 6 boneless, skinless or bone-in chicken breasts or 4 to 6 beef steaks (any kind)

Combine salad dressing, juice, and garlic in a resealable plastic bag or a glass baking dish. Reserve ¼ cup marinade for basting. Marinate chicken breasts or steaks overnight or all day in refrigerator. Grill chicken on medium-high heat, 25 to 30 minutes, until chicken is cooked in center, basting frequently with reserved marinade. Grill steaks 5 to 10 minutes per side, depending on desired degree of doneness.

Serves 4 to 6.

As adults, people remember three kinds of family events with great pleasure—meals, vacations and time outdoors. —MARY PIPHER

Lime Chicken ★ ◡

BETTY DRAPER

Lime and cilantro are often paired in Mexican dishes.

- ½ cup lime juice
- ¼ cup olive oil
- ¼ cup minced cilantro
- ½ teaspoon salt
- ½ clove garlic, minced
- 4 boneless, skinless chicken breasts

Mix lime juice, oil, cilantro, salt, and garlic in a flat dish or a resealable plastic bag. Put chicken in marinade and refrigerate for several hours.

Grill chicken over medium heat 20 to 25 minutes, until center of chicken is no longer pink.

Serves 4.

The universe of my childhood no longer exists. But bits and pieces of that lost world remain with me: the meat grinder I inherited from my mother; my Aunt Anna's recipe for baked beans; the sense of well-being that still warms my heart at the sight of my family gathered around the table.

And when I close my eyes and let my mind wander into the past, I can picture us still, drifting one at a time on a cold winter evening into my mother's kitchen, five separate souls merging into one family, in a timeless celebration of what it means to belong. —DORIS CHRISTOPHER

Grilled Basil Chicken ★ ☻
NIKI JENSEN

Grow basil in a container on your patio or in your garden so that you'll have fresh basil all summer long.

- 3 tablespoons lemon juice
- 2 tablespoons fresh minced basil or 2 teaspoons dried basil
- 1 clove garlic, minced
- ¼ cup olive oil
- 4 skinless chicken breasts

Combine lemon juice, basil, and garlic in blender. Process for 30 seconds. With motor running, gradually add olive oil. Reserve ⅛ cup basil mixture.

Pour basil mixture over chicken in a shallow baking dish or resealable plastic bag. Cover and refrigerate 30 minutes. Cook chicken over medium heat 25 to 30 minutes, or until done, basting twice with reserved basil mixture.

Serves 4.

Grab a menu from the best "fast food" place in town—your kitchen! The price is right, the atmosphere relaxing, and the service couldn't be friendlier nor the guests more appreciative.
—FROM *TASTE OF HOME'S QUICK COOKING, COLLECTOR'S EDITION*

Lemon-Dill Marinated Flank Steak or Chicken
TERRI AVERY

Ask the butcher to run steak through the tenderizer when you purchase it.

- ¼ cup sliced green onions
- ¼ cup water
- ⅛ cup red wine vinegar
- ¼ cup soy sauce
- 3 tablespoons lemon juice
- 2 tablespoons olive oil
- 1 tablespoon fresh dill weed or 1 teaspoon dried dill weed
- 1 tablespoon Worcestershire sauce
- 2 cloves garlic, minced
- ½ teaspoon celery seed
- ½ teaspoon pepper
- 1 to 1½ pounds flank steak (about ¾-inch thick) or 4 to 6 boneless, skinless chicken breasts

In a medium bowl, combine onions, water, vinegar, soy sauce, lemon juice, olive oil, dill, Worcestershire sauce, garlic, celery seed, and pepper. Pour marinade over meat in a glass baking dish or a resealable plastic bag. Marinate 6 to 24 hours in refrigerator. Remove meat from marinade. Grill over medium high heat on an oiled or sprayed grill until desired doneness, about 10 minutes per side.

Serves 4 to 6.

Food not only feeds the body but enhances community, passes on traditions, puts marrow in the funny bone, and connects us with each other and the Divine. —LINDA HOFFMAN KIMBALL

Aloha Grilled Steak and Pineapple
BETTY DRAPER

Grilled pineapple slices and the flavorful steak are superb together.

- 5 tablespoons olive oil
- 2 tablespoons lemon juice
- 2 tablespoons lime juice
- ¼ cup chopped cilantro
- 1 jalapeño pepper, seeded
- 1 teaspoon cumin
- ½ teaspoon pepper
- ½ teaspoon salt
- 1½ pounds steak (sirloin, flank, or New York)
- 1 pineapple, cored and cut into ½-inch slices

Put oil, lemon juice, lime juice, cilantro, jalapeño pepper, cumin, pepper, and salt in a blender or food processor. Puree until smooth. Place steak in a large resealable plastic bag or glass baking dish. Add ¼ cup marinade. Refrigerate and marinate overnight. Reserve remaining marinade.

Remove steak from marinade and discard marinade. Grill steak over medium heat 12 to 15 minutes, turning several times. Season with salt. Let rest 5 minutes before slicing thinly on the diagonal.

Toss pineapple with 2 tablespoons marinade. Grill about 4 minutes, turning once. Serve steak with grilled pineapple slices drizzled with remaining marinade.

Serves 4.

Korean Barbecue Steak ★
NANCY SKAGGS

Sesame seeds, sesame oil, and ginger give this steak its distinctive flavor.

- 4 tablespoons sesame seeds, toasted*
- ⅓ cup soy sauce
- 2 tablespoons sesame oil
- ¼ cup brown sugar
- ¼ cup chopped green onions
- ½ cup chopped onion
- 1 clove garlic, minced
- ¼ teaspoon pepper
- 2 teaspoons minced ginger
- 1½ to 2 pounds steak (sirloin, New York, rib-eye, T-bone, or flank)

*Place sesame seeds in a baking pan and bake 5 to 7 minutes at 350° F., watching so they don't burn.

In a small bowl, combine sesame seeds, soy sauce, sesame oil, sugar, green onions, onion, garlic, pepper, and ginger. Pierce steak with a fork on both sides. Place steak in a glass baking dish or resealable plastic bag. Add marinade. Marinate in refrigerator 4 hours or more.

Remove steak from marinade and grill over medium heat on an oiled or sprayed grill to desired doneness, about 12 to 15 minutes.

Serves 4 to 6.

No one who cooks cooks alone. Even at her most solitary, a cook in the kitchen is surrounded by generations of cooks past, the advice and menus of cooks present, the wisdom of cookbook writers. —LAURIE COLWIN

New York Steak with Tomato Relish and Black-Eyed Peas
BETTY DRAPER

A whole meal! Black-eyed peas are often eaten on New Year's Day to bring good luck the rest of the year. The peas need to be prepared before grilling the steaks.

Black-Eyed Peas

- 2 tablespoons minced bacon (or pancetta)
- ½ cup minced leek or chopped onion
- 1 teaspoon minced garlic
- 2 cups dried black-eyed peas
- 6 cups chicken broth
- 1 bay leaf

In a large saucepan or pot cook bacon until crispy. Remove and set aside. Sauté leek or onion in bacon drippings 5 minutes. Add garlic and cook another minute. Add peas, broth, and bay leaf. Bring to a boil. Reduce heat and simmer 1 hour. Remove bay leaf and add bacon. Season to taste.

Tomato Relish

- 1 cup diced tomatoes
- 1 cup fresh, uncooked corn (cut from cob) or frozen corn, uncooked
- 1 jalapeño pepper, finely chopped (seeds and membranes discarded)
- 1 teaspoon minced garlic
- 2 teaspoons fresh lime juice
- 1 tablespoon olive oil
- Salt and pepper

Combine tomatoes, corn, jalapeño pepper, garlic, lime juice, and oil in a medium bowl. Add salt and pepper.

GRILLING

6 New York steaks
2 cloves garlic, cut in halves
2 tablespoons oil
Salt and pepper to taste

Rub both sides of steaks with garlic and drizzle oil over. Season with salt and pepper. Grill to desired doneness, about 12 to 15 minutes, turning several times. Remove from grill and let rest 2 to 5 minutes. Slice. To serve, fan steak slices over peas and garnish with tomato relish.

Serves 6.

I'll tell you what I cherish most from the past: our family traditions, all those little rituals that bind you together. Folks today tend to be so busy and independent that they abandon the daily habits, like eating meals together, that keep you close. They think they can watch the TV during dinner or grab a bite and rush off. They think it doesn't matter. Well, they are wrong!

When we were growing up, we ate all of our meals together. Supper was the most special time, when we could talk about our day and just enjoy each other's company. It was comforting, and it was fun. . . .

I'd never give up our suppertimes. Folks who let the little rituals go are missing out on a lot. —A. ELIZABETH DELANY

London Broil ★
KATHRYN WADE

For safety, foods should be marinated in the refrigerator only. Don't reuse marinades—discard them after use.

2 to 2½ pounds London broil
Bottled Italian salad dressing
¼ cup soy sauce
¼ to ½ teaspoon minced ginger (optional)

Place meat in a glass baking dish or resealable plastic bag. Pour enough dressing over meat to coat it, but not excessively. Add soy sauce. Add ginger, if desired. Cover and marinate several hours in refrigerator, turning several times. Remove meat from marinade and place on grill over medium heat. Grill about 10 minutes per side, cooking until desired doneness. Slice diagonally in thin slices.

Serves 6 to 10.

Today, with our family of nine children married and gone, the only real "event" at our dinner table is Sunday dinner, when we invite our family back to our home. We still set an elegant table with the best china and silverware, a centerpiece, and napkins. We still love to prepare what we can from scratch—hot rolls or scones, raspberry jam and honey butter, roast beef, mashed potatoes and gravy, and a variety of vegetables and salads. Favorite desserts are homemade pies—banana cream, chocolate cream, apple, and pumpkin—fancy cakes, brownies, and ice cream. We love to make homemade ice cream! Now my beautiful daughters and daughters-in-law bring a fair share of the dinner to make it easier for all of us. We have a wonderful time around our ample dining room table with the best company in the world and food fit for a king! In fact, no king ever ate this well! —PAT MENLOVE

Super Hamburgers ★ ⌣
JANET PETERSON

Sour cream makes these grilled hamburgers very moist.

    2½ pounds ground beef
    ¼ cup sour cream
    2 teaspoons dried parsley
    1 teaspoon thyme
    1 teaspoon salt
    1 teaspoon pepper
    10 hamburger buns

Garnish
    Lettuce leaves
    Sliced cheese
    Sliced onion
    Sliced tomatoes

Mix ground beef, sour cream, parsley, thyme, salt, and pepper in a large bowl. Form into 10 patties. Grill patties over medium heat 5 to 6 minutes per side, until meat is cooked through. Serve on buns with garnishes as desired.

Serves 10.

How true that happy memories are flavored with the foods of childhood. —CLAUDIA BUSHMAN

Chili Burgers ★ ◡
JANET PETERSON

Fun for a backyard picnic.

2 pounds ground beef
2 teaspoons salt
¾ teaspoon freshly ground pepper
1 clove garlic, minced
1½ to 2 teaspoons chili powder
½ teaspoon cumin
2½ to 3 cups meatless chili
6 hamburger buns or sandwich rolls

Garnish
Grated cheddar cheese
Lettuce
Sliced black olives
Sliced onion
Sliced tomatoes
Sour cream

WHETHER THE MEAL IS PREPARED IN A RESTAURANT, A CONDOMINIUM'S KITCHEN, OR A CAMPSITE, MAKE DINNERTIME YOUR FAMILY'S FOCUS.

Combine ground beef, salt, pepper, garlic, chili powder, and cumin in a large bowl. Form into 6 patties. Place patties on an oiled grill, 4 to 6 inches from coals. Grill over high heat, turning once, until patties reach desired doneness, about 10 to 15 minutes. Warm chili in a medium saucepan on side of grill or on stove. Lightly grill opened buns or rolls. Place patties on buns or rolls. Spoon chili over patties. Add garnishes as desired.

Serves 6.

California Burgers
JANET PETERSON

Sophisticated burgers.

- 2 pounds ground beef
- 1 clove garlic, minced
- 2 tablespoons chopped fresh basil or ¾ teaspoon dried basil
- 2 teaspoons salt
- ¾ teaspoon freshly ground pepper
- 2 to 3 tablespoons olive oil
- 6 slices Monterey Jack cheese
- 1 large onion, thickly sliced
- 6 sourdough rolls

Garnishes
- Dijon mustard
- Catsup
- Pesto
- Romaine lettuce leaves
- Sliced tomatoes

Combine ground beef, garlic, basil, salt, pepper, and 1 tablespoon oil in a large bowl. Form into 6 rectangular patties, to fit shape of rolls.

Place patties on grill, 4 to 6 inches from coals. Grill 10 to 15 minutes, turning once, until center of hamburger reaches desired doneness. Place a slice of cheese on each patty 30 seconds before removing from heat.

Brush onion slices with remaining oil. Place on grill, 4 to 6 inches from coals. Grill, turning once, until lightly browned, about 5 minutes.

Place opened rolls on grill and toast until lightly browned. Place burgers and onions in rolls. Garnish as desired.

Serves 6.

Salsa Fish ★

CHERYL PIPER-SNYDER

Your family will put this on their Top 10 list.

4 to 6 white fish fillets (cod, halibut, sole, or haddock), frozen*
3 cloves garlic, minced
Rosemary to taste
Cumin to taste
Curry to taste
Chili powder to taste
3 dashes of Tabasco® sauce
1 onion, sliced
1 (16-ounce) jar medium salsa

GET YOUR FAMILY TO THE DINNER TABLE BY USING A LITTLE CREATIVITY: SEND EACH FAMILY MEMBER PERSONALIZED INVITATIONS TO DINNER.

*The fish needs to be frozen to cook more slowly so that flavors can be fully absorbed.

Lay frozen fish on a sheet of heavy-duty aluminum foil that has been sprayed with cooking spray. Distribute garlic pieces on top of fish. Sprinkle desired amount of rosemary, cumin, curry, and chili powder over fish (use less chili powder than other spices.) Add Tabasco®. Spread onion slices over fish; top with jar of salsa. Seal foil tightly. Place on top rack of grill and cook 45 minutes on medium to medium-low heat. Check fish after 25 minutes; then continue cooking 20 to 25 more minutes, until fish is done.

Serves 4 to 6.

GRILLING

Grilled Shrimp
DIANNA HALL

Fish should be marinated for only a few hours at most, not overnight as meats usually are.

- 4 tablespoons olive oil
- 3 tablespoons red wine vinegar
- 1 clove garlic, minced
- Salt and pepper to taste
- Red pepper or any fresh or dried herbs such as rosemary, basil, oregano, and paprika to taste
- 1½ pounds jumbo shrimp, shelled and deveined

Mix together oil, vinegar, garlic, salt, pepper, and herbs in a small bowl. Pour marinade into a glass baking dish and add shrimp. Refrigerate and marinate shrimp 3 hours.

Put shrimp on an oiled or sprayed rack over grill, or broil in oven. Cook shrimp about 4 to 6 minutes, turning once, until shrimp are pink. Shrimp can also be threaded on wooden skewers that have been soaked in water for 1 hour to prevent burning.

Serves 4 to 6.

When I look back on growing up in my family's house during the 1940s, one room comes most quickly to mind—Mom's kitchen.

Despite its size, this tiny room is where Mom (Sarah Curci) spent most of her time. That made it the heart of our home, especially during the cooler winter months. . . .

I still fondly recall the mouth-watering food and the warmth and comfort of Mom's cozy kitchen. —COOKIE CURCI-WRIGHT

Dill Salmon ★ ◡
NANCY HUGHES

Salmon simply could not be better or easier.

2 to 3 pounds salmon (leave uncut)
Salt and pepper to taste
Fresh or dried dill weed to taste
1 lemon, sliced
½ onion, sliced

Spray a large piece of heavy-duty aluminum foil with cooking spray. Place salmon on foil. Sprinkle salmon with salt, pepper, and dill. Arrange slices of lemon and onion over salmon. Seal foil. Grill over medium heat 20 minutes.

Serves 6 to 8.

Sharing joys with family and friends over a meal resonates deeply within the human consciousness, tracking all the way back to the days when our ancestors gathered around the cooking fires, eating, laughing, telling stories, and reveling in the pleasure of human companionship. Europeans understand; in France, Italy, Spain, and Greece, for example, people linger over meals, not only relishing good food but also recognizing that meals should be enjoyed at many levels. In our fast-paced world, even though you may not be able to do so every evening, we urge you to make time, as often as possible, for the joy of family, good friends, and good food. —MICHAEL R. EADES AND MARY DAN EADES

Teriyaki Salmon
JANET PETERSON

Leftover salmon (if you have any) is just as delicious cold as it is right off the grill.

- 2 teaspoons fresh dill weed or ¾ teaspoon dried dill weed
- ½ teaspoon lemon pepper
- ½ teaspoon salt
- ¼ teaspoon garlic powder
- ¼ cup brown sugar
- ¼ cup oil
- ¼ cup soy sauce
- ¼ cup finely chopped green onions
- 1 (2- to 2½-pound) salmon fillet
- 1 lemon, sliced
- ½ onion, sliced

Hold a "crazy hat dinner." Invite each family member to wear their favorite hat to dinner.

In a medium bowl, combine dill weed, lemon pepper, salt, garlic powder, brown sugar, oil, soy sauce, and green onions. Stir to dissolve sugar. Place salmon in a large flat dish or large resealable plastic bag. Pour marinade over salmon. Cover. Refrigerate 1 hour, turning once. Remove salmon from marinade and place on a large sheet of heavy-duty aluminum foil that has been coated with cooking spray. Place lemon and onion slices on salmon. Fold over foil and seal ends. Place on grill. Cook over medium heat 15 to 20 minutes, or until fish flakes easily. Remove salmon from foil and place on serving platter.

Serves 4 to 6.

Grilled Swordfish with Red Pepper Sauce
BETTY DRAPER

The red pepper sauce is also very good on grilled chicken or pan-fried orange roughy.

6 (6- to 8-ounce) swordfish steaks, 1 inch thick
3 tablespoons oil
Salt and pepper to taste

Brush swordfish with oil. Season with salt and pepper. Grill or broil about 10 minutes. Serve with sauce.

Red Pepper Sauce

2 red bell peppers, chopped
2 shallots, chopped
1 garlic clove, minced
1 serrano chili, minced
2 tablespoons oil
1 cup chicken broth
Salt and pepper to taste

Sauté red peppers, shallots, garlic, and chili in oil in a medium skillet about 5 minutes, until peppers are soft. Add chicken broth and boil until reduced by half. Puree in blender and strain. Season with salt and pepper.

Serves 6.

I never considered my mom's cooking good or bad until Grandma came for dinner one day. "Your mother is such a good cook!" she said. "Oh, this food is delicious." I had to say to myself, "Hmmm. This food is pretty good." Grandma is always so appreciative, and it's contagious.
—HEIDI P. JENSON, GRANDDAUGHTER OF MARJORIE P. HINCKLEY

Grilled Swordfish or Halibut a la Orange
BETTY DRAPER

Most grocery stores offer a wide array of fresh and fresh-frozen fish. Be daring and try something new.

- 8 swordfish or halibut steaks
- 2 teaspoons grated orange peel
- 1½ cups orange juice (preferably fresh)
- 2 tablespoons lemon juice
- 2 tablespoons sesame oil
- 2 tablespoons soy sauce
- Salt and pepper
- 2 oranges, peeled and cut into sections or 1 (11-ounce) can mandarin oranges, drained

Rinse fish and pat dry with paper towels.

Combine grated orange peel, orange juice, lemon juice, sesame oil, and soy sauce in a small bowl. Pour mixture into a resealable plastic bag with fish. Marinate in refrigerator 1 hour, turning several times.

Remove fish from marinade and sprinkle lightly with salt and pepper. Grill 6 to 8 minutes per side, or until fish is opaque and flakes easily. Top with orange sections.

Serves 8.

The key is to look for ways to seize the priceless time we have each day, sitting across the table from one another, to reinforce our bonds of love, to affirm the value of each family member and to acknowledge the importance of our relationship with God—the Provider of every good and perfect gift. —SHIRLEY DOBSON

Grilled Orange Roughy with Salsa ★
BETTY DRAPER

Fresh salsa is unlike anything out of a jar.

2 pounds orange roughy, cut in 6 pieces
Olive oil
¼ cup minced cilantro

Rinse orange roughy and pat dry with paper towels. Brush both sides with oil and sprinkle with ¼ cup cilantro. Place orange roughy in a sprayed or greased fish basket or on a grill screen. Grill over medium heat 5 to 6 minutes per side, or until orange roughy is opaque and flakes easily.

Salsa
4 large tomatoes, chopped
1 medium red onion, chopped
½ cup minced cilantro
3 tablespoons lime juice
1 to 2 jalapeño peppers, seeded and chopped
2 to 3 cloves garlic, minced
¼ teaspoon salt

Turn dinnertime into a cultural experience by preparing ethnic dishes and talking about the particular country or culture from which the food comes. If possible, eat the way people of that culture do: use chopsticks for Japanese cuisine or eat with your fork in your left hand, the way Europeans do.

In a medium bowl, combine tomatoes, onion, cilantro, lime juice, jalapeño peppers, garlic, and salt. Cover and refrigerate. Stir before serving. Serve orange roughy with salsa.

Serves 6.

Sea Bass or Haddock with Black Bean Relish
BETTY DRAPER

Very south-of-the border and very tasty.

- 2 tablespoons chopped cilantro
- 2 tablespoons minced fresh oregano or 1½ to 2 teaspoons dried oregano
- ½ teaspoon grated lime peel
- 2 tablespoons lime juice
- 1 tablespoon olive oil
- 1 clove garlic, minced
- ¼ teaspoon hot pepper sauce
- 1 (15-ounce) can black beans, rinsed and drained
- 1 medium avocado, chopped
- 4 sea bass or haddock fillets

Combine cilantro, oregano, lime peel, lime juice, oil, garlic, and hot pepper sauce in a small bowl. Put 2 tablespoons of cilantro mixture in another bowl. Add beans and avocado to first bowl, stirring to mix. Cover and chill.

Rinse fillets and pat dry with paper towels. Brush reserved cilantro mixture over fillets. Put fillets in an oiled or sprayed fish basket or a grill rack. Grill over medium heat 4 to 6 minutes per side, until fillets flake easily when tested with a fork. Serve fillets with black bean relish.

Serves 4.

Sharing food daily at the table is a powerful ritual that creates and nourishes family and communal life. It teaches us to share, to listen, and to talk with others. It teaches us to be civilized. —MARION CUNNINGHAM

Barbecued Spareribs
LESLIE BETTWIESER

Every backyard chef should have a great barbecue sauce in his or her repertoire.

- 4 pounds spareribs
- 1 large onion, quartered
- 2 teaspoons salt
- ¼ teaspoon pepper

Place ribs in a large pot or Dutch oven (cut ribs in 2 or 3 pieces, if necessary, to fit). Add onion, salt, and pepper. Add water to cover. Bring to a boil. Reduce heat and simmer, covered, 1½ hours.

Barbecue sauce
- ¾ cup cider vinegar
- ½ teaspoon dry mustard
- 2 tablespoons chopped onion
- 1 tablespoon brown sugar
- ¼ cup Worcestershire sauce
- ½ cup catsup
- ¼ cup chili sauce
- 1 tablespoon lemon juice
- 1 clove garlic, minced
- Dash of cayenne

While ribs are cooking, combine vinegar, mustard, onion, brown sugar, Worcestershire sauce, catsup, chili sauce, lemon juice, and garlic in a medium saucepan. Simmer, uncovered, 30 minutes, stirring occasionally. Add cayenne. Remove ribs from pot. Baste with sauce. Place on oiled grill, 6 inches from coals. Grill 30 minutes, basting with sauce several times.

Serves 4 to 6.

GRILLING

Grilled Seasoned Ham ★ ▽
JANET PETERSON

Grilling adds a new dimension to ham.

⅓ cup orange or apricot marmalade
½ cup Dijon mustard
¾ teaspoon Worcestershire sauce
½ cup water
4 (6- to 8-ounce) ham slices, 1-inch thick

In a small bowl, mix marmalade, mustard, Worcestershire sauce, and water. Put in a large glass dish or resealable plastic bag. Add ham slices. Marinate 2 to 3 hours or longer in refrigerator. Remove ham from marinade. Place on an oiled grill. Grill over medium heat, 10 to 15 minutes. Cook until ham is browned on both sides.

Serves 4.

For the Christensen family, the evening meal is always a special time to gather around the dinner table to share good times, plan for the day ahead and enjoy family relationships. One evening, during a busy week for the chief homemaker and chef (Mom), we sat down at the table and noticed that the menu consisted of warmed up leftovers. Our middle son, Stephen, age 5, was invited to offer the blessing on the food. His prayer of thanksgiving was expressed in a traditional LDS way, except rather than giving thanks for the hands that prepared the meal, he gave thanks for the hands that repaired the meal. We all agreed that he was inspired!
—FERREN L. CHRISTENSEN

Grilled Pork Chops with Apples ★
BETTY DRAPER

You'll want to prepare these pork chops again and again.

- 1 cup orange juice
- ¼ teaspoon Worcestershire sauce
- 6 pork chops
- 3 large Granny Smith apples, cored and thickly sliced into rounds
- ¼ cup butter or margarine, melted
- ¼ cup sugar

In a small bowl, mix orange juice and Worcestershire sauce. Brush pork chops with mixture. Place pork chops on a sprayed or oiled grill and cook over medium heat, 8 to 10 minutes per side (depending on thickness), until center is no longer pink.

While pork chops are cooking, brush apple slices with melted butter and place on an oiled or sprayed grill rack. Cook apples 1 to 2 minutes per side, until slightly brown and soft. Remove from grill and sprinkle with sugar. Serve pork chops with apple slices.

Serves 6.

My kitchen is a mystical place, a kind of temple for me. It is a place where the surfaces seem to have significance, where the sounds and odors carry meaning that transfers from the past and bridges to the future. —PEARL BAILEY

Grilled Toast ★

TRINA WEATHERSTON

Better than Sizzlers'.

- ¼ cup butter or margarine, softened
- ¼ cup Parmesan cheese
- 1 tablespoon oil
- 1 teaspoon garlic powder
- Thickly sliced sourdough, French, or white bread

In a small bowl, mix butter, Parmesan cheese, oil, and garlic powder. Spread on bread. Place on top rack of a hot grill, buttered side down. Cook a few minutes until golden brown. Watch so that toast doesn't burn.

Servings variable.

To soften butter, place on a microwave-safe plate and heat in microwave 5 seconds. Repeat until softened.

Hot Bacon Potato Salad
JUDITH NIELSON

An 8-inch-square disposable aluminum pan or heavy-duty aluminum foil can be used to grill these potatoes. Cleanup is easy—just throw the pan away.

- 5 to 6 unpeeled medium potatoes (about 1½ pounds), cooked and sliced into ¼-inch slices
- 8 slices bacon, cooked and crumbled
- 3 green onions, finely chopped
- 2 celery stalks, finely chopped
- ½ cup mayonnaise
- ¼ cup white vinegar
- 2 teaspoons sugar
- 1 teaspoon salt
- 1 teaspoon dry mustard
- ½ teaspoon coarsely ground pepper

Mix potatoes, bacon, onions, and celery in a large bowl. Add mayonnaise, vinegar, sugar, salt, mustard, and pepper. Toss thoroughly. Place mixture in an 8-inch-square aluminum pan. Cover pan with foil. Or place mixture on a double thickness of heavy-duty aluminum foil. Fold foil securely. Grill 4 inches from medium heat 20 minutes, stirring once or turning foil packet over once.

Serves 5 to 6.

In cooking, as in all the arts, simplicity is the sign of perfection. —CURNONSKY

Cheesy Potatoes ⌣

JANET PETERSON

These potatoes are smothered with good taste.

- 6 medium potatoes, peeled and thinly sliced
- 1 medium onion, sliced
- 6 tablespoons butter or margarine
- ½ cup grated cheddar cheese
- 2 tablespoons minced fresh parsley
- 1 tablespoon Worcestershire sauce
- Salt and pepper to taste
- ⅓ cup chicken broth

Arrange potato and onion slices on a 20-inch, double thickness square of heavy-duty aluminum foil. Cut butter in small pieces and distribute over potatoes and onions. Mix cheese, parsley, and Worcestershire sauce in a small bowl. Spread cheese mixture over potatoes. Sprinkle with salt and pepper. Fold foil up around potatoes. Sprinkle chicken broth over potato mixture. Tightly seal foil.

Grill, covered, over medium heat 35 to 40 minutes, or until potatoes are done.

Serves 4 to 6.

HOLD AN INTERNATIONAL CHRISTMAS DINNER AND PREPARE FOOD FROM A DIFFERENT COUNTRY EACH YEAR. TRY CHOOSING A COUNTRY FROM WHICH YOUR ANCESTORS CAME OR A COUNTRY WHERE A FAMILY MEMBER HAS SERVED A MISSION. RESEARCH THE CHRISTMAS FOODS, CUSTOMS, AND TRADITIONS OF THE COUNTRY AND DECORATE THE TABLE WITH ITEMS FROM THAT REGION. A GERMAN CHRISTMAS MIGHT INCLUDE ROULADEN ON THE MENU AND A TABLE DECORATED WITH NUTCRACKERS. A SCOTTISH CHRISTMAS MIGHT CALL FOR EVERYONE TO WEAR PLAID AND EAT LEEK SOUP, SALMON, AND SHORTBREAD.

Parmesan Potato Packets ★ ⬇

JANET PETERSON

You don't even have to peel these potatoes.

- 2 pounds new red or white potatoes, unpeeled and cubed
- ½ cup chopped green onions
- 4 teaspoons olive oil
- 2 tablespoons grated fresh Parmesan cheese
- 2 teaspoons oregano
- 1 teaspoon garlic salt
- ½ teaspoon pepper

Put potatoes, onions, and oil in a large bowl. Toss to coat. Put mixture on a 20-inch square piece of double-thick heavy-duty aluminum foil.

In a small bowl, combine Parmesan cheese, oregano, garlic salt, and pepper. Sprinkle over potatoes. Fold foil and seal tightly. Grill, covered, over medium heat 25 to 30 minutes, or until potatoes are tender.

Serves 8.

BEGIN DINNERTIME DISCUSSION WITH THE QUESTION, "WHAT WAS THE BEST THING ABOUT YOUR DAY?" YOU'LL BE AMAZED AT HOW FAST THE TIME FLIES AS FAMILY MEMBERS SHARE THEIR EXPERIENCES.

❖ VEGETABLES ❖

Vegetables add color, texture, fiber, vitamins, and variety to dinner. If they are cooked well, even the fussiest of eaters can enjoy them. Many vegetables are equally good served hot or cold, cooked or uncooked. Whether plain or enhanced, vegetables are essential to a well-balanced diet.

Asparagus with Lemon Butter/207

Chilled Asparagus Oriental/208

Great Green Beans/209

Extra-Delicious Green Beans/210

Oriental Beans/211

Baked Beans/212

Glazed Almond Broccoli/213

Broccoli with Swiss Cheese/214

Glazed Carrots/215

Chilled Carrots and Peas/216

Lemon Carrots/217

Carrots Lyonnaise/218

Dilly Mustard Cauliflower/219

Holiday Cauliflower/220

Corn on the Cob with Herb or Thyme Butter/221

Dilly Corn and Snow Peas/222

Almond Mushroom Peas/223

Oven-Baked Potato Pie/224

Potato Cakes/225

Savory Mashed New Potatoes/226

Italian-Seasoned Potatoes/227

Oven-Roasted Potatoes/228

Sweet Potato Pudding/229

Summer Squash/230

Zucchini Carrot Casserole/231

Skillet Tomatoes and Zucchini/232

Oriental Vegetables/233

Speedy Mock Hollandaise/234

Glaze for Vegetables/235

Asparagus with Lemon Butter ★
ELIZABETH SORENSEN

Lemon juice enhances the flavor of most vegetables, especially asparagus.

- 1 pound asparagus, cut into 3-inch pieces
- 2 tablespoons butter or margarine, melted
- Juice and grated rind of 1 lemon
- 1 tablespoon chopped fresh parsley (optional)

Steam asparagus in a vegetable steamer about 5 minutes, or until crisp-tender and a vivid green, or cook in boiling water 3 to 4 minutes. Drain asparagus. Return to the pan, add butter, lemon juice, rind, and parsley, if desired. Toss well. Can be served hot or chilled.

Serves 4 to 6.

PLANT A GARDEN. NOT ONLY WILL GROWING YOUR OWN VEGETABLES AND FRUITS YIELD HIGH DIVIDENDS, YOU CANNOT BUY THE TASTE OF A JUST-PICKED TOMATO IN THE GROCERY STORE.

Chilled Asparagus Oriental
JANET PETERSON

Asparagus is appealing either hot or cold, especially when flavored with these ingredients.

1 pound asparagus, cut into 3-inch pieces
2 tablespoons soy sauce
1 tablespoon oil
1 tablespoon vinegar
1½ teaspoons sugar
1½ teaspoons sesame seeds, toasted*
¼ teaspoon ground ginger
⅛ to ¼ teaspoon cumin

Can or freeze fresh produce from your garden or from a produce market.

*Place sesame seeds in a baking pan and bake 5 to 7 minutes at 350° F., watching so they don't burn.

In a medium saucepan or steamer, cook asparagus until crisp-tender, about 3 to 5 minutes. Drain and plunge in cold water to stop cooking process. Drain again and put in a large serving bowl.

In a small bowl, mix soy sauce, oil, vinegar, sugar, sesame seeds, ginger, and cumin. Pour mixture over asparagus, tossing to coat. Cover and refrigerate at least 1 hour. Drain liquid before serving. If preferred, reheat and serve hot.

Serves 4 to 6.

Great Green Beans

JILL SPENCER

For best results, make this early in the day and allow flavors to mellow together. Just reheat.

- 2 tablespoons butter or margarine
- ⅓ cup chopped onion
- 2 tablespoons flour
- 1 teaspoon salt
- ¼ teaspoon pepper
- 1 cup sour cream
- 2 (14½-ounce) cans green beans
- ⅓ cup grated Swiss cheese
- 3 slices bacon, cooked and crumbled

Heat oven to 350° F.

In a medium skillet, melt butter and sauté onion until lightly browned or limp. Slowly add the flour and stir. Add salt and pepper. Cook until flour is absorbed and slightly thickened, 1 to 2 minutes. Stir in sour cream. Heat through, but do not boil. Add green beans and stir. Put mixture in a 7x11-inch pan or 1½- or 2-quart casserole dish. Top with cheese and bacon. If made early in the day, refrigerate until baking time. Bake 15 to 20 minutes.

Serves 6.

USE BABY PICTURES OF FAMILY MEMBERS AS PLACE CARDS AT THE DINNER TABLE. DURING THE MEAL, REMINISCE ABOUT EACH OF THE CHILDREN AND PARENTS AS BABIES AND TODDLERS.

Extra-Delicious Green Beans ★ ▽
JANI STONE

Easy, quick, and extra delicious.

2 (14½-ounce) cans French-cut green beans
⅔ cup grated cheddar cheese (Cracker Barrel® recommended)
1 cup sour cream
2 shakes of dried dill weed

Heat oven to 375° F.

Drain beans. Put beans in a 2-quart casserole dish or 8-inch square baking dish. Stir in cheese, sour cream, and dill. Bake, uncovered, 30 minutes.

Serves 6 to 8.

JUMP-START YOUR DINNER TABLE CONVERSATION BY KEEPING A JAR OF CONVERSATION TOPICS HANDY. EVERY NOW AND THEN, PASS THE JAR AROUND THE TABLE AND HAVE FAMILY MEMBERS DRAW A TOPIC, SUCH AS "WHAT IS YOUR EARLIEST MEMORY OF YOUR GRANDPARENTS?" OR "WHAT WAS YOUR FAVORITE VACATION AND WHY?" OR "WHAT DO YOU REMEMBER ABOUT KINDERGARTEN?"

Oriental Beans ★

JANET PETERSON

Fresh green beans are a must; canned green beans just don't taste the same.

- 1 pound fresh green beans, trimmed
- 1 tablespoon butter or margarine
- 1½ tablespoons soy sauce
- 2½ teaspoons sesame seeds, toasted*

*Place sesame seeds in a baking pan and bake 5 to 7 minutes at 350° F., watching so they don't burn.

Steam beans 10 minutes in a vegetable steamer or cook in boiling water in a medium saucepan 10 to 12 minutes, until beans are crisp-tender. Drain. Put in a serving bowl. Add butter, soy sauce, and sesame seeds. Toss to coat. Serve hot.

Serves 6 to 8.

HOW TO STEAM VEGETABLES

PUT SEVERAL INCHES OF WATER IN THE BOTTOM OF A STEAMER OR SAUCEPAN (MORE IF LONGER STEAMING IS NEEDED). PUT THE STEAMING BASKET IN THE STEAMER OR SAUCEPAN. PLACE VEGETABLES (WHOLE, SLICED, CHOPPED) IN BASKET. COVER STEAMER OR POT. BRING WATER TO A BOIL, THEN REDUCE HEAT. STEAM UNTIL VEGETABLES ARE CRISP-TENDER. LENGTH OF STEAMING TIME VARIES DEPENDING ON THE VEGETABLE AND AMOUNT.

Baked Beans
KATHLEEN MCGUIRE

Easy and great tasting.

2 (31-ounce) cans of pork and beans
½ pound bacon, cooked crisp and cut into small pieces
1 large onion, chopped
1 green pepper, diced
⅔ cup brown sugar
2 teaspoons Worcestershire sauce
¼ cup vinegar
1 cup catsup

Heat oven to 325° F.

Combine pork and beans, bacon, onion, green pepper, sugar, Worcestershire sauce, vinegar, and catsup in a deep baking dish (3-quart or larger). Bake, uncovered, 2 hours. During last part of baking, cover if getting dry.

Serves 12.

Laughter is our favorite recipe. We've always felt like our neighbors could tell when it was dinnertime in the McRae household. Usually, somewhere between the entrée and dessert, someone would tell a funny story . . . , and that would get us started. And of course, once someone started laughing, that would quickly spread to the rest of us, often to the point where one or more would have to leave the table to regain normal breathing and/or composure.

The years have dimmed our recollections and details about when a particular dish was served or a new recipe tried, but we can all remember that the main course recipe most often served was laughter.

—DAVID AND SYLVIA MCRAE

Glazed Almond Broccoli
SUE NELSON

Makes a lovely Sunday-dinner vegetable. Can be made before church, then put in the oven afterwards while other preparations are completed.

- 2 pounds fresh broccoli, trimmed and cut into florets
- ½ cup butter or margarine
- ½ cup flour
- ¾ cup chicken broth
- 1 cup light cream
- 2 tablespoons lemon juice
- ¼ cup grated fresh Parmesan cheese
- ¼ cup slivered almonds

Heat oven to 350° F.

Steam broccoli in a vegetable steamer 5 to 8 minutes, or cook in salted, boiling water 5 to 8 minutes, or cook in microwave in a small amount of salted water. Melt butter in a small saucepan. Mix in flour and stir until well blended. Add chicken broth, cream, and lemon juice. Cook, stirring until thickened. Arrange broccoli in a 9x13-inch glass baking pan. Pour white sauce over broccoli. Sprinkle with cheese and almonds. Bake 25 minutes.

Serves 6 to 8.

To perk up everyday vegetables, thicken ½ cup chicken broth with a little cornstarch; add a little brown sugar, a couple teaspoons of soy sauce, a teaspoon of butter, chopped green onions, and a little pepper. Pour over cooked vegetables and heat through.

Broccoli with Swiss Cheese
JENNIFER OLDROYD

Fresh, not frozen, broccoli is mandatory here.

- 2 pounds fresh (not frozen) broccoli, cut into florets
- 1 cup grated Swiss cheese
- ⅓ cup mayonnaise
- 2 tablespoons finely chopped green onions
- ¼ teaspoon salt
- ⅛ teaspoon pepper
- ½ teaspoon spicy mustard

Heat oven to 350° F.

Steam broccoli in a vegetable steamer 8 minutes or cook broccoli in a large saucepan 8 to 10 minutes, until crisp-tender. Drain. Arrange in a shallow 2½-quart casserole dish or 9x13-inch baking dish. Combine cheese, mayonnaise, green onions, salt, pepper, and mustard in a small bowl. Spoon evenly over broccoli. Bake, uncovered, 20 minutes. Be careful not to overbake.

Serves 6 to 8.

IF YOU PUT TOO MUCH SALT IN VEGETABLES OR SOUP, REMEDY BY ADDING A TEASPOON EACH OF CIDER VINEGAR AND SUGAR OR BY ADDING PEELED AND CUT RAW POTATOES. POTATOES SHOULD BE REMOVED AFTER THEY ARE COOKED AND HAVE ABSORBED THE SALT.

Glazed Carrots ★ ▽

ELAINE JACK

Fresh gingerroot, which can be found in the produce section of the grocery store, has a more intense flavor than ground ginger.

- 5 to 6 carrots, peeled and sliced diagonally in ⅛-inch pieces
- 3 (¼-inch) slices gingerroot
- 1 tablespoon sugar
- 1 teaspoon salt
- ¼ cup butter or margarine
- ½ cup sugar

Put carrots in a medium saucepan with enough water to barely cover them. Add gingerroot, 1 tablespoon sugar, and salt. Boil carrots about 5 to 8 minutes, until crisp-tender. Drain water; discard ginger slices. (Be sure carrots are well drained.) Melt butter and ½ cup sugar in a medium or large saucepan and add carrots. Heat until butter and sugar are melted and carrots are glazed.

Serves 4 to 6.

BUY BABY CARROTS READY FOR USE RATHER THAN PEELING AND CUTTING WHOLE CARROTS.

Chilled Carrots and Peas
KAREN SADLER

Chilled vegetables are a nice change in side dishes.

2 carrots, cut into thin sticks
1 (10-ounce) package frozen peas
½ cup sour cream
1 tablespoon fresh lemon juice
2 teaspoons chopped fresh chives
1 tablespoon minced fresh dill weed or 1 teaspoon dried dill weed
Freshly ground pepper to taste

Boil carrots in salted water about 5 to 8 minutes, until tender. Drain. Rinse in cold water. Cube carrots into pea-sized pieces. Boil peas in salted water about 4 to 5 minutes. Drain. In a serving bowl, mix carrots, peas, sour cream, lemon juice, chives, dill weed, and pepper. Chill.

Serves 4 to 6.

The idea in cooking is to keep the procedure simple and quick, the food flavorful and fresh, and, as often as you can, the experience of eating a convivial delight. —MICHAEL R. EADES AND MARY DAN EADES

Lemon Carrots ★ ◡

JANET PETERSON

A light lemon sauce complements the carrots.

- 8 or 9 large carrots, sliced diagonally
- 3 tablespoons butter or margarine
- 3 tablespoons brown sugar
- ¼ cup fresh lemon juice
- ½ teaspoon salt
- Grated lemon peel

Boil carrots in a large saucepan in salted water about 5 to 8 minutes, until tender. Drain. Place in a serving bowl. Melt butter in a small saucepan. Add brown sugar, lemon juice, and salt. Bring to a boil. Mix lemon sauce with carrots. Sprinkle with lemon peel.

Serves 8.

MAKE AN ORANGE SAUCE TO DRESS UP LEFTOVER COOKED CARROTS (¼ CUP ORANGE JUICE, 1 TEASPOON CORNSTARCH, ¼ TEASPOON GINGER, 2 TABLESPOONS SUGAR, 1 TEASPOON LEMON JUICE, AND 1 TO 2 TABLESPOONS BUTTER).

Carrots Lyonnaise
DEBBIE NELSON

Wonderful with roast beef for Sunday dinner.

5 to 6 carrots, cut into sticks
½ cup water
1 teaspoon chicken bouillon granules or 1 bouillon cube
¼ cup butter or margarine
2 to 3 onions, sliced
1 tablespoon flour
½ cup water
Salt and pepper to taste

B<small>UY WHOLE CARROTS AND WASH AND PARE THEM YOURSELF.</small>

In a large saucepan, simmer carrots in ½ cup water and chicken bouillon 5 to 8 minutes, until crisp-tender. Do not drain. In a medium skillet, melt butter and sauté onions. Mix flour with onions. Add ½ cup water, stirring constantly. Bring to a boil. Add salt and pepper to taste. Simmer over low heat 10 minutes. Add carrots and cooking liquid.

Serves 4 to 6.

Dilly Mustard Cauliflower ★
ELAINE JACK

A favorite of the Jack family.

- 1 head cauliflower
- ½ cup mayonnaise
- 1 teaspoon Dijon mustard
- 1 teaspoon chopped onion
- ½ cup grated cheddar cheese
- 1 teaspoon dill weed

Remove stem of cauliflower. Steam whole cauliflower in a medium saucepan 8 to 10 minutes, or until barely tender. Combine mayonnaise, mustard, and onion in a small bowl. Place cauliflower in an ovenproof serving dish. Spread mayonnaise mixture on hot cauliflower. Sprinkle cheese on top. Broil cauliflower 4 to 5 inches from heat until cheese melts. Garnish by sprinkling dill weed on top.

Serves 6.

Instead of thinking of dinner as just another obligation, think of it as an opportunity for jump-starting your creativity. . . . Like the union of canvas and pigment, cooking is alchemy, a work of Wholeness-in-progress. A paring knife can be as creative as a paintbrush. Scraping, slicing, shredding, stirring, simmering, sautéing, are all sleights of hand that switch your conscious mind onto artistic, automatic pilot. . . . Whenever I don't know what to do—whether it's writing or living, I seek discoveries in the kitchen, such as trying to re-create a great dish I enjoyed somewhere else. The worst that can happen is that the experiment's a flop and we end up eating sandwiches before bed. The best is that my pleasant brainstorming and the supper that results provide a new taste sensation.

—SARAH BAN BREATHNACH

Holiday Cauliflower
AFTON BROULIM

Serve this cauliflower at a special family dinner.

- 1 cauliflower, cut into medium-sized florets
- 1 (4-ounce) can sliced mushrooms or ½ cup fresh sliced mushrooms
- ¼ cup diced green pepper
- ¼ cup butter or margarine
- ½ cup flour
- 2 cups milk
- 1 teaspoon salt
- 1 cup grated Swiss cheese
- 1 teaspoon chopped pimiento

Heat oven to 325° F.

Cook cauliflower in boiling water 8 minutes, until tender. Don't overcook. Drain and set aside.

In a 2-quart saucepan, sauté mushrooms and green peppers in butter. Blend in flour. Gradually stir in milk. Cook, stirring constantly, until thick. Stir in salt, cheese, and pimiento. Place half of cauliflower in a greased or sprayed 2-quart casserole dish and cover with half of the sauce. Add remaining cauliflower and top with remaining sauce. Bake 15 minutes.

Serves 6.

Use undiluted cream soups or cheese soup for quick sauces to go with pasta or vegetables.

Corn on the Cob with Herb or Thyme Butter

DEMETRIA DAVIS/NANCY HUGHES

Not many things can improve freshly picked corn on the cob—but these butters do.

- 4 quarts water
- 1 tablespoon sugar
- 10 ears corn, husked and cleaned

In a large stockpot, bring water and sugar to a boil. Add corn. Cover and reduce heat. Simmer 3 to 5 minutes, or until corn is tender. Remove corn from water.

Herb Butter

- ½ cup butter or margarine, melted
- 1 tablespoon chopped fresh parsley
- 1 tablespoon lemon juice
- ½ teaspoon basil
- ¼ teaspoon garlic powder

While corn is cooking, combine butter, parsley, lemon juice, basil, and garlic. Brush ears with herb butter. Serve with remaining butter.

Thyme Butter

- ½ cup butter or margarine, melted
- 1 teaspoon thyme

Mix butter with thyme. Serve with corn.

Grill Method

Place each ear of corn on a piece of heavy-duty foil. Prepare butter. Brush butter over each ear. Wrap corn securely with double-folded seal. Place corn 4 to 6 inches from medium coals. Cook 20 to 30 minutes, or until tender, turning occasionally. Serve with remaining butter.

Serves 10.

Dilly Corn and Snow Peas ★
JANET PETERSON

Attractive as it is tasty.

2 cups snow peas
2 cups fresh or frozen corn
1 small red pepper, thinly sliced
⅓ cup water
1 tablespoon butter or margarine
1 teaspoon fresh dill weed or ¼ teaspoon dried dill weed
Salt and pepper to taste

In a medium saucepan, put peas, corn, pepper, and water. Bring to a boil and cook 3 to 4 minutes, until vegetables are crisp-tender. Drain. Add butter, dill weed, salt, and pepper, stirring to coat.

Serves 6 to 8.

IF YOU'RE REALLY PRESSED FOR TIME, ORDER YOUR GROCERIES ONLINE OR BY PHONE FOR DELIVERY OR PICKUP. MOST STORES OFFERING THIS SERVICE CHARGE A SMALL FEE.

Almond Mushroom Peas ★ ⌒

JANET PETERSON

Almonds and mushrooms provide a contrast in color and texture to the peas.

- 1 (16-ounce) package frozen peas
- 3 tablespoons butter or margarine
- ½ cup fresh sliced mushrooms or 1 (4-ounce) can sliced mushrooms, drained
- ¼ cup chopped onion
- ¼ cup sliced almonds
- ½ teaspoon salt
- ¼ teaspoon pepper

Cook peas in boiling water in a medium saucepan, 4 to 5 minutes, or in microwave. Drain. Melt butter in a small skillet. Sauté mushrooms, onion, and almonds. Add to peas. Add salt and pepper.

Serves 8.

I remember when Kenny, our oldest son, was in the first grade. I was teaching half days at two different schools, so I had time to come home and fix lunch for him even though we had to move fast. I used to look out the window when it was time for him to come down the street. He had the kindest heart in the world; and if someone didn't have a lunch, he would always bring that child home with him. And sometimes there were more than one! I'd count heads quickly and make a few more sandwiches or open another can of soup. Kenny was always amazed that I always had the right number of places set on the table and enough food for all. And I was always amazed that his heart was big enough for everyone who needed help. The best part for me was that my son knew I'd be willing to help and share. —CHIEKO OKAZAKI

Oven-Baked Potato Pie
IDALINA DUNN

"This is my mom's own recipe from Paraguay. Serve with ham, steak, or chicken."

    2 pounds potatoes, washed
    6 eggs
    1 cup milk
    1 cup chopped green onions
    1 cup grated cheddar cheese
    1 teaspoon salt

Heat oven to 350° F.

Boil whole potatoes in salted water. Drain, peel, and cut into 1-inch cubes. Beat eggs. Add milk, onions, cheese, salt, and potatoes. Pour into a buttered and floured 9x13-inch baking dish. Bake 20 minutes, or until golden brown.

Serves 8 to 10.

POTATOES ARE MUCH EASIER TO PEEL IF YOU BOIL THEM WITH THEIR SKINS ON AND REMOVE THE PEELS AFTER COOKING.

Potato Cakes ★

LINDA LOSCHER

"This is a recipe my mother's family in Chicago used during the Depression."

> Leftover mashed potatoes
> Flour (same amount as potatoes)
> ½ to 1 teaspoon salt (according to taste)
> Butter or margarine
> Salt and pepper to taste

Heat oven to 350° F.

In a medium or large bowl, combine potatoes, flour, and salt. Mix until it forms a dough. Roll out about ¾-inch thick on a floured board. Cut into rectangles about 2x3 inches. Bake on a greased cookie sheet 30 to 45 minutes. Split cakes with knife and add butter. Sprinkle with salt and pepper.

Variable servings.

HOW TO PREPARE MASHED POTATOES

WASH POTATOES THOROUGHLY. CUT AWAY ANY EYES ON THE POTATOES. PEEL WITH A VEGETABLE PEELER OR KNIFE. QUARTER OR HALVE POTATOES, PLACE IN A SAUCEPAN LARGE ENOUGH TO COVER POTATOES WITH WATER. ADD WATER AND 1 TEASPOON OF SALT. BRING TO A BOIL, THEN REDUCE HEAT AND COOK 15 TO 20 MINUTES, UNTIL POTATOES ARE TENDER. DRAIN.

PUT POTATOES INTO A LARGE, DEEP BOWL. USE A MANUAL POTATO MASHER, ELECTRIC MIXER, OR RICER. DO NOT PUT POTATOES IN A FOOD PROCESSOR, AS THEY WILL TURN OUT GUMMY. ADD A SMALL AMOUNT OF MILK (ABOUT ¼ TO ½ CUP, DEPENDING ON NUMBER OF POTATOES AND CREAMINESS DESIRED), BUTTER (SEVERAL TABLESPOONS OR MORE), AND SALT AND PEPPER TO TASTE. (WARMING THE MILK WITH THE BUTTER MAKES CREAMIER POTATOES.) WHIP UNTIL SMOOTH.

IF DESIRED, SEASON POTATOES WITH ROASTED GARLIC, CHOPPED CHIVES, PARMESAN CHEESE, OR ANY SPICES OR HERBS.

Savory Mashed New Potatoes ★
BEVERLY BLUNCK

Brown potatoes aren't the only kind that makes great mashed potatoes.

> 2 pounds small red new potatoes
> 1 teaspoon salt
> ½ cup whipping cream or half-and-half
> ¼ cup, or more, butter or margarine, softened
> Salt and pepper to taste
> 2 tablespoons chopped fresh parsley

Put unpeeled potatoes in a large saucepan or pot. Cover with water. Add salt to water. Boil potatoes until tender, about 15 to 20 minutes. Drain potatoes. Coarsely mash potatoes while adding cream and butter. Season to taste with salt and pepper. Stir in chopped parsley.

Serves 6.

MAKE LEFTOVER MASHED POTATOES INTO POTATO CAKES OR USE IN MAKING BREAD DOUGH.

Italian-Seasoned Potatoes ★
MARCIA STOSICH

A much tastier version of traditional fries.

2 tablespoons olive oil
½ teaspoon Italian seasoning
¼ teaspoon salt
¼ teaspoon pepper
¼ teaspoon paprika
4 to 5 large potatoes, peeled and cut in wedges

Heat oven to 350° F.

In a small bowl, mix oil, Italian seasoning, salt, pepper, and paprika. Brush surfaces of potato wedges with oil mixture or place part of potatoes in bowl and toss to coat. Place potatoes on an ungreased cookie sheet. Bake 30 to 40 minutes until soft, depending on size of potatoes. Remove from oven, turn over, and brush with remaining seasoning mixture.

Serves 4 to 5.

IMITATE TIME-CONSUMING TWICE-BAKED POTATOES BY ADDING CHOPPED GREEN ONIONS OR WHITE ONION AND GRATED CHEDDAR CHEESE TO MASHED POTATOES AND THEN BAKING AT 350° F. 15 TO 20 MINUTES, OR UNTIL HEATED THROUGH.

Oven-Roasted Potatoes
DEBBIE NELSON

Start a new potato tradition with these oven-roasted red potatoes.

1½ pounds or 4½ cups red potatoes, cut in ½-inch pieces
¼ cup olive oil
1 pound fresh mushrooms, cut in half
1 cup red peppers, cut in ½-inch pieces
2 to 3 cloves garlic, minced
½ cup chopped green onions
½ teaspoon thyme
1 teaspoon salt
¼ teaspoon pepper

SHRED OR SLICE LEFTOVER POTATOES, WHOLE OR IN CHUNKS, FOR HASH BROWNS.

Heat oven to 450° F.

Mix potatoes with oil in a 9x13-inch baking pan. Bake 10 minutes. Add mushrooms and peppers. Bake 15 minutes. Mix in garlic, green onions, thyme, salt, and pepper. Bake 10 minutes.

Serves 6 to 8.

Sweet Potato Pudding

BETH ROSE

"Sweet Potato Pudding is a very old Southern recipe from my Great-grandmother Rolf, who lived in Richmond, Virginia. This was a favorite dish of mine as a child and just making it brings back wonderful memories of the holidays spent with my family. This pudding can also be baked in a pie shell to make sweet potato pie."

- 1 (40-ounce) can sweet potatoes or 5 to 6 sweet potatoes or yams, cooked
- 1 (12-ounce) can evaporated milk
- ½ cup brown sugar
- 1 egg
- ¼ cup butter or margarine, melted
- 2 teaspoons cinnamon
- ½ teaspoon nutmeg
- ¼ teaspoon cloves
- Dash salt
- ½ cup chopped walnuts or pecans

Heat oven to 450° F.

Mash sweet potatoes or yams well in a large bowl, blender, or food processor. Add evaporated milk, brown sugar, egg, melted butter, cinnamon, nutmeg, cloves, and salt. Mix until very smooth.

Pour sweet potato mixture into a sprayed or greased 9x13-inch baking dish or 3-quart casserole. Sprinkle top with chopped walnuts or pecans.

Bake at 450° F. for 15 minutes, then at 350° F. for 50 minutes. A knife inserted in the center should come out clean.

Serves 10 to 12.

Summer Squash ★
NANCY SIMPSON

Zucchini, always abundant at the end of summer, could be used instead of squash.

> 2 to 3 crookneck squash or zucchini, cut into 1-inch pieces
> 1 (4-ounce) can chopped green chilies
> ½ medium onion, finely chopped
> ½ cup grated Monterey Jack cheese
> ¼ cup Parmesan cheese

Heat oven to 350° F.

In a medium bowl, combine squash or zucchini, chilies, and onion. Put into a 10-inch square or 9x13-inch pan or other baking dish. Top with cheeses. Bake 45 minutes.

Serves 8 to 10.

When my mother, Camilla, died, we divided up her belongings. Among the things I chose for myself was her file box of three-by-five-inch recipe cards. Thumbing through them takes me back to mother-as-cook.

Born in 1894, she was by training and choice a homemaker. As a young woman she taught home economics at the LDS Church academies in Hinckley, Utah, and Thatcher, Arizona, and even had a plan to study dietetics at Johns Hopkins University, until marriage intervened and made her own kitchen the focus of her skills. A great cook, she offered nothing fancy in her meals, but they satisfied. Her father said her cooking was "salubrious!". . .

The kitchen table served as the center of the home. There we studied our lessons, played games, ate meals. . . .

(Continued on pg. 231)

Zucchini Carrot Casserole

JANET PETERSON

Often maligned, zucchini is actually a versatile vegetable.

- 6 cups sliced zucchini
- 1 cup grated or sliced carrots
- 1½ cups seasoned croutons or stuffing mix
- 1 (10¾-ounce) can cream of chicken soup
- 1 cup sour cream
- ½ cup onion, chopped

Heat oven to 350° F.

Cook zucchini and carrots in salted water until just tender, about 5 minutes. Drain and reserve liquid. Add water to make 1 cup. Toss croutons or stuffing in this liquid.

In a large bowl, mix soup and sour cream. Stir in carrots, zucchini, and onion. Put half of the croutons in a buttered or sprayed 3-quart casserole dish or 9x13-inch. Spoon vegetable mixture over dressing and top with remaining dressing. Bake, uncovered, 30 minutes.

Serves 8 to 10.

(Continued from pg. 230)

We looked forward eagerly to baking days, when we could come home from school to the tempting aroma of fresh bread and cinnamon rolls, dough spread thin, filled generously with raisins, cinnamon, and brown sugar. No one has ever made them better than my mother. . . .

Grandfather was right; those who sat at my mother's table enjoyed truly salubrious eating.

—EDWARD L. KIMBALL, SON OF SPENCER W. KIMBALL AND CAMILLA EYRING KIMBALL

Skillet Tomatoes and Zucchini ★
DEMETRIA DAVIS

These flavors are so amazing together. Be sure to use flavored croutons.

For a change, spread the food out on the counter like a buffet and let each family member line up to dish out his or her own dinner.

2 tablespoons butter or margarine
2 small zucchini, thinly sliced
1 medium onion, thinly sliced
2 medium tomatoes, sliced
½ teaspoon garlic salt
½ teaspoon basil
Dash of pepper
1 cup grated mozzarella cheese
1 cup seasoned croutons

Melt butter in a large skillet. Add zucchini and onion. Cook over medium heat until crisp-tender. Gently stir in tomatoes, garlic salt, basil, and pepper. Cover; cook 3 to 5 minutes until tomatoes are tender. Remove from heat; sprinkle with cheese and croutons. Cover; let stand 2 to 3 minutes until cheese is melted.

Microwave Method

Place butter in a 2½-quart casserole dish or 9-inch square dish. Microwave on high 1 minute. Add zucchini and onion. Cook on high 3 minutes. Stir. Gently stir in tomatoes and seasonings. Cover and cook on high 3 to 5 minutes. Sprinkle with cheese and croutons. Cover. Let stand 3 minutes, until cheese is melted.

Serves 4.

Oriental Vegetables
CLAUDIA BOONE

Prepare all vegetables first and work quickly. Vegetables should be thinly cut for best results.

- 3 slices bacon, cut in ½-inch pieces
- 2 cups finely chopped or shredded cabbage
- 1 cup diagonally sliced celery
- 1 to 2 carrots, diagonally sliced
- ¼ cup sliced fresh mushrooms
- ½ medium onion, finely sliced
- ½ tablespoon sugar
- Salt and freshly ground pepper to taste

Cook bacon in a hot skillet until barely crisp. Add cabbage, celery, carrots, mushrooms, and onion. Sprinkle with sugar, salt, and pepper. Stir-fry 4 to 5 minutes, until vegetables are crisp-tender. Serve immediately.

Serves 4 to 6.

HOLD AN "ANCESTOR DINNER." DISPLAY PHOTOS AND MEMORABILIA OF ONE OF YOUR ANCESTORS, SERVE FOOD FROM HIS COUNTRY OF ORIGIN OR ERA, AND GATHER AROUND THE TABLE TO TELL STORIES ABOUT HIS LIFE.

Speedy Mock Hollandaise
MARDY EREKSON

Wonderful on cauliflower and broccoli when hot. Use leftover sauce chilled as a sandwich spread.

½ cup mayonnaise (low fat, if preferred)
2 teaspoons Dijon mustard
1 teaspoon lemon juice

Combine mayonnaise, mustard, and lemon juice in a small saucepan. Heat over low heat (or microwave carefully) until heated through. Do not boil.

Makes about ½ cup sauce.

Here in my hands are not one, but two of my intimate sources of belonging. They tell me food is indeed love. In one hand I hold my mother's recipe book, with its spine gone and pages dog-eared. In the other is my 4 x 6 holder, its flap long since missing, worn thin and soggy from handling. . . .

Handling these cards might be what handling my mother's recipe book is to me—a gift of remembering, of savoring, of being connected, of the grace of handling the beginnings of a feast tendered into bowl and pan and oven and onto tables surrounded by the love that has made it and me and them. Out of each spills what flows in my veins and theirs.

—EMMA LOU THAYNE

Glaze for Vegetables ★
LORRAINE DAY

For carrots, snow peas, water chestnuts . . .

- 1 cup orange juice
- 1 tablespoon cornstarch
- ¼ teaspoon ginger
- ¼ teaspoon poppy seeds or celery seeds
- 1 to 2 tablespoons brown sugar or honey

Put orange juice, cornstarch, ginger, poppy seeds or celery seeds, and brown sugar or honey in a small saucepan and bring to a boil. Pour over cooked vegetables.

Makes about 1 cup sauce.

HOW TO ROAST VEGETABLES

SPRAY A ROASTING PAN, BAKING SHEET, OR DISH WITH COOKING SPRAY OR LINE IT WITH PARCHMENT PAPER. PLACE WHOLE OR CUT VEGETABLES, SUCH AS SWEET POTATOES, MUSHROOMS, GREEN BEANS, AND ONIONS (ONE KIND OR MIXED), IN THE PAN OR DISH. DRIZZLE VEGETABLES WITH OLIVE OIL AND SPRINKLE WITH HERBS OR SPICES.

HEAT OVEN TO 425° F. ROAST VEGETABLES, UNCOVERED, 20 TO 45 MINUTES, DEPENDING ON KIND OF VEGETABLES AND SIZE. TOMATOES SHOULD BE ADDED ONLY DURING THE LAST 10 TO 15 MINUTES OF ROASTING. STIR VEGETABLES ONCE OR TWICE WHILE THEY ARE ROASTING.

✚ RICE, PASTA, ✚ AND LIGHT SUPPERS

Rice is exceptionally easy to cook—no peeling, chopping, or slicing—and can be prepared plain or combined with myriad other ingredients.

Likewise, a wide array of pastas—enhanced by a variety of meats, vegetables, and cheeses—provide healthy and enticing side dishes and main courses.

In addition to delicious rice dishes and pastas, this section will arm you with light supper ideas and recipes for those days when you don't feel like preparing a full-scale meal.

Rice-Cheese Dish/*239*

Rice and Mushrooms/*240*

Mexican Rice/*241*

Fried Rice/*242*

Broccoli Rice Quiche/*243*

Parmesan Pasta/*244*

Macaroni and Cheese/*245*

My Best Lasagne/*246*

Easy Lasagne/*248*

Vegetable Lasagna/*249*

Manicotti/*250*

Pasta Primavera Pie/*251*

Spaghetti Sauce/*252*

Simple Spaghetti Sauce/*253*

Baked German Pancakes/*254*

French Bread Pizza/*255*

Puffy Apple Pancake/*256*

Egg Burritos/*257*

Oven Omelet/*258*

Rice-Cheese Dish ★

SALLY BLACK

Rice with a perky flavor.

- 1½ cups rice, uncooked
- 3 cups water
- 1 (4-ounce) can diced green chilies
- 1 pint sour cream
- Salt and pepper
- ½ pound cheddar or Monterey Jack cheese, grated

Heat oven to 350° F.

Cook rice in water in a rice cooker or medium saucepan. In a medium bowl, combine chilies and sour cream. Salt and pepper to taste. Add rice and half of the cheese. Mix. Grease or spray a 3-quart casserole dish with cooking spray. Spoon rice mixture into dish. Sprinkle with remaining cheese. Bake, uncovered, 30 minutes.

Serves 6.

TURN MONDAY NIGHT INTO A SPECIAL, ONCE-A-WEEK FAMILY HOME EVENING DINNER. TAKE TURNS, BEGINNING WITH DAD AND WORKING DOWN TO THE YOUNGEST CHILD, CHOOSING THE MENU FOR DINNER. THE "SPECIAL" PERSON GETS TO CHOOSE WHATEVER HE OR SHE WANTS FOR DINNER AND, WITH MOTHER'S HELP, PREPARE THE MEAL.

Rice and Mushrooms ★
PATTI WITTWER

Rice makes a terrific side dish.

2 teaspoons beef bouillon granules or 2 bouillon cubes

2 cups water

1 cup rice

½ cup sliced fresh mushrooms or 1 (4-ounce) can sliced mushrooms

2 to 3 green onions, chopped

⅓ cup butter or margarine

Cook more rice than needed for a recipe and keep the rice (one week in the refrigerator and six months in the freezer) to use when preparing a quick dinner.

In a large saucepan, dissolve bouillon in water. Add rice, bring to a boil, and reduce heat. Cook 15 to 20 minutes. Sauté mushrooms and onions in butter in a small skillet. Add to cooked rice and mix well.

Serves 4.

Mexican Rice

CAMMY FULLER

This is easy to make and really completes a Mexican dinner.

- 2 teaspoons olive oil
- ½ teaspoon minced garlic
- ½ cup chopped onion
- 1 large tomato, chopped
- 1 cup rice (not instant)
- 1 small green pepper, diced
- Dash of red pepper
- ½ teaspoon oregano
- ½ teaspoon salt
- 1 (14½-ounce) can chicken broth

Heat oven to 400° F.

Heat oil in an ovenproof saucepan or Dutch oven over moderate heat. Add garlic, onion, and tomato. Cook, covered, 3 minutes, or until onion is soft. Add rice and cook 2 minutes, stirring until shiny and hot. Stir in green pepper, red pepper, oregano, and salt. Add chicken broth. Bring to a boil. Bake, covered, 15 to 20 minutes.

Serves 4 to 5.

HOW TO COOK RICE

RICE CAN BE COOKED IN A SAUCEPAN ON A STOVETOP OR IN AN ELECTRIC RICE COOKER. MEASURE RICE AND PUT IN A SAUCEPAN OR RICE COOKER. ADD 2 CUPS OF WATER TO EVERY CUP OF RICE. ADD 1 TEASPOON (OR LESS) SALT PER CUP OF RICE. IF COOKING IN A SAUCEPAN, BRING WATER TO A BOIL, THEN REDUCE HEAT AND COVER PAN. COOK RICE 15 TO 20 MINUTES, UNTIL ALL WATER IS ABSORBED AND RICE IS TENDER. AN ELECTRIC RICE COOKER MONITORS HEAT AND SIGNALS WHEN RICE IS DONE.

Fried Rice ★
TERE WEIR

A fast dinner when you haven't a lot of time. A great way to use leftover rice from another meal.

3 to 4 green onions, or ½ small onion, chopped
½ cup sliced celery
2 tablespoons butter or oil
1 cup cubed ham
1 cup frozen peas
4 to 5 cups cooked white rice
2 to 3 eggs, beaten well
Salt and pepper to taste
Soy sauce to taste

AFTER CHILDREN HAVE LEFT THE NEST, OCCASIONALLY INVITE ONLY ONE FAMILY AT A TIME TO DINNER SO THAT RELATIONSHIPS CAN BE NURTURED IN SMALL NUMBERS.

In a large skillet sauté onion and celery in butter or oil. Add ham and peas. Stir in precooked rice. Cook over medium heat 2 to 3 minutes. Add eggs. Season with salt, pepper, and soy sauce to taste. Heat about 10 minutes, stirring frequently.

Serves 6 to 8.

Broccoli Rice Quiche
JAN MARTIN

Looking for a new idea? Try this quiche made with rice.

- 1½ cups milk
- 3 eggs
- 1 tablespoon Dijon mustard
- ¼ cup finely chopped onion
- ¾ cup grated Swiss cheese
- 1 (2-ounce) jar diced pimientos, drained
- 1½ cups chopped fresh broccoli
- ¾ cup instant brown or white rice, uncooked

Heat oven to 350° F.

Spray a 9-inch pie pan with cooking spray. In a large saucepan, heat milk until very hot but not boiling. In a small bowl, beat eggs and mustard until well blended. Add onion, cheese, and pimientos to eggs. Mix well. Stir broccoli and rice into hot milk. Slowly add egg mixture, stirring constantly. Pour into pie pan. Bake 30 to 35 minutes, or until a knife inserted in center of quiche comes out clean. Let stand 5 minutes before serving.

Serves 6.

USE LEFTOVER RICE TO MAKE DESSERT BY ADDING SWEETENED WHIPPED CREAM OR COOL WHIP®, SLICED OR DICED BANANAS, CRUSHED OR CHUNK PINEAPPLE, AND RASPBERRIES.

Parmesan Pasta ★
BETTY DRAPER

A super side dish to serve with fish, beef, ham, or chicken or a light main course served with a green salad and a vegetable.

- 1 pound pasta of choice, cooked according to package directions and drained
- ½ cup butter or margarine (or less)
- 1½ cups grated fresh Parmesan or Romano cheese
- 2 to 3 tablespoons light cream
- Salt and freshly ground pepper to taste

Heat oven to 250° F.

While pasta is cooking, cut butter into several pieces and put in an ovenproof bowl. Place bowl in oven with door ajar. Drain pasta when it is cooked *al dente*. Take bowl out of oven, put pasta into bowl, and coat pasta with softened butter. Add cheese and mix. Add cream, a tablespoon at a time, to help distribute cheese evenly. Sprinkle with salt and pepper.

Serves 4.

HOW TO COOK PASTA

NEARLY ALL PACKAGES OF PASTA GIVE COOKING DIRECTIONS, INCLUDING AMOUNT OF WATER AND LENGTH OF COOKING TIME. MOST PASTAS COOK IN ABOUT 5 TO 14 MINUTES.

COOK PASTA IN A LARGE SAUCEPAN OR POT (8 QUARTS OR LARGER). PUT ENOUGH WATER IN PAN (FILL ABOUT ¾ FULL) TO ALLOW PASTA TO MOVE AROUND DURING BOILING. ADD 1 TABLESPOON SALT. BRING WATER TO A FULL ROLLING BOIL. TO PREVENT PASTA FROM STICKING TOGETHER AND TO KEEP WATER FROM BOILING OVER, ADD ONE TABLESPOON OF OIL TO COOKING WATER. ADD PASTA TO PAN AND BRING TO A BOIL AGAIN. REDUCE HEAT SO THAT PASTA DOES NOT BOIL OVER BUT MAINTAINS A

(Continued on pg. 245)

Macaroni and Cheese ★ ⌣

PAT MENLOVE

Wonderful macaroni and cheese. Serve with crusty bread, stewed tomatoes, and spinach salad.

- 1½ cups macaroni, uncooked
- ½ teaspoon onion salt
- 1 teaspoon Worcestershire sauce
- 1½ cups cubed cheese (mild or medium cheddar or combination)
- Milk

Heat oven to 325° F.

Cook macaroni until fairly tender. Drain and put in a greased 2- or 2½-quart casserole dish. Add onion salt and Worcestershire sauce and stir. Stir cheese cubes into macaroni, distributing them evenly. Pour milk into casserole dish to the top of the macaroni. Bake, uncovered, until set, about 1 hour. Test by inserting a knife in the center. If it comes out clean, macaroni and cheese is done.

Serves 6.

(Continued from pg. 244)

ROLLING BOIL. COOK, UNCOVERED, STIRRING OCCASIONALLY. COOK FOR DESIGNATED TIME, OR UNTIL PASTA REACHES DESIRED SOFTNESS. REMOVE A PIECE OF PASTA FROM THE PAN WITH A FORK OR TONGS AND TEST BY BITING INTO IT. PASTA *AL DENTE* IS TENDER BUT OFFERS SOME RESISTANCE WHEN BITTEN INTO OR HAS SOME DEGREE OF FIRMNESS. IT IS EASY TO OVERCOOK PASTA AND HAVE IT BECOME TOO SOFT. DRAIN PASTA IN A COLANDER OVER THE SINK. DO NOT RINSE PASTA. SERVE OR MIX WITH OTHER INGREDIENTS.

My Best Lasagne
SHARON MARTIN

This lasagne does take extra time—but it is worth the effort. It is the best lasagne.

- 1 pound mild Italian sausage
- 1 pound ground beef
- Pinch of nutmeg
- 48 ounces homemade or prepared spaghetti sauce
- 16 ounces lasagne noodles
- 2 to 4 tablespoons butter
- 2 to 4 tablespoons flour
- 1½ cups milk
- 8 ounces sharp cheddar cheese, grated
- ¾ cup grated fresh Parmesan cheese
- 8 ounces mushrooms or zucchini (or other fresh vegetables), sliced or chopped
- 1 clove garlic, minced
- Olive oil
- 8 ounces mozzarella cheese, grated

Heat oven to 350° F.

In a large skillet, brown sausage and ground beef together. Add nutmeg. When cooked, drain grease and set meat aside. Warm spaghetti sauce in a large saucepan. Boil lasagne noodles in salted water for only a few minutes, just until noodles are softened. Do not cook as long as package directions indicate. This allows for easier handling.

Prepare cheese sauce by melting butter in a medium saucepan; add flour and stir until thickened. Add milk, stir again; add cheddar and Parmesan cheeses. Cook until the sauce thickens to pouring consistency. In a small skillet, sauté mushrooms with garlic in a little oil about 2 minutes.

RICE, PASTA, AND LIGHT SUPPERS

Spread 2 cups of spaghetti sauce over the bottom of a 10x14-inch or 4-quart baking dish. Layer a row of noodles. Layer some meat over noodles. Add some red sauce. Cover with another layer of lasagne noodles. Add the rest of the meat and the red sauce. Place mushrooms or other vegetables over the sauce. Layer any remaining noodles. Spread the cheese sauce, the final layer, evenly over entire pan. Sprinkle with mozzarella cheese. Bake 40 to 50 minutes, until bubbly. Allow to cool a little before cutting.

Serves 10.

HOW TO MINCE GARLIC

SEPARATE INDIVIDUAL GARLIC CLOVES FROM THE GARLIC BULB. THE CLOVES USUALLY PULL AWAY FROM THE BULB QUITE EASILY. WITH A SHARP KNIFE, CUT OFF BOTH ENDS. REMOVE THE PAPERY OUTER LAYER OF THE GARLIC CLOVE BY RUBBING OR PEELING. MASH THE GARLIC CLOVE WITH THE END OF A KNIFE OR LARGE SPOON, MINCE OR FINELY CHOP WITH A SHARP KNIFE, OR USE A GARLIC PRESS (PUT GARLIC CLOVE INTO PRESS AND SQUEEZE HANDLES).

Easy Lasagne ★ ⌣
KAYLENE REDD

The lasagne noodles don't even have to be precooked.

½ pound ground beef
1 (32-ounce) jar spaghetti sauce
¾ cup water
1 (8-ounce) package lasagne noodles
1 (16-ounce) carton ricotta cheese or cottage cheese
12 ounces mozzarella cheese, grated or sliced
¼ cup Parmesan cheese

LOW-FAT COTTAGE CHEESE CAN BE SUBSTITUTED FOR MORE EXPENSIVE RICOTTA CHEESE. FREEZE COTTAGE CHEESE, THEN THAW AND DRAIN WELL.

Heat oven to 375° F.

Brown ground beef in a large skillet. Drain grease. Add spaghetti sauce and water. Simmer. In a 9x13-inch baking pan layer sauce, uncooked lasagne noodles, ricotta or cottage cheese, then mozzarella cheese. Sprinkle with Parmesan cheese. Repeat layers, ending with sauce. Cover with foil and bake 1 hour. Remove foil. Let stand 10 minutes before cutting.

Serves 8 to 10.

Vegetable Lasagna

KATHRYN WADE

Herb-seasoned ricotta cheese can be used in place of plain ricotta cheese, onion, basil, and garlic powder.

- 2 (16-ounce) cartons ricotta cheese or cottage cheese
- 1 (8-ounce) package cream cheese, softened
- ½ cup chopped onion
- 2 teaspoons basil
- 1 teaspoon garlic powder
- 1 (15-ounce) package lasagne noodles, cooked according to package directions and drained
- 4 cups fresh vegetables (any combination, such as broccoli florets; grated carrots; sliced zucchini; chopped green, red, or yellow bell peppers; sliced fresh or canned mushrooms)
- 4 cups grated mozzarella cheese
- ¾ cup grated Parmesan cheese
- 1 (14-ounce) jar spaghetti sauce

Heat oven to 375° F.

Mix ricotta cheese, cream cheese, onion, basil, and garlic powder together in a large bowl. Spray or grease a 9x13-inch baking pan or lasagne pan. Spread a third of cheese mixture in pan; layer a third of noodles, vegetables, and mozzarella cheese. Repeat layers. Sprinkle with Parmesan cheese. Bake 50 to 60 minutes. Heat spaghetti sauce in a medium saucepan. Serve atop baked lasagne.

Serves 8 to 10.

Manicotti
LISA COWAN

Use a narrow spoon to stuff manicotti, or make a slit in the manicotti and fill through it; arrange in pan cut side down.

2 pounds meat (all ground beef or 1 pound ground beef and 1 pound Italian sausage)

1 to 2 tablespoons olive oil

2 eggs

½ pound mozzarella cheese, grated

½ cup milk

4 slices bread, diced (crusts removed)

2 tablespoons chopped fresh parsley (stems removed)

1 cup rinsed, chopped spinach (optional)

Salt and pepper to taste

2 (8-ounce) packages manicotti shells

3 to 4 cups spaghetti sauce

1 cup V-8® or tomato juice (optional)

Grated fresh Parmesan cheese

WHEN MAKING LASAGNE OR MANICOTTI, THIN THE SAUCE WITH A CUP OF V-8® JUICE OR TOMATO JUICE. THIS ELIMINATES THE NEED TO BOIL THE PASTA BEFORE LAYERING THE LASAGNE OR FILLING THE MANICOTTI; THE NOODLES WILL COOK AND SOFTEN DURING THE BAKING PROCESS.

Heat oven to 350° F.

In a large skillet, break up ground beef and sausage and sauté in oil. Drain grease. Cool. In a large bowl, thoroughly mix meat, eggs, mozzarella cheese, milk, bread, parsley, and spinach, if desired. Season with salt and pepper.

If using uncooked manicotti, thin spaghetti sauce with juice. If not, boil manicotti in salted water until shells are softened but not fully cooked. Fill with meat mixture. Spread at least 1 cup spaghetti sauce in a lasagna pan or a 9x13-inch baking dish. Arrange manicotti in pan. Top with remaining sauce. Sprinkle Parmesan cheese over sauce. Bake, uncovered, about 45 minutes, until bubbly and cheese is melted.

Serves 8 to 12.

Pasta Primavera Pie
JANET PETERSON

Bright, colorful, and filling.

- 1 egg, beaten
- ¾ cup grated fresh Parmesan cheese
- 3 tablespoons butter or margarine
- 4 ounces spaghetti or linguini, cooked according to package directions and drained
- 2 cups broccoli florets
- 1 small green or red pepper, cut into strips
- 1 small onion, sliced
- 2 cups diced, cooked chicken
- ¾ teaspoon Italian seasoning
- ¼ teaspoon salt
- 2 eggs, beaten
- ½ cup light cream

Heat oven to 350° F.

Combine 1 egg, ¼ cup Parmesan cheese, and 1 tablespoon butter in a medium bowl. Add cooked spaghetti or linguini. Mix well. Press mixture into a greased or sprayed 9-inch pie pan.

Melt 2 tablespoons butter in a large skillet. Sauté broccoli, green or red pepper, and onion. Add chicken, ¼ cup Parmesan cheese, Italian seasoning, and salt. Put mixture into pasta crust.

In a small bowl, mix together 2 eggs and cream. Pour mixture over vegetables and chicken. Bake, covered with foil, 25 minutes. Remove foil. Sprinkle with ¼ cup Parmesan cheese. Bake an additional 10 minutes. Let stand 10 minutes before cutting into wedges and serving.

Serves 6.

Too much salt, pepper, oregano, or any seasoning in a casserole, soup, vegetable, or dish with combined ingredients can be remedied by increasing the quantities of some or all ingredients but the seasoning.

Spaghetti Sauce
KATHY CRAWFORD

This sauce tastes even better the second day.

1 pound ground beef
¾ pound (1 roll) mild or hot ground pork sausage
1 to 2 large onions, chopped
1 tablespoon olive oil
2 (28-ounce) cans whole tomatoes, drained
1 (15-ounce) can tomato sauce
1 (6-ounce) can tomato paste
2 to 4 cloves garlic, minced
1 to 2 teaspoons Italian seasoning
2 to 3 bay leaves
Spaghetti or other pasta, cooked according to package directions and drained

SEASONED GROUND BEEF IS THE MAIN INGREDIENT IN MANY RECIPES, SUCH AS CHILI, SOUPS, TACOS, AND VARIOUS CASSEROLES. COOK SEVERAL POUNDS OF GROUND BEEF MIXED WITH ONIONS AND SEASONINGS AT ONCE. STORE IN THE FREEZER FOR LATER USE.

Brown ground beef and sausage together in a large skillet. When cooked, drain thoroughly and put in a large pot. In a small skillet, sauté onion in oil and add to meat. Add tomatoes, tomato sauce, tomato paste, garlic, and Italian seasoning, stirring to mix well. Add bay leaves. Simmer 1 to 1½ hours. Discard bay leaves. Serve over cooked spaghetti or pasta.

Serves 8.

Simple Spaghetti Sauce ★ ⬯
KRISTEN CARPENTIER

Put water on to boil for spaghetti noodles while you cook the sauce; they will be done at the same time.

- 1 pound mild or hot Italian sausage or ½ pound sausage and ½ pound ground beef
- 1 green pepper, chopped
- 1 small onion, chopped
- 3 cloves garlic, minced
- 1 small tomato, cut in wedges
- Sliced mushrooms to taste
- 1 (15-ounce) can Hunt's® Chunky Special Sauce
- 2 (15-ounce) cans Hunt's® Italian Sauce
- Spaghetti noodles, cooked according to package directions and drained

USE BOTTLED MINCED GARLIC RATHER THAN MINCING YOUR OWN.

Brown sausage in a large skillet. Remove sausage and drain all but 1 to 2 tablespoons grease. Sauté green pepper, onion, garlic, tomato, and mushrooms in same skillet. Add sausage and sauces. Cook on medium-low heat 15 minutes. Serve over cooked spaghetti.

Serves 6 to 8.

Baked German Pancakes ★
MARJORIE TALL

Breakfast foods—which are often bypassed on busy mornings—make excellent suppers.

½ cup butter or margarine
1½ cups milk
1½ cups flour
6 eggs, beaten
¼ teaspoon salt

Heat oven to 425° F.

Melt butter in a 9x13-inch pan in oven. Mix milk, flour, eggs, and salt in a blender and pour into pan. Bake 20 to 25 minutes. Remove from oven, cut into serving slices.

Fruit Topping

1 (8-ounce) can pineapple chunks, drained
2 sliced bananas
1 cup sliced fresh or frozen strawberries or raspberries (thawed)

In a medium bowl, mix together pineapple chunks, bananas, and berries.

Additional Toppings

Sour cream
Brown sugar
Lemon wedges
Powdered sugar

Spread sour cream and fruit topping over pancake and sprinkle with brown sugar. Or serve with lemon wedges and powdered sugar.

Serves 4 to 6.

RICE, PASTA, AND LIGHT SUPPERS

French Bread Pizza ★
TERE WEIR

Instead of making pizza dough or purchasing expensive pizza crusts, simplify with a loaf of French bread or English muffins.

- 1 loaf French bread or 1 (12.5-ounce) package English muffins
- 1 (14-ounce) jar pizza sauce
- 1 cup grated cheese (mozzarella, cheddar, or combination of cheeses)

Pizza Toppings
- Cooked sausage
- Diced onion
- Ham
- Olives
- Pepperoni
- Pineapple chunks
- Sliced mushrooms
- Sliced olives
- Sliced tomatoes

Every so often, listen to each other's music during dinner. Put a portable tape or CD player in the kitchen and have each family member play a favorite song.

Heat oven to 425° F.

Cut French bread lengthwise and spread pizza sauce over each half of bread or on individual muffins. Sprinkle with cheese, then add desired pizza toppings. Bake 15 minutes, until cheese is melted. Cook on a broiler pan or baking stone for crisper crust.

Serves 4 to 6.

Puffy Apple Pancake
LIZ OLSEN

When this fun pancake is baked, it puffs into a shell shape. Good for a light weekend supper.

- 2 tablespoons butter or margarine
- 2 tablespoons brown sugar
- ¼ teaspoon cinnamon
- 1 cup thinly sliced, peeled apples (1 to 2 apples)
- 2 large eggs
- ½ cup flour
- ½ cup milk
- ¼ teaspoon salt

Heat oven to 400° F.

Melt butter in a 9-inch pie pan. Brush butter around sides of pie pan. Sprinkle brown sugar and cinnamon over butter or margarine. Arrange apple slices over sugar.

Beat eggs slightly in a medium bowl with a whisk. Stir in flour, milk, and salt until just mixed (do not overbeat). Pour over apples. Bake 30 to 35 minutes. Remove from oven and immediately loosen edges of pancake and turn upside down onto a serving plate.

Serves 2 to 4.

IF A PIECE OF EGGSHELL FALLS INTO YOUR MIXTURE, DIP A LARGER PIECE OF SHELL INTO THE BOWL.. IT ADHERES INSTANTLY.

Egg Burritos
LORRAINE DAY

Eggs with a south-of-the-border flair make a fun family night dinner.

- 16 eggs
- 2 tablespoons milk
- 2 tablespoons chopped onion or green onions
- 1 (4-ounce) can diced green chilies (reserve 1 teaspoon for sauce)
- ½ (2-ounce) jar pimientos, diced
- ¼ cup grated Monterey Jack cheese
- Salt and pepper to taste
- 8 flour tortillas
- Sour cream
- Salsa

Thoroughly beat eggs with milk in a large bowl. Add onions, green chilies, pimientos, cheese, salt, and pepper. Spray a large skillet with cooking spray or melt 1 tablespoon butter in skillet. Pour egg mixture in skillet and cook until eggs are scrambled and done. Prepare sauce.

Sauce

- 2 tomatoes, chopped
- 2 avocados, chopped
- 1 tablespoon chopped onion
- 1 teaspoon green chilies
- 1 tablespoon salsa
- Minced garlic to taste

In a medium bowl, combine tomatoes, avocados, onion, chilies, salsa, and garlic.

Place an inverted pie pan inside a large skillet. Add water so that it fills the skillet about 1 inch. Place tortillas on top of pie pan, cover, and steam 5 minutes to soften and heat them. Fill tortillas with eggs and top with sauce, sour cream, and salsa.

Serves 8.

Oven Omelet ★ ⬯
KRISTY OLSEN

An easy supper when you have no time for fancy stuff. Substitute or eliminate ingredients in the omelet to suit individual tastes.

1 cup diced ham, bacon, or sausage, cooked
1 (4-ounce) can sliced mushrooms
1 tomato, chopped
2 to 3 green onions, chopped
½ cup sliced black olives
1 cup grated cheddar cheese
1 cup grated mozzarella cheese
6 eggs
1 cup sour cream
Salt and pepper to taste
Sliced black olives (optional)
Chopped fresh parsley (optional)
1 cup salsa

Heat oven to 350° F.

Spray a 9x13-inch pan with cooking spray. Spread ham (or bacon or sausage), mushrooms, tomato, onions, olives, and cheeses in pan. Beat eggs well. Add sour cream and mix well. Add salt and pepper. Pour egg mixture over ham and other ingredients. Bake 30 to 40 minutes, or until center is set. To test, insert knife in center of omelet. If it comes out clean, omelet is done. Cut into squares and garnish with olives and parsley, if desired. Serve with salsa.

Serves 9 to 12.

SING WHILE YOU PREPARE DINNER OR DO THE DISHES TOGETHER.

DESSERTS

Desserts are the ultimate comfort food, each bite kindling memories of special times at home with family and friends. Many families have a favorite dessert, something sweet and delicious that has become a family tradition—pies, cookies, cakes, puddings, or ice cream. Dessert is often the reason we eat dinner in the first place! The simple pleasures that come from tasting something sweet and rich and the memories made while sharing it really are worth the indulgence every now and then.

Best-Ever Frosted Brownies/261

Brownies/262

Carmel Pecan Brownies/263

Infallible Chocolate Chip Cake/264

Texas Sheet Cake/265

Grasshopper Cake/266

Lemon Cake/267

Spiced Peach Cake/268

Oatmeal Cake/269

Mud Squares/270

Piña Colada Cake/271

Chocolate Chunk Cookies/272

Applesauce Oatmeal Cookies/273

Oatmeal Chocolate Chip Cookies/274

Chocolate Mint Cookies/276

Chocolate Rolo® Cookies/277

Chocolate Crinkles/278

Gingersnaps/279

Snickerdoodles/280

Peanut Butter Cookie Bars/281

Almost Candy Bars/282

Fudge Jumbles/283

Oh Henry Bars/284

Sunday Pudding/285

Brownie Trifle/286

Frosty Dog Dessert/287

Apple or Peach Crisp/288

Baked Apple/289

Apple Slump/290

Salt Lake City Dessert/291

Angel's Delight/292

Raspberry Banana Sherbet/293

Orange Sherbet Dessert/294

Raspberry Danish Dessert/295

Cool Lime Dessert/296

Velvet Fudge Sauce/297

Never-Fail Pie Crust/298

Easy Apple Pie/299

Quick Lemon Pie/300

Oreo® Ice Cream Pie/301

Banana Cream Pie (Chocolate or Lemon Variations)/302

Frosty Pumpkin Pie/303

Fresh Strawberry Pie/304

Fresh Peach Pie/305

Tutti Frutti Ice Cream/306

Fresh Peach or Berry Ice Cream/307

Chocolate Ice Cream/308

Fruit and Yogurt Ice Cream/309

DESSERTS

Best-Ever Frosted Brownies
JENNIFER OLDROYD

"My grandma is a brownie expert, and this is her all-time favorite recipe!"

- 1 cup butter or margarine, softened
- ½ cup plus 1 tablespoon cocoa
- 2 cups sugar
- 4 eggs
- 1⅔ cups flour
- ½ tablespoon baking powder
- 2 teaspoons vanilla
- ½ teaspoon salt
- ½ cup chopped nuts (optional)

Heat oven to 350° F.

Blend butter and cocoa in a large bowl. Add sugar. Cream together. Add eggs, one at a time. Add flour, baking powder, vanilla, salt, and nuts, if desired. Blend. Put batter into a greased 9x13-inch baking pan and a 5x9-inch bread pan. (As this is a very thick brownie, use a bread pan for part of batter.) Or put batter into a 10x14-inch baking pan.

Bake for the following times:

5x9-inch pan: 15 minutes

9x13-inch or 10x14-inch pan: 20 to 22 minutes

Frosting

- 2½ to 3 cups powdered sugar (adjust according to stiffness desired in frosting)
- ⅓ cup cocoa
- ½ cup butter or margarine, softened or melted
- ½ cup evaporated milk, cream, or milk

Mix powdered sugar and cocoa together. Add butter and milk and beat until smooth. Frost cooled brownies.

Makes 2½ to 3 dozen brownies.

Brownies
KATHY CRAWFORD

An original recipe for which Kathy is famous, especially in Baldham, Germany, where her family lived for several years.

½ pound unsalted butter (not margarine)
1 cup cocoa, preferably Dutch process, sifted
2 cups sugar
4 eggs at room temperature*
1 teaspoon vanilla
½ teaspoon salt
1 cup flour
2 cups chopped walnuts

MAKE YOUR VALENTINE'S DAY DINNER A CELEBRATION OF LOVE. ASK EVERYONE TO WEAR RED AND TO BRING RED FOOD. BAKE HEART-SHAPED COOKIES WITH EACH PERSON'S NAME WRITTEN IN FROSTING AND SET THE COOKIES ON THE TABLE AS PLACE CARDS. DURING THE DINNER, HAVE EACH FAMILY MEMBER SHARE A THOUGHT, POEM, SCRIPTURE, OR SONG ON LOVE.

*If eggs are at room temperature, the batter will flow more evenly into the baking pan.

Heat oven to 350° F.

Melt butter in a 3-quart saucepan. Mix in cocoa. Add sugar and mix well. Add eggs one at a time, mixing thoroughly after each addition. Add vanilla and salt. Stir in flour until thoroughly mixed. Add walnuts. Line a 9x13-inch baking pan with parchment paper (preferably) or buttered foil. Pour brownie batter into pan, being careful to spread it evenly into the corners. Bake 30 to 35 minutes, or until a toothpick inserted into the center comes out clean. Cool thoroughly and chill in refrigerator overnight (or in freezer if pressed for time), before cutting into small squares. To cut, peel off parchment paper and use a sharp serrated knife to cut while brownies are chilled. These brownies keep well in the refrigerator if left uncut, or they may be frozen for future use.

Variation

Use 1 cup chopped macadamia nuts and ½ cup chopped crystallized ginger in place of the walnuts.

Makes 4 dozen small brownies or 2 dozen large brownies.

Carmel Pecan Brownies

JANET PETERSON

Beginning with a cake mix reduces preparation time.

- 1 (18.25-ounce) package devil's food cake mix
- 1 cup chopped pecans
- ¾ cup butter or margarine, melted
- 1 (16-ounce) package caramels
- ⅓ cup evaporated milk
- 1 (12-ounce) package chocolate chips

Heat oven to 350° F.

Mix cake mix, pecans, and butter in a large bowl with a wooden spoon. Press half of batter into a 9x13-inch glass baking pan. Bake 8 minutes. Remove from oven.

Melt caramels in microwave or in the top of a double boiler. Stir in evaporated milk and mix well. Pour caramel mixture over brownie layer. Sprinkle on chocolate chips. Pat rest of brownie batter on top. Return to oven and bake 18 more minutes. Remove and cool. Cut into squares.

Makes 2 dozen brownies.

CREATE A FAMILY COOKBOOK BY INVITING CHILDREN, GRANDCHILDREN, AND GREAT-GRANDCHILDREN OF ONE COMMON ANCESTOR TO CONTRIBUTE RECIPES. SHARING YOUR FAVORITE RECIPES, WRITING ABOUT TRADITIONS INVOLVED WITH THE RECIPES, AND COOKING FROM THE COOKBOOK CAN BRING YOUR FAMILY CLOSER TOGETHER WHEN DISTANCE SEPARATES YOU.

Infallible Chocolate Chip Cake ★
HEATHER CLAYTON

Even if you've ruined cake recipes before, try this one. It's impossible to get wrong!

1 cup sour cream
⅓ cup oil
⅓ cup water
4 eggs
1 (18.25-ounce) package chocolate cake mix
1 (3-ounce) instant chocolate pudding mix
1 (12-ounce) package chocolate chips
Powdered sugar (optional)

Heat oven to 350° F.

In a large bowl, mix sour cream, oil, water, eggs, cake mix, and pudding mix. Stir in chocolate chips. Pour batter into a well-greased and floured 10-inch bundt pan. Bake 40 to 45 minutes, or until a toothpick inserted in the center comes out clean. Remove from pan and sprinkle powdered sugar over the top of cake, if desired.

Serves 10 to 12.

WHEN TAKING A CAKE OUT OF THE OVEN, PLACE THE PAN ON A DAMP KITCHEN TOWEL FOR A FEW MINUTES. THIS HELPS COOL THE CAKE AND KEEPS IT FROM STICKING TO THE PAN.

Texas Sheet Cake

KATHLEEN MCGUIRE

Big—just like Texas!

- 2½ cups flour
- 2 cups sugar
- 1 teaspoon salt
- 1 cup butter or margarine
- 1 cup water
- 2 tablespoons cocoa
- 4 eggs
- 1 cup milk
- 1 teaspoon baking soda
- 1 teaspoon vanilla

Heat oven to 375° F.

In a large bowl combine flour, sugar, and salt. In a large saucepan, combine butter, water, and cocoa. Heat, stirring until butter is melted and mixture is smooth. Pour cocoa mixture over flour mixture, mixing until smooth. Add eggs, milk, baking soda, and vanilla. Beat again. Spray or grease a 12x17-inch cookie sheet (must have at least a ½-inch side). Spread batter on cookie sheet. Bake 20 minutes. Cool and frost.

Frosting

- ½ cup butter or margarine
- 3 tablespoons milk
- 2 tablespoons cocoa
- 2 to 2½ cups powdered sugar

Combine butter, milk, and cocoa in a saucepan. Heat, stirring until smooth. Put powdered sugar in a medium bowl. Add cocoa mixture and beat to a frosting consistency. Spread on surface of cooled cake.

Serves 16.

Grasshopper Cake ★

MAUREEN SHUMWAY

A cool and inviting dessert.

1 (18.25-ounce) package white cake mix
½ to 1 teaspoon peppermint extract
Green food coloring
1 (8-ounce) carton Cool Whip® or vanilla or chocolate mint ice cream, softened
½ to 1 teaspoon peppermint extract (optional)
1 (12-ounce) jar hot fudge topping

HOLD A MONTHLY BIRTHDAY DINNER TO CELEBRATE THE BIRTHDAYS OF ALL EXTENDED FAMILY MEMBERS WHO WERE BORN THAT MONTH. ROTATE HOSTS AND MAKE THE DINNER POTLUCK FOR SIMPLICITY.

Mix cake according to package directions. Add ½ to 1 teaspoon peppermint extract and several drops of green food coloring to the batter. The food coloring will make it "look" minty. Bake in a sprayed or greased 9x13-inch pan. Cool. Mix thawed Cool Whip® topping with a few drops of green food coloring and ½ to 1 teaspoon peppermint extract, if desired. Spread Cool Whip® or ice cream on top of cooled cake layer. Top with softened hot fudge (warmed in microwave). Refrigerate leftovers.

Serves 12.

DESSERTS

Lemon Cake ★
KRISTEN LEE

"This is a family favorite. Simple, but good!"

- 1 (18.25-ounce) package yellow cake mix
- 1 (3-ounce) package lemon Jell-O®
- 1 cup water
- ½ cup oil
- 4 eggs
- 2 cups powdered sugar
- Grated rind of 1 lemon
- Juice of 2 lemons

Heat oven to 350° F.

With an electric beater, mix cake mix with Jell-O®, water, oil, and eggs in large bowl. Pour into a greased 9x13-inch pan. Bake 50 minutes. Punch holes in cake with meat fork when baked. Make glaze of powdered sugar, lemon rind, and lemon juice. Pour over cake and place in oven with the heat turned off. Let glaze set in oven 5 minutes.

Serves 12.

When I was serving as Relief Society president, I brought home work from the office nightly. In those days dinner was never elaborate. If it took more than fifteen minutes to prepare, we didn't have it, and Joe never complained. Although there were two rooms in our home fitted with desk and workplace, my work was always done at one end of the kitchen table, right after dinner. That was my "place." . . .

Life centered around the kitchen. Rarely was a meal prepared where everyone liked everything, but even when half-eaten food was put down the disposal, the sense of family was pervasive and treasured. —ELAINE L. JACK

Spiced Peach Cake
MARIE GALBRAITH

You'd never know this wonderful cake started out as a mix in a box.

- 1 (16-ounce) can sliced peaches
- 1 (18.25-ounce) package white or yellow cake mix
- 1 teaspoon cinnamon
- ½ teaspoon allspice
- ½ cup light molasses
- ½ teaspoon salt
- ⅓ cup oil
- 3 eggs
- 1 cup chopped walnuts

Heat oven to 350° F.

Drain peaches; pat dry on paper towel. Coarsely chop peaches. Combine cake mix, cinnamon, allspice, molasses, salt, oil, and eggs in a large bowl. Stir in peaches and walnuts. Pour batter into a greased or sprayed bundt pan. Bake 1 hour, or until an inserted toothpick comes out with fine crumbs. (Check cake while baking and cover with foil if browning too quickly.) Remove cake from pan to cool on a wire rack.

Frosting

- 1 (3-ounce) package cream cheese
- ½ cup powdered sugar
- 1 tablespoon milk
- 2 teaspoons fresh lemon juice
- 1 teaspoon vanilla
- 2 tablespoons chopped walnuts

Beat cream cheese in a medium bowl until smooth. Beat in powdered sugar, milk, lemon juice, and vanilla. Spoon over cake. Top with walnuts. Dusting cake with powdered sugar may substitute for frosting.

Serves 10 to 12.

Oatmeal Cake

MARJORIE TALL

A New Zealand favorite.

> 1 cup oatmeal
> 1¼ cups boiling water
> ½ cup butter or margarine
> 1 cup sugar
> 1 cup brown sugar
> 1 teaspoon vanilla
> 2 eggs
> 1½ cups flour
> 1 teaspoon baking soda
> ½ teaspoon salt
> ¾ teaspoon cinnamon
> ¼ teaspoon nutmeg

Heat oven to 350° F.

Put oatmeal in a medium bowl. Pour boiling water over oatmeal and cover. Let stand 10 minutes. In a large bowl, cream butter and sugars together. Add vanilla, eggs, softened oatmeal, flour, baking soda, salt, cinnamon, and nutmeg. Mix. Pour batter into a sprayed or greased and floured 9-inch square pan. Bake 50 to 55 minutes.

Frosting

> ¼ cup butter or margarine, melted
> ½ cup brown sugar
> 3 tablespoons half-and-half or evaporated milk
> ⅓ cup chopped nuts
> ¾ cup coconut

In a medium bowl, mix butter, brown sugar, and half-and-half. Stir in nuts and coconut. Frost warm cake. Place cake under broiler and brown until bubbly, watching carefully so that it does not burn.

Serves 9.

Mud Squares
JUDITH NIELSON

These ingredients can be easily kept on hand for a great Sunday-evening, spur-of-the-moment treat. Serve with Canadian vanilla ice cream.

1¾ cups boiling water
1 cup oatmeal (not instant)
½ cup butter or margarine
1 cup brown sugar
1 cup sugar
2 eggs, slightly beaten
1¾ cups flour
1 teaspoon baking soda
½ teaspoon salt
2 to 4 tablespoons cocoa (according to taste)
1 (12-ounce) package chocolate chips
¾ cup coarsely chopped walnuts or pecans

Heat oven to 350° F.

In a large bowl, pour boiling water over oatmeal and butter. Let stand 10 minutes. Stir in sugars and eggs.

Combine flour, baking soda, salt, and cocoa in a small bowl. Add to oatmeal mixture. Stir in half of the chocolate chips. Pour batter into a greased and floured 9x13-inch pan. Sprinkle remaining chocolate chips and nuts over cake. Bake 40 minutes, or until toothpick comes out clean.

Serves 12.

Mealtimes provide an opportunity for families to gather together as a group and develop a sense of belonging with each other. The images of family mealtimes may be passed down across generations and may represent what it means to be a member of MY family. —BARBARA FIESE

Piña Colada Cake ★ ▽

KAYLENE REDD

This cake tastes best when made the night before and refrigerated.

- 1 (18.25-ounce) package white or yellow cake mix
- 1 (8-ounce) can cream of coconut (*not* coconut milk)
- 1 (20-ounce) can crushed pineapple, drained
- 1 (16-ounce) carton Cool Whip® or 1 pint whipping cream, whipped and sweetened

Heat oven to 350° F.

Make cake mix according to package directions. Pour batter into a sprayed or greased and floured 9x13-inch pan. Bake 30 to 35 minutes. Remove cake from oven and immediately punch holes in it with the handle of a wooden spoon or with a meat fork. While cake is hot, pour cream of coconut over the entire surface. Spoon a layer of crushed pineapple over cake. Refrigerate. When ready to serve cake, top with Cool Whip® or whipped cream.

Serves 12 to 15.

My two grandmothers were important in my childhood, and some of my fondest memories of them are mingled with the tastes and smells of their kitchens. My Grandmother Fischer, who cooked on a wood stove, produced savory Thanksgiving feasts and at Christmas made stöllen, the recipe brought from her native Germany. My Grandmother Matheson, who shared the bounties of her garden—peas, beans, and tomatoes—until age 90, baked unusually good bread. Her chiffon pumpkin pie was legendary.

—JANET PETERSON

Chocolate Chunk Cookies
CAROL GARDNER

Make the chocolate chunks as big as you like.

- 1 cup butter (not margarine), softened
- 1 cup brown sugar
- 1 cup sugar
- 2 eggs
- 1 teaspoon vanilla
- ½ teaspoon salt
- 1 teaspoon baking powder
- 1 teaspoon baking soda
- 3 cups flour
- 2 (7-ounce) milk chocolate bars, chopped or 1 (12-ounce) package chocolate chips
- 1½ cups chopped nuts
- 1 cup coconut (optional)

MAKE A LARGE BATCH OF COOKIES OR SEVERAL KINDS AT THE SAME TIME. PUT BALLS OF COOKIE DOUGH ON A BAKING SHEET AND PLACE THEM IN THE FREEZER. WHEN DOUGH IS FROZEN, TRANSFER TO A FREEZER CONTAINER AND KEEP IN FREEZER. BAKE AS NEEDED FOR FRESH, HOMEMADE COOKIES.

Heat oven to 375° F.

Cream butter and sugars. Add eggs and vanilla and beat well. Mix in salt, baking powder, baking soda, and flour. Add chocolate, nuts, and coconut, if desired. Mold into golf-size balls and place 2 inches apart on an ungreased cookie sheet. Press slightly. Bake 7 minutes. Cookies will be very soft. Remove immediately from cookie sheet. When cool, they will firm. (If cooked until firm, they will be dry and hard when cool.)

Makes 2½ dozen cookies.

Applesauce Oatmeal Cookies
JUDY SHIMMIN

A soft, spicy cookie.

- 1 cup sugar
- 1 cup brown sugar
- 1 cup shortening
- 2 eggs
- 1 cup applesauce
- ½ teaspoon baking soda
- 2 cups oatmeal
- 1 teaspoon vanilla
- ½ teaspoon salt
- 2 tablespoons baking powder
- 1 teaspoon cinnamon
- ½ teaspoon ground cloves
- ½ teaspoon allspice
- ½ teaspoon nutmeg
- 3 cups flour
- 1 cup raisins
- 1 cup chopped nuts

Heat oven to 375° F.

Cream sugars and shortening. Add eggs and mix well. Add applesauce, baking soda, oatmeal, and vanilla and mix. Add salt, baking powder, cinnamon, cloves, allspice, and nutmeg and mix. Add flour and mix. Stir in raisins and nuts. Drop by heaping tablespoonfuls onto a greased cookie sheet. Bake 12 minutes.

Makes 3 to 4 dozen cookies.

Laughter is the brightest where food is best. —IRISH PROVERB

Oatmeal Chocolate Chip Cookies
NATALIE WILSON

This is an all-time-favorite chocolate chip cookie recipe. It makes a huge batch. You can cut the recipe in half, but you probably won't want to.

- 2 cups butter or margarine, softened
- 2 cups sugar
- 2 cups brown sugar
- 4 eggs
- 2 teaspoons vanilla
- 4 cups flour
- 5 cups oatmeal*
- 1 teaspoon salt
- 2 teaspoons baking powder
- 2 teaspoons baking soda
- 2 (12-ounce) packages chocolate chips
- 2 to 3 cups chopped nuts (optional)
- 1 (8-ounce) Hershey® bar, grated (optional)

*Measure oatmeal, then put in a blender or food processor in small amounts. Blend until oatmeal is the texture of a fine flour.

Heat oven to 375° F.

In a very large bowl, cream butter and sugars. Add eggs and vanilla. Mix well. Add flour, oatmeal, salt, baking powder, and baking soda. Mix well. Add chocolate chips. Add nuts and grated Hershey® bar, if desired. Stir gently to mix. Roll into 1½-inch balls or drop by heaping tablespoons onto an ungreased cookie sheet 2 inches apart. Bake 8 to 10 minutes.

DESSERTS

Variation

- 1 (10-ounce) package chipped toffee
- ½ cup coconut (optional)
- 1 cup raisins (optional)
- ½ cup dried cherries (optional)
- Unprocessed oatmeal (this makes for a more traditional cookie)

Heat oven to 400° F.

Follow recipe as above, adding toffee, coconut, raisins, and dried cherries, if desired, with chocolate chips. Drop by spoonful on an ungreased cookie sheet. Bake 6 minutes, just until slightly golden.

Makes 8 to 9 dozen cookies.

Might it be possible to trace female inheritance through recipes? I thought about the Danish pancakes my Grandmother Thatcher used to make, huge dinner-plate-sized crepes, fried in butter, then filled with stewed gooseberries, warm from the pan, a bulging pocket of buttery tartness. . . . I am thinking of another family recipe, a wonderfully pink soup made with strained rhubarb, sweetened and thickened with cornstarch. I got the recipe from Sunset magazine when we lived in California a number of years ago. Only after it had become a springtime perennial at our house did I learn that my Grandma Thatcher had also made it. She didn't call it "Rabarbergrod," as the magazine did, or even "Danish Dessert," though it bears a faint resemblance to the packaged variety. She called it "Barn Paint." By that name the recipe will be passed down (or lost) to my children's children's children. —LAUREL THATCHER ULRICH

Chocolate Mint Cookies
NANCY TIBBITTS

Chocolate and mint are a winning combination.

1 (18.25-ounce) package devil's food cake mix
2 eggs
⅓ cup oil

Heat oven to 350° F.

In a large bowl, combine cake mix, eggs, and oil. Knead to make dough. Roll into 1-inch balls. Place on an ungreased cookie sheet. Flatten slightly. Bake 8 to 10 minutes. Cool.

Frosting

1 (3-ounce) package cream cheese, softened
¼ cup butter or margarine, softened
1 tablespoon hot water
3 cups powdered sugar
½ teaspoon mint extract (more if desired)
3 to 4 drops green food coloring

Mix cream cheese, butter, water, and powdered sugar in a large bowl until smooth. Add mint extract and food coloring. Mix. Frost cookies.

Makes 2 to 2½ dozen cookies.

Like many other cooking enthusiasts, I've discovered that good food pleases the palate and soothes the soul! —DAVID COLLIN

DESSERTS

Chocolate Rolo® Cookies
STEPHANIE SANTIAGO

Watch out! These cookies are addicting.

- 1 (18.25-ounce) chocolate cake mix, any variety
- ½ cup butter or margarine, softened
- 1 egg
- 1 (13-ounce) package Rolo® candies

Heat oven to 375° F.

In a large bowl, mix together cake mix, butter, and egg. It will seem dry but keep mixing. Form dough around a Rolo® and make into a ball that just covers the Rolo®. Place on a greased or sprayed cookie sheet and bake 9 to 10 minutes. Do not overbake!

Makes 4½ to 5 dozen cookies.

On the wall over the kitchen table hung a large map of the world. As youngsters, we sisters would eat our toasted cheese sandwiches and imagine aloud to each other what the children in exotic places around the world were having for lunch. Geography a la carte! —JANET PARBERRY

Chocolate Crinkles

JANET PETERSON

"Our family discovered these brownie-like cookies years ago and still loves them."

> 4 ounces (4 squares) unsweetened baking chocolate
> ½ cup oil
> 2 cups sugar
> 4 eggs
> 2 teaspoons vanilla
> 2 cups flour
> 2 teaspoons baking powder
> ½ teaspoon salt
> 1 cup powdered sugar

DISCUSS BOOKS DURING MEALTIME. ASK FAMILY MEMBERS TO SHARE THEIR CURRENT AND LONG-TIME FAVORITES.

Put chocolate and oil in a heavy saucepan, double boiler, or microwave dish. Melt. Pour into a large bowl. Cool.

Add sugar and mix. Blend in eggs, one at a time, until well mixed. Add vanilla. Mix in flour, baking powder, and salt. Cover bowl and chill 4 or more hours in refrigerator or 30 minutes in freezer.

Heat oven to 350° F.

Put powdered sugar in a small bowl. Roll a heaping teaspoon of dough in powdered sugar. Place 2 inches apart on a sprayed or greased cookie sheet. Bake 12 minutes.

Makes 3½ dozen cookies.

Gingersnaps
LISA DALTON

"My grandma always had these delicious cookies baked for us when we saw her. She was an amazing cook!"

1½ cups butter or margarine, softened
2 cups sugar
2 eggs
½ cup light molasses
2 teaspoons cinnamon
1 teaspoon ginger
1 teaspoon allspice
4 cups flour
1 teaspoon baking soda
2 teaspoons baking powder
1 teaspoon salt
⅓ cup sugar

Heat oven to 350° F.

Cream together butter and 2 cups sugar in a large bowl. Add eggs, molasses, cinnamon, ginger, and allspice and mix well. Mix in flour, baking soda, baking powder, and salt. Form into balls. Put ⅓ cup sugar in a small bowl. Roll balls in sugar. Bake about 12 minutes.

Makes 5 dozen cookies.

Cookie dough that is too soft or runny can be remedied by adding equal amounts of flour and sugar. Adding only flour will make cookies too dry.

Snickerdoodles
CAMILLE RICKS

Try this innovation: Put a Hershey's® kiss in the middle of each cookie about 2 minutes before cookies are done and continue baking for remainder of time.

½ cup butter or margarine, softened
½ cup shortening
1½ cups sugar
2 eggs
2¾ cups flour
2 teaspoons cream of tartar
1 teaspoon baking soda
¼ teaspoon salt
2 teaspoons cinnamon
2 tablespoons sugar

WHEN MAKING SNICKERDOODLES OR OTHER COOKIES THAT ARE ROLLED IN SUGAR, PUT SUGAR MIXTURE IN A SMALL COVERED CONTAINER OR RESEALABLE PLASTIC BAG. ADD A FEW BALLS AND SHAKE.

Heat oven to 400° F.

In a large bowl, cream butter, shortening, and 1½ cups sugar. Add eggs and mix well. Blend in flour, cream of tartar, baking soda, and salt.

Shape dough by rounded teaspoonfuls into balls. Mix cinnamon and 2 tablespoons sugar in a small bowl. Roll balls in sugar mixture. Place 2 inches apart on an ungreased cookie sheet. Bake 8 to 10 minutes. Cookies should be soft when removed from oven.

Makes 3 dozen cookies.

Peanut Butter Cookie Bars

CAMILLE RICKS

Bars are the easiest form of cookies to make.

1½ cups butter or margarine, softened
1 cup sugar
1¼ cups brown sugar
2 eggs
1 cup peanut butter
¾ teaspoon salt
1½ teaspoons baking soda
1½ cups flour
1 teaspoon vanilla
6 cups oatmeal
Chocolate frosting*

Heat oven to 350° F.

Cream butter and sugars together in a large bowl. Add eggs and peanut butter. Mix well. Add salt, baking soda, and flour and mix well. Stir in vanilla and oatmeal. Spread dough in a sprayed or greased 9x13-inch pan. Bake 15 minutes. Do not overbake. Remove from oven and spread additional peanut butter over bars. When cool, frost with favorite chocolate frosting. Cut into bars.

Makes 2 dozen bars.

*See page 261 for chocolate frosting recipe.

SHAKE THINGS UP A BIT AT DINNERTIME. INSTEAD OF HAVING FAMILY MEMBERS SIT IN THEIR TRADITIONAL PLACES, PLAY MUSICAL CHAIRS AND SIT SOMEWHERE NEW DURING DINNER.

Almost Candy Bars
SHELLEY SCHENCK

Almost decadent.

½ cup butter or margarine
1 (18.25-ounce) package devil's food cake mix
1 (6-ounce) package butterscotch chips
1 (6-ounce) package chocolate chips
1 cup chopped nuts
1 cup coconut (optional)
1 (14-ounce) can sweetened condensed milk

Heat oven to 350° F.

In a large bowl, cut butter into cake mix with a pastry blender or fork until crumbly. Sprinkle evenly over the bottom of an ungreased 9x13-inch baking dish or 10x15-inch cookie sheet. Press lightly. Sprinkle with butterscotch chips, chocolate chips, nuts, and coconut, if desired. Spread sweetened condensed milk evenly over top of mixture. Bake 30 minutes, or until light golden brown. Cool completely.

Makes 4 dozen small bars.

When guests in our home compliment me on a great meal, I share some of the credit with my mom. . . . She's my inspiration in the kitchen. . . . Mom has a talent for making guests feel welcome. She's warm and cheerful as she dances around the kitchen putting the finishing touches on a meal.
She laughs when everyone crowds around the counter as she works instead of sitting in comfortable living room chairs just a few steps away. They've discovered what I've known for years—the best spot in the house is the kitchen when Mom's cooking. —LISA KIVIRIST

DESSERTS

Fudge Jumbles
GAYLEN BYWATER

This creamy chocolate filling melts in your mouth.

- 1 cup butter or margarine, softened
- 1½ cups brown sugar
- 1 egg
- 1 teaspoon vanilla
- 1 teaspoon baking soda
- 1 teaspoon salt
- 2 cups flour
- 2½ cups oatmeal

Heat oven to 350° F.

Cream together butter and brown sugar. Add egg and vanilla. Mix well. Add baking soda, salt, flour, and oatmeal and mix. Press half of dough in a sprayed or greased 9x13-inch pan.

Filling

- 1 (12-ounce) package chocolate chips
- 1 (14-ounce) can sweetened condensed milk
- 2 tablespoons butter or margarine
- ½ teaspoon salt
- 1 teaspoon vanilla
- 1 cup chopped nuts (optional)

Melt chocolate chips, sweetened condensed milk, butter, and salt together in a heavy saucepan. Stir in vanilla and nuts, if desired. Spread filling over oatmeal mixture. Crumble remaining oatmeal mixture over the top of filling. Bake 20 minutes. Mixture will set up as it cools.

Makes 2 dozen bars.

Oh Henry Bars ★
CESSILY DUKE

A new version of Rice Krispie® Treats.

- 1 cup sugar
- 1 cup light corn syrup
- 1 cup creamy peanut butter
- 1 cup chopped salted peanuts
- 3 cups Rice Krispies®
- 1 cup chocolate chips
- 1 cup butterscotch chips

In a heavy saucepan, bring sugar and corn syrup to a boil. Remove from heat and add peanut butter, peanuts, and Rice Krispies®. Stir well and press into a greased 9x13-inch pan. Melt chocolate chips and butterscotch chips together in a small saucepan or in microwave. Spread over top of peanut butter mixture. Cool and cut into bars.

Makes 2 dozen small or 1 dozen large bars.

I have become increasingly aware in recent years of the fact that very few people are really cooking at home. There are all kinds of reasons given—lack of time, other demands at the family dinner hour, anxiety about wasting ingredients not eaten up, the ease of eating in a restaurant, the lure of take-out foods. But the main reason nobody's in the kitchen, I began to suspect, was that people today are uneasy about cooking. They don't enjoy it, and many actually fear it. And that is very troubling to me, because I feel they are missing one of the greatest pleasures in life.

—MARION CUNNINGHAM

DESSERTS

Sunday Pudding ★
STEPHANIE SANTIAGO

A crispy pudding/cake with a caramel sauce. Serve hot with ice cream and sauce drizzled over top.

- 1 cup brown sugar
- 2 cups water
- ½ cup butter or margarine
- ½ cup sugar
- 1 teaspoon baking powder
- ½ cup cold water
- 1 cup flour
- ½ teaspoon salt

Heat oven to 375° F.

In a medium saucepan, combine brown sugar, 2 cups water, and butter. Bring to a boil. Pour into a 9x13-inch pan.

Combine ½ cup sugar, baking powder, ½ cup cold water, flour, and salt in a medium bowl. Mix well. Dough will be sticky. Drop by spoonfuls into caramel mixture until pan is covered. Bake 30 minutes.

Serves 8 to 12.

Few things are more personal than the foods we love and the ways we have learned to prepare them. When we let others see our recipes, we're often sharing a part of our lives about which we feel passionately.

—SARA PITZER

Brownie Trifle ★
TAMMY MCFARLAND

This trifle tastes as if it took all day to prepare.

- 1 (19.8-ounce) package fudge brownie mix
- 1 (3.5-ounce) package instant chocolate mousse mix
- 8 (1.4-ounce) Heath® bars, crushed
- 1 (12-ounce) carton Cool Whip®, thawed

Prepare brownie mix and bake according to package directions in a 9x13-inch pan. Cool and crumble. Prepare chocolate mousse according to package directions, but do not chill.

Place half of the crumbled brownies in a 3-quart trifle dish or large glass bowl. Top with half the mousse, half the crushed candy bars, and half the Cool Whip®. Repeat layers with remaining ingredients, ending with Cool Whip®. Garnish with chocolate curls, if desired. Chill 8 hours.

Serves 16 to 18.

The best day of the week started with bacon and eggs and ended with Ed Sullivan. In between were fat newspapers and heavenly choirs, droning lawn mowers and sweet ice cream cones. And right in the middle, the centerpiece of it all, was our family's Sunday dinner, a meal that did for our spirits what the morning sermon had done for our souls. Even now, more than forty years later, I still marvel at how seamlessly one ceremony flowed into the other; how natural it felt to walk home from church and take our seats at the family table. And so one week ended and another began, in an atmosphere of reflection and renewal. —DORIS CHRISTOPHER

Frosty Dog Dessert
KAYLENE REDD

"When I was a little girl, the ice-cream man would come through our neighborhood in the summer. He sold an ice-cream bar called the 'Frosty Dog.' When my mother made this dessert, it tasted just like those yummy ice-cream bars, so our family has always called it 'Frosty Dog Dessert.'"

Crust

> 12 graham crackers, crushed
> ½ cup butter or margarine, melted

Combine cracker crumbs and butter to form crust. Press into a 9x13-inch pan.

Chocolate Sauce

> ½ cup butter or margarine, melted
> 6 tablespoons cocoa
> 2 cups powdered sugar
> 3 egg yolks, beaten
> 3 egg whites, whipped stiff

In a medium saucepan, blend butter, cocoa, powdered sugar, and egg yolks. Cook until slightly thickened. Cool and fold in egg whites. Pour over crust.

Filling

> ½ gallon vanilla ice cream or any flavor ice cream, softened
> 6 graham crackers, crushed

Scoop ice cream over top of sauce. Top with additional cracker crumbs. Freeze overnight. Soften 10 to 15 minutes before serving.

Serves 12.

IF YOU'RE PRESSED FOR TIME, USE PURCHASED GRAHAM CRACKER OR CHOCOLATE COOKIE CRUMB CRUSTS INSTEAD OF MAKING YOUR OWN.

Apple or Peach Crisp ★
GERTRUDE MUECKE

The aroma of apples (or peaches) baking will gather your family to the kitchen.

8 large apples or peaches, peeled and sliced
1 to 2 tablespoons lemon juice
⅔ cup sugar
2 teaspoons cinnamon
¼ to ½ teaspoon nutmeg

Heat oven to 350° F.

Place apples or peaches in a buttered 9x13-inch pan. Sprinkle with lemon juice. In a small bowl, mix sugar, cinnamon, and nutmeg. Sprinkle mixture over apples or peaches.

Topping

1½ cups flour
½ cup oatmeal
1 cup brown sugar
½ cup butter or margarine, softened

Combine flour, oatmeal, brown sugar, and butter. Mix with a fork, cutting the butter into the dry ingredients. Spread over apples or peaches. Bake 1 hour.

Serves 12.

TAKE AN ANNUAL FAMILY PHOTO OF A FOOD TRADITION IN YOUR FAMILY, SUCH AS PREPARING THANKSGIVING DINNER, EATING OUT ON THE PATIO DURING THE SUMMER, OR WARMING UP WITH CHILI AFTER A DAY OF SKIING. KEEP THE PHOTOS TOGETHER IN A SMALL ALBUM SO THAT YOU CAN ENJOY SEEING THE CHANGES IN YOUR FAMILY OVER THE YEARS.

DESSERTS

Baked Apple ★
JANET PETERSON

Almost any variety of apple bakes deliciously. Include as many ingredients listed below as desired. Serve with a splash of heavy cream, ice cream, or whipped cream.

- 6 apples
- ⅓ cup brown sugar
- ⅓ cup nuts, chopped
- ⅓ cup raisins
- ¼ cup oatmeal
- ¼ teaspoon cinnamon
- ⅛ teaspoon nutmeg
- ¼ cup butter or margarine, softened
- 2 teaspoons lemon juice
- 1 cup apple juice

WHEN LEMON AND ORANGE PEELS ARE FROZEN, THEY ARE EASIER TO GRATE. PLACE PEELS IN A PLASTIC BAG IN THE FREEZER SO THEY'LL BE READY WHEN YOU NEED ZEST OR CITRUS PEEL.

Heat oven to 350° F.

Core apples, being careful not to break through bottom of apple. In a small bowl, mix brown sugar, nuts, raisins, oatmeal, cinnamon, nutmeg, butter, and lemon juice. Using a spoon, fill each apple with brown sugar mixture. Place apples in a shallow baking pan. Pour apple juice around apples. Bake 40 to 45 minutes, until apples are fork-tender.

Serves 6.

Apple Slump ★
JANET PETERSON

Apples don't always require cinnamon—you'll enjoy the pure apple flavor of this slump. Serve warm with vanilla ice cream or whipped cream.

> 4 to 5 large apples, peeled and thinly sliced
> 1⅓ cups sugar
> 1 cup plus 2 tablespoons flour
> 1 teaspoon baking powder
> ½ teaspoon salt
> 1 egg
> ½ cup butter or margarine (slightly less)

Heat oven to 375° F.

Mix apples with ⅔ cup sugar in a large bowl, stirring to coat. Add more sugar if desired. Stir in 2 tablespoons flour, mixing evenly. Place apples in an ungreased 8-inch square pan or 9- or 10-inch pie pan.

Mix together 1 cup flour, ⅔ cup sugar, baking powder, and salt. Beat egg in a separate dish, then add to flour mixture. Stir with fork until egg and flour are crumbly. Sprinkle over apples. Melt butter and pour evenly over topping. Bake 30 minutes or until golden brown.

Serves 8 to 9.

I could tell Mom was making chili sauce from a block away. Walking from school on an autumn afternoon, I could literally follow my nose home. Nutmeg, curry, clove, garlic, ginger, cinnamon were piquant enticement. Tonight we'd be having pot roast—with Mom's fresh chili sauce on it! —JANET PARBERRY

Salt Lake City Dessert
BETTY DRAPER

"This dessert is practically an institution in my family. Mom made it; Aunt Maurine Parry made it. I don't know the original source but will testify it is chocolatey-rich!"

12 graham crackers, crushed
¼ cup butter or margarine, melted
⅔ cup miniature marshmallows
6 ounces Hershey's® chocolate syrup
½ cup butter or margarine, softened
¾ cup powdered sugar
3 egg yolks
1 teaspoon vanilla
1 cup chopped nuts
3 egg whites, whipped stiff
1 cup whipping cream, whipped stiff

SEPARATE THE EGG YOLK FROM THE WHITE QUICKLY WITH A FUNNEL OR EGG SEPARATOR. CRACK THE EGG INTO THE FUNNEL OVER A BOWL. THE WHITE WILL DROP INTO THE BOWL AND THE YOLK WILL REMAIN IN THE FUNNEL.

Mix cracker crumbs with melted butter and press into a 9x13-inch pan. Combine marshmallows and chocolate syrup in a medium bowl. Let stand ½ hour or longer, stirring often. In a large bowl, beat butter and powdered sugar together until fluffy.

Add egg yolks, 1 at a time, beating well after each addition. Add vanilla and chopped nuts. Combine with marshmallow mixture.

Beat egg whites until stiff. Combine with stiffly beaten whipped cream. Fold into other mixtures. Spread mixture over crust. Refrigerate overnight. May serve with additional whipped cream.

Serves 12 to 16.

Angel's Delight ★ 🥣
BETTY DRAPER

This recipe is unbelievably easy.

1 (5½-ounce) package instant vanilla pudding
3 cups milk
1 (16-ounce) carton sour cream
1 large angel food cake, broken into pieces
1 (21-ounce) can cherry pie filling

Mix pudding and milk as directed on package. Blend with sour cream. Alternate layers of cake first, pudding second, and cherry filling third in a 9x13-inch pan or trifle bowl. Chill to set.

Serves 8 to 12.

You're likely to eat more nutritious meals when you eat with someone else. Do you remember the "It's just me—I'll have popcorn and soda for dinner" stage? If you add the kids, your spouse, a dinner guest, the menu likely takes on a different look. Maybe a few more vegetables or fruits? Maybe a fresh salad along with the take-out food, or something grilled? Healthy doesn't have to be hard, and it tastes better than popcorn.

—SUSAN DOSIER AND JULIA DOWLING RUTLAND

Raspberry Banana Sherbet ★ ⬇

JANET PETERSON

"I made this dessert for a stake priesthood meeting years ago. A number of men requested the recipe so they could have it at home. The leader in charge of several subsequent meetings served it each time."

- ½ gallon pineapple or raspberry sherbet, softened
- 2 bananas, diced
- 1 (10-ounce) package frozen raspberries and juice, thawed, or 2 cups fresh raspberries
- ½ to 1 cup chopped pecans

Transfer sherbet from carton to a large bowl or large plastic container. Stir in bananas, raspberries, and pecans. Cover and freeze. Soften slightly before serving.

Serves 10 to 12.

Don't wash fresh berries until you are ready to use them. To store them, keep in refrigerator in a single layer on a cookie sheet or other large, level surface to keep them from being crushed.

Orange Sherbet Dessert ★ ⬡
SHERI CALDWELL

This frozen, melt-in-your-mouth treat will create fond family memories.

1 quart vanilla ice cream, softened
1 pint orange sherbet, softened
2 to 3 bananas, diced
2 cups cashews, salt rinsed off and chopped

Transfer sherbet and ice cream to a large bowl or large plastic container. Stir in bananas and cashews. Serve immediately or return to freezer. Allow dessert to soften before serving.

Serves 8 to 10.

As . . . a new millennium begins, we seem to be coming back to our senses with more of us recognizing the importance of combining nurturing with nutrition. Across the land, Americans are coming back to the table, in a nightly celebration of family life. We're coming back for a taste of the old-fashioned values that hold families together through difficult times; for the comfort of sharing life's ups and downs with our loved ones; for the chance to honor the mealtime traditions that brighten our days and form the basis for memories that will last forever. We're coming back because in a world that is moving too fast, families tend to drift apart, and because there's no better vehicle than the table for bringing them back together.

—DORIS CHRISTOPHER

Raspberry Danish Dessert

KATHLEEN MCGUIRE

Serve in beautiful glass goblets or dishes. Delicious with angel food cake cut up in small squares. Pour pudding and sauce over the cake.

- 1 cup rice
- 1 quart milk
- 2 to 2½ cups whipping cream (adjust to taste)
- ¼ cup sugar
- ½ cup sliced almonds (optional)

Place rice and milk in a large heavy saucepan. Bring to a boil, stirring constantly. Reduce heat to low, put on lid, and leave wooden spoon in pan, stirring occasionally. When rice has absorbed all the milk and is cooked, pour rice mixture into a metal mixing bowl and cool in refrigerator. Whip cream. Add sugar. Fold into cooled rice. Add almonds, if desired.

Sauce

- 1 (4¾-ounce) package raspberry Danish® dessert
- 2½ cups water
- 1 (10-ounce) package frozen raspberries, thawed, or 2 cups fresh raspberries

Make Danish® dessert according to package directions using 2½ cups water. Cool. Add raspberries to sauce. Serve rice with sauce. Garnish with almonds, if desired.

Serves 6 to 8.

CHILL CREAM BEFORE WHIPPING. TRY CHILLING THE BOWL AND BEATERS, TOO. THE COLDER THEY ARE, THE QUICKER THE CREAM WHIPS.

Cool Lime Dessert ★
D. LOUISE BROWN

This dessert can also be made with cherry or other flavors of Kool-Aid®.

- 1 (12-ounce) can evaporated milk
- ¾ cup sugar
- 1 (0.15-ounce) package lemon-lime unsweetened Kool-Aid®
- 12 graham crackers, crushed or 2 cups crushed vanilla wafers or 2 ready-made crumb pie crusts

Chill can of evaporated milk 1 hour. Pour evaporated milk into a deep bowl and beat with electric mixer until frothy. Add sugar and Kool-Aid®. Beat until thick and pour into a 9x13-inch pan lined with a graham cracker or vanilla wafer crumb crust. Freeze 2 to 3 hours. Soften 10 to 15 minutes before serving.

Serves 9 to 12.

START DINNER CONVERSATION WITH THE QUESTION, "DO YOU REMEMBER WHEN?" AND SPECIFY A PARTICULAR ENJOYABLE EVENT OR EXPERIENCE THAT THE FAMILY CAN DISCUSS (FOR EXAMPLE, LAST SUMMER'S CAMP OUT WHEN YOU COOKED YOUR DINNER IN A DUTCH OVEN).

Velvet Fudge Sauce ★
ANN PAINTER

This sauce is great over ice cream or brownies.

- 2 cups powdered sugar
- 1 cup evaporated milk
- ½ cup butter or margarine
- 1 tablespoon light corn syrup
- 1 cup chocolate chips
- 1 teaspoon vanilla

In a large saucepan, combine powdered sugar, evaporated milk, butter, corn syrup, and chocolate chips. Cook over medium heat until mixture boils. Reduce heat to low. Cook 8 minutes, stirring constantly. Remove from heat. Stir in vanilla.

Makes 2½ cups sauce.

TAKE THE TIME TO OCCASIONALLY READ A STORY OR ARTICLE ALOUD TO EACH OTHER AT THE DINNER TABLE. YOU'LL LIKELY FIND THAT DINNER IS FINISHED, BUT FAMILY MEMBERS ARE LINGERING AROUND THE TABLE TO HEAR THE END OF THE STORY.

Never-Fail Pie Crust
JANET PARBERRY

The key to making pie crusts is to roll the dough out lightly, starting from the center and rolling outwards. Roll the dough large enough to extend beyond the pie pan. Stretching dough will result in shrinkage during baking.

2½ cups flour
1 teaspoon salt
1 cup shortening
1 egg, beaten
1 tablespoon apple cider vinegar
¼ cup cold water

Combine flour and salt in a large bowl. With fork or pastry blender, cut shortening into flour until it resembles coarse cornmeal. In a small bowl, mix egg, vinegar, and water. Combine egg mixture with flour mixture. Blend well. Chill.

Heat oven to 450° F.

Roll piecrusts out between wax paper sheets or on a floured pastry cloth or breadboard. Bake unfilled pie shells 12 to 15 minutes. For filled pies, bake according to recipe directions.

Makes 2 (10-inch) pie crusts or 1 double-crust (10-inch) pie.

When I was a child, people sat around kitchen tables and told their stories. We don't do that so much anymore. Sitting around the table telling stories is not just a way of passing time. It's the way the wisdom gets passed along, the stuff that helps us to live a life worth remembering.
—RACHEL NAOMI REMEN

Easy Apple Pie
JENNIFER OLDROYD

No rolling pin needed!

Crust
- 1½ cups flour
- 1½ teaspoons sugar
- 1 teaspoon salt
- ½ cup oil (slightly less)
- 2 tablespoons milk

Heat oven to 350° F.

Mix flour, sugar, salt, oil, and milk in a medium bowl. If crust looks too oily, add a little more flour. Press into a 9- or 10-inch pie pan.

Filling
- 5 cups apples, peeled and sliced
- 1 to 2 tablespoons lemon juice
- ½ cup sugar
- 2 tablespoons flour
- ½ teaspoon nutmeg
- ½ teaspoon cinnamon

Put sliced apples in a medium bowl. Add lemon juice to apples. Mix sugar, flour, nutmeg, and cinnamon in a small bowl. Add to apples and toss to coat. Pour apples in crust.

Topping
- ½ cup flour
- ½ cup sugar
- ½ cup butter or margarine, firm

Put flour and sugar in a medium bowl. Cut in butter with a fork or pasty blender. Drop mixture on top of apples so that apples are mostly covered. Bake 1 hour.

Serves 6.

Quick Lemon Pie ★
LYNDA COOPER

Lemony and cold—very refreshing on a hot summer day.

1 quart vanilla ice cream
1 (6-ounce) can frozen lemonade concentrate
1 prepared 8- or 9-inch graham cracker pie crust

Soften ice cream and mix with lemonade concentrate. Spoon into pie crust and refreeze. Soften 10 to 15 minutes before serving.

Serves 6.

There are many reasons to make family mealtime a priority:

Stronger Family Bonds. Sharing meals promotes unity and a family sense of belonging.

Better Communication. Family mealtime gives families a chance to reconnect with each other after school or work.

Social Skills. Family mealtime gives an opportunity to learn [social] skills. . . .

Shared Learning. Family mealtime can provide the setting to intellectual discussion and teaching. Studies show that elementary children who eat with their families have a larger vocabulary and read better than those who don't eat with their families.

Family Unity and Love. Therapists say family conflict is usually less in a family who eats together regularly.

Economics. When meals are planned and shared, money can be saved.

—MARY MATHEWS

DESSERTS

Oreo® Ice Cream Pie ★

DEMETRIA DAVIS

"This is my husband's favorite dessert from his childhood. I have to make it every year for his birthday."

- ½ (1-pound 4-ounce) package double-stuffed Oreo® cookies
- ½ gallon mint chocolate chip ice cream, softened
- Mrs. Richardson's® Fudge topping
- Chopped nuts (optional)

Crush Oreos® in a blender or food processor. Press into a greased or sprayed 10-inch glass pie pan. Microwave on high 1½ minutes. Spread softened ice cream over cookies. Freeze until firm. Soften 10 minutes before serving. Pour fudge topping over ice cream. Sprinkle with Oreo® crumbs or nuts, if desired.

Serves 6 to 8.

Unfortunately, most fast food falls short as far as healthy nutrition goes; on most menus the items consist of starch, sugar, and trans fats that take various forms, with numbers for names. For many people the traditional family dinner, with the whole bunch (whether friends or family) sitting down together and enjoying a leisurely meal and talking to one another, has slipped into history. And with it, one of the great joys of life—the social aspect of a meal. Too often people bemoan its passing but say there's just no time for that nowadays. We say, Baloney! —MICHAEL R. EADES AND MARY DAN EADES

Banana Cream Pie (Chocolate or Lemon Variations) ★
NANCY FLAMM

Creamy and smooth and very easy.

1 (3-ounce) package instant vanilla pudding
1½ cups milk
½ pint whipping cream, whipped
1 to 2 bananas, sliced
1 prepared 9-inch pie crust (pastry, graham cracker, or cookie crumb)
Coconut (optional garnish)

Add a dash of salt to cream or eggs to make them whip faster.

Combine instant pudding with milk, stirring until well mixed and thick. Fold half the whipped cream into pudding. Arrange banana slices on the pie crust. Pour pudding mixture into pie crust. Refrigerate until set. Top with remaining whipped cream that has been sweetened. Garnish with coconut and additional banana slices.

Chocolate Cream or Lemon Cream Variation

Prepare with chocolate or lemon pudding as above, omitting bananas. Garnish with whipped cream, coconut, chocolate curls, or lemon zest.

Serves 6.

Frosty Pumpkin Pie
EVA TALL

Better than cooked pumpkin pie! Top with whipped cream and toasted coconut or unsweetened whipped cream and 1 teaspoon warm honey per slice.

- 1 (9-inch) graham cracker crust or baked pie shell
- 1 pint vanilla ice cream, softened
- ½ cup canned pumpkin
- ½ cup sugar
- ½ teaspoon ginger
- ½ teaspoon cinnamon
- ¼ teaspoon nutmeg
- ⅛ teaspoon ground cloves
- Pinch of salt
- 1 cup whipping cream, whipped

Line pie shell with vanilla ice cream. Mix pumpkin, sugar, ginger, cinnamon, nutmeg, cloves, and salt together in a medium bowl. Fold whipped cream into pumpkin mixture. Spread over ice cream. Freeze 2 to 4 hours until firm. Soften 10 to 20 minutes before serving.

Serves 6.

DURING DINNER, TALK ABOUT MEMORABLE FAMILY VACATIONS. YOU'LL FIND THAT STRESSFUL INCIDENTS CAN EVEN BE LAUGHABLE IN RETROSPECT—LIKE THE TIME MOM DIDN'T HAVE PHOTO ID AT THE AIRPORT OR THE ALL-NIGHT, SLEEPLESS TRAIN RIDE FROM FLORENCE TO BERN.

Fresh Strawberry Pie
STEPHANIE BYWATER

While the local growing season for strawberries may be short, fresh strawberries are available in grocery stores at a reasonable price many months of the year.

1½ cups water
¾ cup sugar
1 (3-ounce) package strawberry Jell-O®
3 heaping tablespoons cornstarch
1 baked 9-inch pie crust
1 quart (or more) strawberries, sliced or left whole
Whipped cream or Cool Whip®

Bring water, sugar, Jell-O®, and cornstarch to a boil in a medium saucepan, stirring constantly until thickened. Cool. Pour some of the Jell-O® mixture into the pie crust. Arrange berries in pie crust. Pour remaining Jell-O® mixture over berries. Refrigerate to set up. Serve with whipped cream or Cool Whip®.

An even simpler method is to prepare 1 (4¾-ounce) package of strawberry Danish® dessert in place of the Jell-O® mixture.

Serves 6.

Going out to dinner on a regular basis or bringing home takeout wasn't an option in my family. With three hungry boys involved in sports, the amount of food would have broken the bank and might not have been good for us, even if we could have afforded it. Quick, healthful meals at home were what we needed. —LINDA GASSENHEIM

Fresh Peach Pie
TERRI AVERY

Tree-ripened peaches are a world apart from those purchased at a grocery store. In the fall, locate a fruit stand, visit an orchard, or grow your own.

- 6 peaches, peeled and sliced
- 1 cup sugar
- ½ cup water
- 3 tablespoons cornstarch
- 2 tablespoons butter or margarine
- ½ teaspoon almond extract
- 1 baked 9- or 10-inch pie crust
- 1 cup whipped cream or vanilla ice cream (optional)

In a small saucepan, mash 2 peaches. Add sugar, water, and cornstarch. Stir and cook about 5 minutes. Add butter and almond extract. Arrange remaining peach slices in pie crust. Pour sauce over peaches. Cool. Serve with whipped cream or ice cream, if desired.

Serves 6.

LURE YOUR FAMILY TO THE TABLE WITH NEW RECIPES EVERY NOW AND THEN. SEARCH THE INTERNET FOR DIFFERENT AND EXOTIC RECIPES.

*Note: The following recipes are for traditional 4- or 5-quart ice cream makers in which ice cream is frozen with ice and salt. The recipes can be adjusted for smaller, on-the-counter ice cream makers that do not use ice.

Tutti Frutti Ice Cream
JEAN MULLINER

Ripen homemade ice cream to enhance its flavor and texture by keeping it in the ice cream freezer packed with ice and salt or putting it in the freezer for several hours.

Juice of 3 oranges
Juice of 3 lemons
3 bananas
3 cups sugar (or less)
3 cups milk
3 cups cream

Heat lemons or oranges in microwave for one minute before squeezing. They will yield more juice.

Blend orange and lemon juices, bananas, sugar, and part of milk in a blender or food processor. Pour into freezer container. Add remaining milk and cream. Freeze in ice cream maker as directed until fairly firm.

Makes about 2½ to 3 quarts.

Fresh Peach or Berry Ice Cream
REBECCA OLAVESON

Homemade ice cream is the best!

- 2 cups sliced peaches or berries (strawberries, raspberries, or boysenberries)
- 2½ cups sugar
- 6 tablespoons lemon juice
- 6 tablespoons orange juice
- 2 cups whipping cream
- 1 (14-ounce) can sweetened condensed milk
- 1 teaspoon vanilla
- ½ teaspoon almond flavoring
- Milk

Put peaches or berries and ½ cup sugar in a food processor or blender and lightly puree. Transfer fruit to freezer container. Add 2 cups sugar, lemon juice, orange juice, whipping cream, sweetened condensed milk, vanilla, and almond flavoring, if desired. Stir to dissolve sugar. Fill freezer container to ⅔ full with milk. Freeze ice cream according to manufacturer's directions.

Makes 3 to 4 quarts.

TO QUICKLY PEEL FRESH PEACHES OR TOMATOES, DIP THEM IN BOILING WATER; PEELING IS ONLY A MATTER OF PULLING OFF THE SKINS.

Chocolate Ice Cream
JANET PETERSON

Variations can be created with nuts, chocolate minichips, miniature marshmallows, or fruit.

- 1 quart half-and-half
- 3 cups sugar
- ¾ to 1 cup cocoa
- 1½ to 2 teaspoons vanilla
- 1 quart whipping cream or part cream and part milk

Blend 3 cups half-and-half, sugar, and cocoa in a blender or food processor until smooth. Transfer to freezer container. Add remaining half-and-half, vanilla, and whipping cream or milk. Freeze as directed.

Makes about 3 to 3½ quarts.

As I struggle each night to get dinner on my kitchen table and round up my children from the four corners of our neighborhood, I wonder why I just don't send them to their rooms with a chicken pot pie and "Wheel of Fortune." I don't because I am giving them the gift of the kitchen table.

In all of the treatises on parenting, in all of the psychological studies on child development, and in all of the data on self-esteem, this humble key to rearing children is overlooked. —MARIANNE M. JENNINGS

Fruit and Yogurt Ice Cream

PAT MENLOVE

Homemade ice cream tastes best the day it is made. Make sure you have enough eaters to polish off a batch.

- 3 cups fresh apricots or peaches, pureed, or 1 quart bottled apricots or peaches, drained and pureed
- Juice of 2 lemons
- 3 to 4 cups sugar
- 1 (8-ounce) carton yogurt, plain or fruit-flavored
- 1 quart half-and-half
- Milk

Other fruits as desired

- 1 banana, pureed in blender
- Crushed pineapple
- Fresh or frozen raspberries, mashed
- Fresh or frozen strawberries, pureed

In the freezer container, stir together apricots or peaches, lemon juice, sugar, and yogurt. Add half-and-half. Add other fruits, as desired. Add milk to fill line. Freeze as directed.

Makes about 3 to 4 quarts.

HOLD A FUN DINNER EVERY MONTH OF THE YEAR. START OFF WITH SOMETHING SPECIAL ON NEW YEAR'S DAY.

COOKING RESOURCES

Cookbooks

- *Better Homes and Gardens New Cook Book.* 11th ed. Des Moines, Iowa: Better Homes and Gardens Books, 1996.

    The new cookbook is an updated version of the familiar red-and-white-checked cookbook. Features include cooking basics; glossaries; detailed instructions (often with accompanying photographs); sidebars with cooking tips and hints; and twelve hundred recipes, many of which are low fat or fast to prepare.

- *Betty Crocker's Cookbook: Everything You Need to Know to Cook.* 9th ed. Foster City, Calif.: IDG Books Worldwide, 2000.

    This cookbook provides detailed basic cooking instructions; an extensive glossary; a list of pantry items; and numerous photos illustrating cooking procedures. Recipes are family oriented.

- Bittman, Mark. *The Minimalist Cooks at Home: Recipes That Give You More Flavor from Fewer Ingredients in Less Time.* New York: Broadway Books, 1999.

    Mark Bittman, author of the "Minimalist" column in the *New York Times,* proposes that good food need not be complicated nor time-consuming. Most recipes are accompanied by a page of commentary and instruction, as well as variations. Each recipe includes details about work and preparation time and whether it can be prepared in advance or easily multiplied.

- Cunningham, Marion. *Learning to Cook with Marion Cunningham.* New York: Alfred Knopf, 1999.

    Author of the *Fanny Farmer* cookbooks, Marion Cunningham explains many basic cooking procedures and ingredients in a friendly, chatty style. Included are detailed and homestyle recipes.

- Dosier, Susan, and Julia Dowling Rutland. *Discover Dinnertime: Your Guide to Building Family Time around the Table.* Memphis, Tenn.: Tradery House, 1998.

    This cookbook suggests ways to improve family communication and provides quick-cooking recipes. Ideas are given for conversation starters (If you could be any character in a book, who would it be?) and reasons for families to eat dinner together (children will read better by participating in mealtime conversations).

- McCullough, Fran, and Suzanne Hamlin. *The Best American Recipes 2000: The Year's Top Picks from Books, Magazines, Newspapers, and the Internet.* Boston: Houghton Mifflin, 2000.

Each year, these authors sift through myriad sources of recipes, try hundreds of them, and publish those they deem to be the best. The book includes notes to cooks, serving suggestions, variations, and a number of top ten lists (comeback, spice, novelty, dessert, fruit of the year, and so on).

- Rombauer, Irma S., Marion Rombauer Becker, and Ethan Becker. *All New All Purpose Joy of Cooking.* New York: Scribner, 1997.

  This well-known classic has been expanded to more than one thousand pages and uses the "rules for" approach (rules for vegetables, for example). Especially helpful are the menu suggestions of what to serve with what. *Joy of Cooking* relies on line drawings (no photos) and lots of detailed text.

- Ungaro, Susan Kelliher, ed. *Family Circle All-Time Favorite Recipes.* New York: Doubleday, 1999.

  This book contains six hundred recipes selected from the popular grocery store rack magazine. Recipe format is easy to follow. Helpful cooking tips are given as well as an extensive appendix (party planning, spices and herbs, food safety, and kitchen math).

Books about Cooking

- Christopher, Doris. *Come to the Table: A Celebration of Family Life.* New York: Warner Books, 1999.

  Pampered Chef president Doris Christopher recalls childhood memories of dinner, describes the state of dinner today, and urges readers to come back to the dinner table. She illustrates her points with stories of her family and friends' dinner experiences.

- Kimball, Linda Hoffman, ed. *Saints Well-Seasoned: Musings on How Food Nourishes Us: Body, Heart, and Soul.* Salt Lake City: Deseret Book, 1998.

  Saints Well-Seasoned is a collection of delightful, nostalgic personal essays that focus on food experiences by well-known LDS writers, with some recipes included.

- Mendelson, Cheryl. *Home Comforts: The Art and Science of Keeping House.* New York: Scribner, 1999.

  Written by a philosopher-lawyer/mother, this book has an excellent section on food, with insights on the role of good food in the home and detailed suggestions on how to handle and prepare food, in the "Whys and Wherefores of Home Cooking."

Magazines

- *Better Homes and Gardens.* 1716 Locust St., Des Moines, IA 50309–3023.

  Better Homes and Gardens publishes a monthly magazine as well as speciality issues, such as *Holiday Cooking*. All recipes are tested and approved and deemed "practical, reliable," with "high standards of taste appeal." Food photos are attractive and recipes are family-oriented.

- *Cook's Illustrated.* Boston Common Press. P.O. Box 7446, Red Oak, IA 51591–0446.

    The subtitle of *Cook's Illustrated* is "Home of America's Test Kitchen," and recipes and cooking methods are tested extensively by the staff. Illustrations and text are as significant as food in this bimonthly magazine. Detailed line drawings and fairly lengthy articles accompany recipes and how-to cooking techniques (Pie 101, for example, details the steps of making basic pie crust). The magazine reviews equipment, books, and products (it rates, for example, brand-name cornbread mixes), and gives quick tips and kitchen notes.

- *Family Circle.* 375 Lexington Ave. New York, NY 10017

    Family Circle, published monthly, is available only on the rack, not as a subscription magazine. The food section has family-oriented recipes geared toward busy cooks (sections include Quick Cooks, Tricks of the Trade, 30 Minutes Max, and 5 Ingredients or Less). Photo-illustration cooking instructions are helpful.

- *Fine Cooking.* Taunton Press. 63 South Main St., P.O. Box 5506, Newtown, CT 06470–5506.

    Published bimonthly, *Fine Cooking* is a luscious cooking magazine. Departments include Q&A, Technique Class, Basics, and Quick and Delicious. Feature articles are by professional cooks, food writers, restaurant owners, and cooking instructors.

- *Good Housekeeping.* P.O. Box 7186, Red Oak, IA 51591–0186

    While food is only one section of many in the magazine, *Good Housekeeping* offers a variety of good recipes, a Q&A with the food editor, food tips and instructions, and reports on equipment.

- *Martha Stewart Living.* P.O. Box 60001, Tampa, FL 33660–0001.

    Martha's magazine provides a cooking section, recipes from her television shows, and an "Ask Martha" section, in which she responds to queries about food and cooking.

- *Taste of Home.* Reiman Publications. P.O. Box 5278, Harlan, IA 51593–0778.

    Taste of Home, a bimonthly magazine, has wonderful homestyle recipes gathered from cooks around the United States. Recipes are for "people who love practical cooking." The company publishes an annual cookbook with the previous year's recipes.

- *Taste of Home's Quick Cooking.* Reiman Publications. P.O. Box 5278, Harlan, IA 51593–0778.

    Also a bimonthly magazine, *Quick Cooking* offers "rapid recipes with homemade taste." Recipes are grouped by meals, including breakfast, lunch, dinner, and special events. Time-saving Tips, 10-minute Meals, and 5-Ingredient Dinners are regular features.

Web sites

- allrecipes.com

    This Web site has multiple features, including an extensive cooks' encyclopedia, a create-your-own-recipe collection, and shopping list. Useful features for each recipe include adjustments to the number of servings desired, nutritional statistics, printing to recipe card size, reviews, and metric conversion. Allrecipes also has a recipe exchange and tip of the day with archives.

- aol.com/webcenters/food/home.adp

    This site primarily provides links to tons of other food sites. Recipes can be searched by category (quick recipes, seasonal recipes) and are most frequently drawn from *Better Homes and Gardens* and cooking.com.

- bettycrocker.com

    Betty Crocker offers recipes, weekly menus, ingredients-to-recipes (what to make with what's in your pantry), shopping lists, advice from newspaper columns, the company's radio show, FAQs, and an interactive "talk to Betty."

- bhg.com/food

    Better Homes and Gardens' Web site includes features to create your own recipe file, shopping lists, and menus; to share recipes with other members; and to search for recipes using ingredients you have on hand. It also includes a section on quick and easy recipes and a food encyclopedia.

- cooking.com

    Cooking.com offers recipes by the course, cuisine, advanced search, and menus (of the day or planner). Also included are a chef's roundtable and cook's reference (glossary of techniques, ingredients, and equipment).

- epicurious.com

    Epicurious offers thousands of recipes from *Bon Appetit, Gourmet,* and *House and Garden,* field reports on cookbooks, markets, and ethnic foods, seasonal meals, today's recipe, and shopping.

- familycircle.com (food)

    Family Circle provides fifteen thousand recipes that can be accessed through searching by meal, ingredient, preparation time, or course. Readers' recipes and a "get cooking" segment (cookbooks, shopping list, recipe box, food checklist, and so on) are helpful.

- internet.epicurean.com

    internet.epicurean.com contains a recipe archive (with editors' favorites marked), numerous categories of recipes (chili pepper, worldwide, ridiculously easy), E-zines (online magazines), recipe collections, featured menu, and food-related links.

- marthastewart.com (cooking)

    Registration (free) is required to access this site. Included are recipes from Martha Stewart's television and radio shows, weekly menus, transcripts of Q&A Hour (with Martha, editors of *Martha Stewart Living*, and guest hosts), a recipe finder, and recommendations of "good things" on the market.

- pillsbury.com

    All recipes use at least one Pillsbury product. The site offers winning Pillsbury Bake-Off recipes, general recipes, tips and basics, bulletin board for readers to share tips and recipes, and planning for events such as family reunions and buffets. Pillsbury will E-mail recipes and ideas with registration.

- soar.berkeley.edu/recipes

    SOAR stands for searchable online archive of recipes and has sixty-seven thousand recipes gathered from published sources and Web contributors. Extensive search features are helpful.

- yahoo.com (living/food)

    A major search engine, Yahoo provides links to a multitude of recipe and cooking Web sites. A recipe search engine, weekly picks, a feature from *Cook's Illustrated and Fine Cooking,* a recipe exchange, and a marketplace are incorporated into the site.

Note: Nearly every local newspaper has a food section and most have material on the Web. Utah's *Deseret News,* for example allows a six-month archives search with no charge at deseretnews.com (food). Recipes, articles, and columns, both locally written and nationally syndicated, are included.

Large metropolitan papers, such as the *Los Angeles Times (*latimes.com) and the *New York Times* (newyorktimes.com) offer a wide array of ethnic cuisines as well as advice from renowned food columnists, Marion Cunningham and Mark Bittman, respectively.

Most local television stations have a cooking segment and put recipes on the Internet; for example, ksl.com/TV/recipes/recipes.htm. Recipes from Salt Lake City's KSL News at Noon date back to 1996; features include recent recipes, various categories of recipes, and an index to all recipes. Recipes come from KSL's cooking specialist as well as guest chefs from local restaurants.

Many companies, such as Kraft®, Hersheys®, Bertolli®, and so on, have Web sites with recipes that use their products.

BIBLIOGRAPHY

"My Mom's Best Meal," in *1998 Taste of Home Annual Recipes*. Greendale, WI: Reiman Publications, 1997.

"My Mom's Best Meal," in *1999 Taste of Home Annual Recipes*. Greendale, WI: Reiman Publications, 1998.

"My Mom's Best Meal," in *2000 Taste of Home Annual Recipes*. Greendale, WI: Reiman Publications, 1999.

"My Mom's Best Meal," in *2001 Taste of Home Annual Recipes*. Greendale, WI: Reiman Publications, 2000.

[Beckham], Janette C. Hales. Young Women President's Message, Open House, April 1993.

Branch, Susan. *Days from the Heart of the Home*. Boston: Little, Brown and Co., 1996.

Branch, Susan. *Heart of the Home: Notes from a Vineyard Kitchen*. Boston: Little, Brown and Co., 1986.

Breathnach, Sarah Ban. *Simple Abundance: A Daybook of Comfort and Joy*. New York: Warner Books, 1995.

Christensen, Ferren L. *Church News*. 29 July 2000, 2.

Christopher, Doris. *Come to the Table: A Celebration of Family Life*. New York: Warner Books, 1999.

Cunningham, Marion. *Learning to Cook with Marion Cunningham*. New York: Alfred A. Knopf, 1999.

Curtis, LeGrand R. "A Table Encircled with Love," *Ensign*. May 1995, 82, 83.

Delany, Sarah and A. Elizabeth with Amy Hill Hearth. *The Delany Sisters' Book of Everyday Wisdom*. New York: Kodansha International, 1994.

Dobson, Shirley. "Coming Home," *Focus on the Family with Dr. James Dobson*, November 2000, 6–7.

Dosier, Susan and Julia Dowling Rutland. *Discover Dinnertime: Your Guide to Building Family Time Around the Table*. Memphis, TN: Tradery House, 1998.

Eades, Michael R. and Mary Dan Eades. *The Protein Power LifePlan*. New York: Warner Books, 2000.

Engelbreit, Mary. *Mary Engelbreit's Queen of the Kitchen Cookbook*. Kansas City, MO: Andrews McMeel, 1998.

"In Praise of Time Together." *Good Housekeeping*. Janurary 2000.

Jennings, Marianne M. "Kitchen Table Vital to Family Life," *Deseret News*, 9 February 1997, AA4.

Bibliography

La Ferle, Cynthia. "Teaching My Son to Cook," *Mary Engelbreit's Home Companion*, October and November 2000, 116.

Lund, Joanna M. *Make a Joyful Table*. New York: G.P. Putnam's Sons, 1999.

Martin, Coleen. *Quick Cooking*, Collector's Edition 2000.

Matthews, Mary. "Table Talk: Strengthening Families at Mealtime" (pamphlet), March 2000.

Mendelson, Cheryl. *Home Comforts: The Art and Science of Keeping House*. New York: Scribner, 1999.

Okazaki, Chieko N. *Cat's Cradle*. Salt Lake City: Bookcraft, 1993.

Pearce, Virginia H. *Glimpses into the Life and Heart of Marjorie Pay Hinckley*. Salt Lake City: Deseret Book, 1999.

Peterson, Janet. "It's Your Night to Cook," *Ensign*, January 1987, 64.

Peterson, Janet and LaRene Gaunt. *The Children's Friends*. Salt Lake City: Deseret Book, 1996.

Pipher, Mary. *The Shelter of Each Other: Rebuilding Our Families*. New York: Ballantine Books, 1997.

Pitzer, Sara. *How to Write a Cookbook and Get It Published*. Cincinnati, Ohio: Writers' Digest Books, 1984.

Remen, Rachel Naomi. *Kitchen Table Wisdom* (audiotape), San Bruno, CA: Audio Literature, 1996.

Saints Well Seasoned. Linda Hoffman Kimball, ed. Salt Lake City: Deseret Book, 1998.

Thayne, Emma Lou. *As for Me and My House*. Salt Lake City: Bookcraft, 1989.

Ulrich, Laurel Thatcher and Emma Lou Thayne. *All God's Critters Got a Place in the Choir*. Salt Lake City: Aspen Books, 1995.

"Where to Eat," *Consumer Reports*, July 2000.

INDEX

al dente, definition of, 13
Almond Mushroom Peas, 223
Almost Candy Bars, 282
Aloha Grilled Steak and Pineapple, 182
Angel Hair Pasta and Shrimp, 153
Angel's Delight, 292
Apple Avocado Salad, 62
Apple or Peach Crisp, 288
apples
    Apple Avocado Salad, 62
    Apple or Peach Crisp, 288
    Apple Slump, 290
    Baked Apple, 289
    Carrot Apple Salad, 54
    Easy Apple Pie, 299
    Grilled Pork Chops with Apples, 200
    Puffy Apple Pancake, 256
Applesauce Oatmeal Cookies, 273
Apple Slump, 290
Apricot Glaze, 174
asparagus
    Asparagus with Lemon Butter, 207
    Chilled Asparagus Oriental, 208
    Asparagus with Lemon Butter, 207
avocados
    Apple Avocado Salad, 62

bacon
    Bacon, Cauliflower, and Lettuce Salad, 55
    Bacon and Tomato Salad, 64
    Hot Bacon Potato Salad, 202
Bacon, Cauliflower, and Lettuce Salad, 55
Bacon and Tomato Salad, 64
Baked Apple, 289
Baked Beans, 212
Baked German Pancakes, 254
Baked Salmon, 155
Baking Powder Biscuits, 84
Banana Cream Pie, 302

Banana Nut Bread or Muffins, 95
bananas
    Banana Cream Pie, 302
    Banana Nut Bread or Muffins, 95
    Raspberry Banana Sherbet, 293
barbecue. *See* grilled foods
Barbecue Chicken Breasts, 144
Barbecued Spareribs, 198
Barbecue Sauce, 198
bars
    Almost Candy Bars, 282
    Fudge Jumbles, 283
    Oh Henry Bars, 284
    Peanut Butter Cookie Bars, 281
Basic Vinaigrette, 76
Bean and Salsa Soup, 39
beans
    Baked Beans, 212
    Bean and Salsa Soup, 39
    Beans and Beef, 107
    Chili, 36
    Cilantro, Chicken, and Black Bean Salad, 71
    Easy Minestrone Soup, 40
    Quick and Easy Chili, 35
    Sea Bass or Haddock with Black Bean Relish, 197
    White Chili, 37
beans, green
    Extra-Delicious Green Beans, 210
    Great Green Beans, 209
    Oriental Beans, 211
    Red Potato and Green Bean Salad, 57
Beans and Beef, 107
beat, definition of, 13
beef
    Aloha Grilled Steak and Pineapple, 182
    Beef Stroganoff, 103
    Chop Suey, 117

Index

Cola Roast, 114
Dilled Pot Roast, 115
Fajita Stir-Fry, 116
Italian Chicken Breasts or Steaks, 178
Korean Barbecue Steak, 183
Lemon-Dill Marinated Flank Steak or Chicken, 181
London Broil, 186
New York Steak with Tomato Relish and Black-Eyed Peas, 184–85
Oven Stew, 38
Pot Roast in Foil, 111
Pot Roast with Vegetables, 112–13
Roast Beef Sandwiches, 120
Salsa Beef, 118
Stir-Fry Steak Sandwiches, 119
Vegetable Beef Soup, 28
beef, ground
    Beans and Beef, 107
    Beef Noodle Casserole, 109
    Beef Taco Bake, 104
    California Burgers, 189
    Chili, 36
    Chili Burgers, 188
    Classic Meatloaf, 106
    Easy Lasagne, 248
    Easy Meatballs, 110
    Easy Minestrone Soup, 40
    Quick and Easy Chili, 35
    Scout Dinners, 105
    Sloppy Joes, 108
    Spaghetti Sauce, 252
    Super Hamburgers, 187
    Taco Salad, 72
    Taco Soup, 30
Beef Noodle Casserole, 109
Beef Stroganoff, 103
Beef Taco Bake, 104
berries
    Fresh Peach or Berry Ice Cream, 307
    See also specific berries
Best-Ever Frosted Brownies, 261
biscuits
    Baking Powder Biscuits, 84
    Crispy Cheese Biscuits, 83

Garlic Cheese Biscuits, 85
Black-Eyed Peas, 184–85
blanch, definition of, 13
blend, definition of, 13
Blueberry Muffins, 96
boil, definition of, 13
Bow-Tie Pasta and Chicken Salad, 75
braise, definition of, 13
Bran Muffins, 97
breads
    Baked German Pancakes, 254
    Baking Powder Biscuits, 84
    Banana Nut Bread or Muffins, 95
    Blueberry Muffins, 96
    Bran Muffins, 97
    Breadsticks, 87
    Cinnamon Pull-Aparts, 81
    Corn Muffins, 98
    Crispy Cheese Biscuits, 83
    Flour Tortillas, 93
    Frosted Half-Time Rolls, 89
    Garlic Cheese Biscuits, 85
    Grilled Toast, 201
    Italian Pull-Aparts, 82
    Orange Rolls, 90
    Puffy Apple Pancake, 256
    Pumpkin Muffins, 99
    Ranch Bread, 88
    Seasoned Rolls, 86
    Tennessee-Style Cornbread, 94
    Two-Hour Rolls, 91
    White Bread, 92
Breadsticks, 87
Breadstick Spread, 87
broccoli
    Broccoli Rice Quiche, 243
    Broccoli with Swiss Cheese, 214
    Glazed Almond Broccoli, 213
Broccoli Rice Quiche, 243
Broccoli with Swiss Cheese, 214
broil, definition of, 13
broths
    Chicken Broth, 26–27
brown, definition of, 13
Brownies, 262

Index

brownies
    Best-Ever Frosted Brownies, 261
    Brownies, 262
    Brownie Trifle, 286
    Carmel Pecan Brownies, 263
    Brownie Trifle, 286
butters
    Herb Butter, 221
    Thyme Butter, 221

cabbage
Coleslaw, 66
Caesar Salad, 61
cakes
    Angel's Delight, 292
    Grasshopper Cake, 266
    Infallible Chocolate Chip Cake, 264
    Lemon Cake, 267
    Oatmeal Cake, 269
    Piña Colada Cake, 271
    Spiced Peach Cake, 268
    Sunday Pudding, 285
    Texas Sheet Cake, 265
California Burgers, 189
California Salad, 59
Carmel Pecan Brownies, 263
Carrot Apple Salad, 54
carrots
    Carrot Apple Salad, 54
    Carrots Lyonnaise, 218
    Chilled Carrots and Peas, 216
    Glazed Carrots, 215
    Lemon Carrots, 217
    Zucchini Carrot Casserole, 231
Carrots Lyonnaise, 218
cashews
    Chicken Cashew Stir-Fry, 147
    Iceberg Salad with Cashews, 60
casseroles
    Beef Noodle Casserole, 109
    Beef Taco Bake, 104
    Broccoli with Swiss Cheese, 214
    Chicken Pot Pies, 137
    Creole Pork Chops, 169
    Extra-Delicious Green Beans, 210
    Glazed Almond Broccoli, 213
    Great Green Beans, 209
    Holiday Cauliflower, 220
    Macaroni and Cheese, 245
    Mexican Fiesta Biscuit Bake, 125
    Poppy Seed Chicken, 132
    Rice-Cheese Dish, 239
    Summer Squash, 230
    Tex-Mex Chicken and Rice Casserole, 138
    Zucchini Carrot Casserole, 231
cauliflower
    Dilly Mustard Cauliflower, 219
    Holiday Cauliflower, 220
Cheddar Tuna Pie, 164
cheese
    Cheddar Tuna Pie, 164
    Cheesy Potatoes, 203
    Cheesy Vegetable Soup, 32
    Crispy Cheese Biscuits, 83
    Easy Lasagne, 248
    French Bread Pizza, 255
    Garlic Cheese Biscuits, 85
    Macaroni and Cheese, 245
    Manicotti, 250
    My Best Lasagne, 246–47
    Rice-Cheese Dish, 239
    Vegetable Cheese Soup, 33
    Vegetable Lasagna, 249
Cheese Sauce, 173
Cheesy Potatoes, 203
Cheesy Vegetable Soup, 32
cherries
    Cherry Pie Salad, 48
    Roast Pork with Cherry Sauce, 170
    Cherry Pie Salad, 48
chicken
    Barbecue Chicken Breasts, 144
    boiling, 126
    Bow-Tie Pasta and Chicken Salad, 75
    broiling, 126
    Chicken Broth, 26–27
    Chicken Cashew Stir-Fry, 147
    Chicken Dumplings, 131
    Chicken Enchiladas, 128

Index

Chicken Pot Pies, 137
Chicken Provence, 123
Chicken Salad Supreme, 67
Chicken Tacos, 145
Chicken Waikiki, 134
Chinese Chicken Salad, 68–69
Cilantro, Chicken, and Black Bean Salad, 71
Cranberry Chicken, 127
Crispy Herb Chicken, 136
frying, 126–27
Garden Chicken Salad, 70
Grilled Basil Chicken, 180
grilling, 127
Haystacks, 130
Hearty Cream of Chicken Soup, 25
Imperial Baked Chicken, 139
Italian Chicken Breasts or Steaks, 178
Italian-Seasoned Chicken with Noodles, 140
Lemon Chicken, 141
Lemon-Dill Marinated Flank Steak or Chicken, 181
Lime Chicken, 179
Mandarin Chicken, 124
Mexican Fiesta Biscuit Bake, 125
microwaving, 127
Old-Fashioned Chicken Noodle Soup, 26–27
Orange Chicken, 143
Parmesan Chicken, 135
Peanut Chicken, 133
Poppy Seed Chicken, 132
Quick Chicken a la King, 146
Ranch Chicken, 142
roasting, 127
Salsa Chicken Enchiladas, 129
Sopa de Tortilla con Naranja, 31
Sweet and Sour Chicken Kabobs, 177
Swiss Chicken, 126
Tex-Mex Chicken and Rice Casserole, 138
Tortilla Soup with Orange, 31
White Chili, 37
Chicken Broth, 26–27
Chicken Cashew Stir-Fry, 147
Chicken Dumplings, 131
Chicken Enchiladas, 128
Chicken Pot Pies, 137
Chicken Provence, 123
Chicken Salad Supreme, 67
Chicken Tacos, 145
Chicken Waikiki, 134
Chili, 36
chili
    Chili, 36
    Chili Burgers, 188
    Mexican Chow Mein, 73
    Quick and Easy Chili, 35
    White Chili, 37
Chili Burgers, 188
Chili-Crusted Salmon and Roasted Scalloped Potatoes, 157
Chilled Asparagus Oriental, 208
Chilled Carrots and Peas, 216
Chinese Chicken Salad, 68–69
Chinese foods
    Chinese Chicken Salad, 68–69
    Chop Suey, 117
    Imperial Baked Chicken, 139
    Mandarin Chicken, 124
chocolate
    Best-Ever Frosted Brownies, 261
    Brownies, 262
    Brownie Trifle, 286
    Chocolate Chunk Cookies, 272
    Chocolate Crinkles, 278
    Chocolate Ice Cream, 308
    Chocolate Mint Cookies, 276
    Chocolate Rolo® Cookies, 277
    Frosty Dog Dessert, 287
    Grasshopper Cake, 266
    Oreo® Cream Pie, 301
    Salt Lake City Dessert, 291
    Texas Sheet Cake, 265
chocolate chips
    Almost Candy Bars, 282
    Carmel Pecan Brownies, 263
    Fudge Jumbles, 283
    Infallible Chocolate Chip Cake, 264

Index

Mud Squares, 270
Oatmeal Chocolate Chip Cookies, 274–75
Oh Henry Bars, 284
Chocolate Chunk Cookies, 272
Chocolate Cream Pie, 302
Chocolate Crinkles, 278
Chocolate Ice Cream, 308
Chocolate Mint Cookies, 276
Chocolate Rolo® Cookies, 277
Chocolate Sauce, 287
chop, definition of, 13
Chop Suey, 117
Chunky Baked Potato Soup, 41
Cilantro, Chicken, and Black Bean Salad, 71
Cinnamon Pears, 49
Cinnamon Pull-Aparts, 81
Citrus Dressing for Fresh Fruits, 78
Clam Chowder, 34
Classic Meatloaf, 106
coconut
    Piña Colada Cake, 271
Cola Roast, 114
Coleslaw, 66
Company Fish, 160
cookies
    Almost Candy Bars, 282
    Applesauce Oatmeal Cookies, 273
    Chocolate Chunk Cookies, 272
    Chocolate Crinkles, 278
    Chocolate Mint Cookies, 276
    Chocolate Rolo(r) Cookies, 277
    Fudge Jumbles, 283
    Gingersnaps, 279
    Oatmeal Chocolate Chip Cookies, 274–75
    Peanut Butter Cookie Bars, 281
    Snickerdoodles, 280
cool, definition of, 13
Cool Lime Dessert, 296
corn
    Corn Muffins, 98
    Corn on the Cob with Herb or Thyme Butter, 221
    Corn Salad, 53
    Dilly Corn and Snow Peas, 222
    Tennessee-Style Cornbread, 94
Corn Muffins, 98
Corn on the Cob with Herb or Thyme Butter, 221
Corn Salad, 53
cranberries
    Cranberry Chicken, 127
    Cranberry Salad, 50
Cranberry Chicken, 127
Cranberry Salad, 50
cream, definition of, 14
Creole Pork Chops, 169
Crepes Ensenada, 173
crisps
    Apple or Peach Crisp, 288
crisp-tender, definition of, 14
Crispy Cheese Biscuits, 83
Crispy Herb Chicken, 136
crusts
    for Frosty Dog Dessert, 287
    See also pie crusts
cube, definition of, 14

desserts
    Almost Candy Bars, 282
    Angel's Delight, 292
    Apple Crisp, 288
    Applesauce Oatmeal Cookies, 273
    Apple Slump, 290
    Baked Apple, 289
    Banana Cream Pie, 302
    Best-Ever Frosted Brownies, 261
    Brownies, 262
    Brownie Trifle, 286
    Carmel Pecan Brownies, 263
    Chocolate Chunk Cookies, 272
    Chocolate Cream Pie, 302
    Chocolate Crinkles, 278
    Chocolate Ice Cream, 308
    Chocolate Mint Cookies, 276
    Chocolate Rolo® Cookies, 277
    Cool Lime Dessert, 296
    Easy Apple Pie, 299

Index

Fresh Peach or Berry Ice Cream, 307
Fresh Peach Pie, 305
Fresh Strawberry Pie, 304
Frosty Dog Dessert, 287
Frosty Pumpkin Pie, 303
Fruit and Yogurt Ice Cream, 309
Fudge Jumbles, 283
Gingersnaps, 279
Grasshopper Cake, 266
Infallible Chocolate Chip Cake, 264
Lemon Cake, 267
Lemon Cream Pie, 302
Mud Squares, 270
Oatmeal Cake, 269
Oatmeal Chocolate Chip Cookies, 274–75
Oh Henry Bars, 284
Orange Sherbet Dessert, 294
Oreo® Cream Pie, 301
Peach Crisp, 288
Peanut Butter Cookie Bars, 281
Piña Colada Cake, 271
Quick Lemon Pie, 300
Raspberry Banana Sherbet, 293
Raspberry Danish Dessert, 295
Salt Lake City Dessert, 291
Snickerdoodles, 280
Spiced Peach Cake, 268
Sunday Pudding, 285
Texas Sheet Cake, 265
Tutti Frutti Ice Cream, 306
dice, definition of, 14
Dilled Pot Roast, 115
Dill Salmon, 192
Dilly Corn and Snow Peas, 222
Dilly Mustard Cauliflower, 219
dissolve, definition of, 14
dressings, salad. *See* salad dressings
dumplings
Chicken Dumplings, 131

Easy Apple Pie, 299
Easy Baked Fish, 161
Easy "Homemade" Soup, 29
Easy Lasagne, 248
Easy Meatballs, 110
Easy Minestrone Soup, 40
Egg Burritos, 257
eggs
Egg Burritos, 257
hard boiling, 58
Oven Omelet, 258
separating whites and yolks, 291
Extra-Delicious Green Beans, 210

Fajita Stir-Fry, 116
fat, removing, 111
fish
Angel Hair Pasta and Shrimp, 153
Baked Salmon, 155
Cheddar Tuna Pie, 164
Chili-Crusted Salmon and Roasted Scalloped Potatoes, 157
Company Fish, 160
Dill Salmon, 192
Easy Baked Fish, 161
Grilled Orange Roughy with Salsa, 196
Grilled Shrimp, 191
Grilled Swordfish or Halibut a la Orange, 195
Grilled Swordfish with Red Pepper Sauce, 194
Halibut with Mustard Sauce, 158
Mediterranean-Style Salmon, 156
Orange Roughy in Salsa, 163
Portuguese Fish, 162
Salmon with Papaya-Mango-Pineapple Salsa, 154
Salsa Fish, 190
Sautéed Halibut with Nectarine Salsa, 159
Sea Bass or Haddock with Black Bean Relish, 197
Shrimp Linguini, 152
Shrimp Stroganoff, 151
Teriyaki Salmon, 193
Flour Tortillas, 93
fold, definition of, 14
French Bread Pizza, 255
Fresh Fruit with Raspberry Dip, 46

Index

Fresh Peach or Berry Ice Cream, 307
Fresh Peach Pie, 305
Fresh Strawberry Pie, 304
Fried Rice, 242
Frosted Half-time Rolls, 89
frostings
    for brownies, 261
    for Chocolate Mint Cookies, 276
    for Frosted Half-Time Rolls, 89
    for Oatmeal Cake, 269
    for Spiced Peach Cake, 268
    for Texas Sheet Cake, 265
    See also glazes
Frosty Dog Dessert, 287
Frosty Pumpkin Pie, 303
fruit
    Apple Avocado Salad, 62
    Cherry Pie Salad, 48
    Cinnamon Pears, 49
    Citrus Dressing for Fresh Fruits, 78
    Cranberry Salad, 50
    Fresh Fruit with Raspberry Dip, 46
    Fruit and Yogurt Ice Cream, 309
    Fruit Sauce, 78
    Fruit Topping, 254
    Nectarine Salsa, 159
    Spring Salad with Orange Dressing, 65
    Summer Fruit Salad, 45
    Strawberry and Melon Salad with Lime Dressing, 47
    Tutti Frutti Ice Cream, 306
    See also specific fruits
Fruit and Yogurt Ice Cream, 309
Fruit Sauce, 78
Fruit Topping, 254
fry, definition of, 14
Fudge Jumbles, 283

Garden Chicken Salad, 70
Garlic Cheese Biscuits, 85
garlic, mincing, 247
Gingersnaps, 279
Glazed Almond Broccoli, 213
Glazed Carrots, 215
Glazed Ham, 174

Glaze for Vegetables, 235
glazes
    Apricot Glaze, 174
    Glaze for Vegetables, 235
    Honey Mustard Glaze, 174
    See also frostings
Grasshopper Cake, 266
grate, definition of, 14
grease
    definition of, 14
    removing, 111
Great Green Beans, 209
grill, definition of, 14
Grilled Basil Chicken, 180
grilled foods
    Aloha Grilled Steak and Pineapple, 182
    Barbecued Spareribs, 198
    California Burgers, 189
    Cheesy Potatoes, 203
    Chili Burgers, 188
    Corn on the Cob with Herb or Thyme Butter, 221
    Dill Salmon, 192
    Grilled Basil Chicken, 180
    Grilled Orange Roughy with Salsa, 196
    Grilled Pork Chops with Apples, 200
    Grilled Seasoned Ham, 199
    Grilled Shrimp, 191
    Grilled Swordfish or Halibut a la Orange, 195
    Grilled Swordfish with Red Pepper Sauce, 194
    Grilled Toast, 201
    Hot Bacon Potato Salad, 202
    Italian Chicken Breasts or Steaks, 178
    Korean Barbecue Steak, 183
    Lemon-Dill Marinated Flank Steak or Chicken, 181
    Lime Chicken, 179
    London Broil, 186
    New York Steak with Tomato Relish and Black-Eyed Peas, 184–85
    Parmesan Potato Packets, 204
    Salsa Fish, 190

Index

Sea Bass or Haddock with Black Bean Relish, 197
Super Hamburgers, 187
Sweet and Sour Chicken Kabobs, 177
Teriyaki Salmon, 193
Grilled Orange Roughy with Salsa, 196
Grilled Pork Chops with Apples, 200
Grilled Seasoned Ham, 199
Grilled Shrimp, 191
Grilled Swordfish or Halibut a la Orange, 195
Grilled Swordfish with Red Pepper Sauce, 194
Grilled Toast, 201

Haddock with Black Bean Relish, 197
halibut
    Grilled Swordfish or Halibut a la Orange, 195
    Halibut with Mustard Sauce, 158
    Sautéed Halibut with Nectarine Salsa, 159
Halibut with Mustard Sauce, 158
ham
    Glazed Ham, 174
    Grilled Seasoned Ham, 199
Haystacks, 130
Hearty Cream of Chicken Soup, 25
Herb Butter, 221
Holiday Cauliflower, 220
Honey Mustard Glaze, 174
Hot Bacon Potato Salad, 202

Iceberg Salad with Cashews, 60
ice cream
    Chocolate Ice Cream, 308
    Fresh Peach or Berry Ice Cream, 307
    Frosty Dog Dessert, 287
    Frosty Pumpkin Pie, 303
    Fruit and Yogurt Ice Cream, 309
    Orange Sherbet Dessert, 294
    Oreo® Cream Pie, 301
    Quick Lemon Pie, 300
    Tutti Frutti Ice Cream, 306
Imperial Baked Chicken, 139

Infallible Chocolate Chip Cake, 264
Italian Chicken Breasts or Steaks, 178
Italian Pull-Aparts, 82
Italian-Seasoned Chicken with Noodles, 140
Italian-Seasoned Potatoes, 227

Japanese foods
    Peanut Chicken, 133

knead, definition of, 14
Korean Barbecue Steak, 183

lasagnas
    Easy Lasagne, 248
    My Best Lasagne, 246–47
    Vegetable Lasagna, 249
Lemon Cake, 267
Lemon Carrots, 217
Lemon Chicken, 141
Lemon Cream Pie, 302
Lemon-Dill Marinated Flank Steak or Chicken, 181
Lemon Sauce, 141
Lemon Vinaigrette, 77
Lime Chicken, 179
London Broil, 186

Macaroni and Cheese, 245
Mandarin Chicken, 124
Manicotti, 250
marinate, definition of, 14
meat. *See* specific meats
Mediterranean-Style Salmon, 156
melon
    Strawberry and Melon Salad with Lime Dressing, 47
Mexican Chow Mein, 73
Mexican Fiesta Biscuit Bake, 125
Mexican foods
    Beef Taco Bake, 104
    Chicken Enchiladas, 128
    Chicken Tacos, 145
    Cilantro, Chicken, and Black Bean Salad, 71

Index

Egg Burritos, 257
Fajita Stir-Fry, 116
Lime Chicken, 179
Mexican Chow Mein, 73
Mexican Fiesta Biscuit Bake, 125
Mexican Rice, 241
Salsa Chicken Enchiladas, 129
Sopa de Tortilla con Naranja, 31
Taco Salad, 72
Taco Soup, 30
Tex-Mex Chicken and Rice Casserole, 138
Tortilla Soup with Orange, 31
Mexican Rice, 241
mince, definition of, 14–15
mix, definition of, 15
Mud Squares, 270
muffins
   Banana Nut Bread or Muffins, 95
   Blueberry Muffins, 96
   Bran Muffins, 97
   Corn Muffins, 98
   Pumpkin Muffins, 99
mushrooms
   Rice and Mushrooms, 240
Mustard Sauce, 158
My Best Lasagne, 246–47

Nectarine Salsa, 159
Never-Fail Pie Crust, 298
New England Ribs, 172
New York Steak with Tomato Relish and Black-Eyed Peas, 184–85
Noodles, 27

oatmeal
   Applesauce Oatmeal Cookies, 273
   Oatmeal Cake, 269
   Oatmeal Chocolate Chip Cookies, 274–75
Oatmeal Cake, 269
Oatmeal Chocolate Chip Cookies, 274–75
Oh Henry Bars, 284
Old-Fashioned Chicken Noodle Soup, 26–27

omelets
   Oven Omelet, 258
Orange Chicken, 143
Orange Rolls, 90
orange roughy
   Grilled Orange Roughy with Salsa, 196
   Orange Roughy in Salsa, 163
   Orange Roughy in Salsa, 163
oranges
   Orange Chicken, 143
   Orange Sauce, 217
   Orange Sherbet Dessert, 294
Oreo® Cream Pie, 301
Oriental Beans, 211
Oriental Dressing, 68–69
Oriental Vegetables, 233
Oven-Baked Potato Pie, 224
Oven Omelet, 258
Oven-Roasted Potatoes, 228
Oven Stew, 38

pancakes
   Baked German Pancakes, 254
   Puffy Apple Pancake, 256
parboil, definition of, 15
pare, definition of, 15
Parmesan Chicken, 135
Parmesan Pasta, 244
Parmesan Potato Packets, 204
pasta
   Angel Hair Pasta and Shrimp, 153
   Beef Noodle Casserole, 109
   cooking, 244–45
   Easy Lasagne, 248
   Italian-Seasoned Chicken with Noodles, 140
   Macaroni and Cheese, 245
   Manicotti, 250
   My Best Lasagne, 246–47
   Noodles, 27
   Old-Fashioned Chicken Noodle Soup, 26–27
   Parmesan Pasta, 244
   Pasta Primavera Pie, 251
   Pasta-Vegetable Salad, 74

Index

Shrimp Linguini, 152
Simple Spaghetti Sauce, 253
Spaghetti Sauce, 252
Vegetable Lasagna, 249
Pasta Primavera Pie, 251
Pasta-Vegetable Salad, 74
Peach Crisp, 288
peaches
    Apple or Peach Crisp, 288
    Fresh Peach or Berry Ice Cream, 307
    Fresh Peach Pie, 305
    Spiced Peach Cake, 268
Peanut Butter Cookie Bars, 281
Peanut Chicken, 133
pears
    Cinnamon Pears, 49
peas
    Almond Mushroom Peas, 223
    Chilled Carrots and Peas, 216
    Dilly Corn and Snow Peas, 222
peas, black-eyed
    New York Steak with Tomato Relish and Black-Eyed Peas, 184–85
pecans
    Carmel Pecan Brownies, 263
peel, definition of, 15
peppers
    cutting and seeding, 69
    Red Pepper Sauce, 194
pie crusts
    for Easy Apple Pie, 299
    Never-Fail Pie Crust, 298
pies
    Banana Cream Pie, 302
    Chocolate Cream Pie, 302
    Easy Apple Pie, 299
    Fresh Peach Pie, 305
    Fresh Strawberry Pie, 304
    Frosty Pumpkin Pie, 303
    Lemon Cream Pie, 302
    Oreo® Cream Pie, 301
    Quick Lemon Pie, 300
    Piña Colada Cake, 271
pizza
    French Bread Pizza, 255

Poppy Seed Chicken, 132
Poppy Seed Dressing, 76
pork
    Barbecued Spareribs, 198
    Creole Pork Chops, 169
    Crepes Ensenada, 173
    Glazed Ham, 174
    Grilled Pork Chops with Apples, 200
    Grilled Seasoned Ham, 199
    New England Ribs, 172
    Pork Chops with Brown Rice, 168
    Pork Tenderloin, 171
    Red Pork Chops, 167
    Roast Pork with Cherry Sauce, 170
Pork Chops with Brown Rice, 168
Pork Tenderloin, 171
Portuguese Fish, 162
Potato Cakes, 225
potatoes
    Cheesy Potatoes, 203
    Chili-Crusted Salmon and Roasted Scalloped Potatoes, 157
    Chunky Baked Potato Soup, 41
    Hot Bacon Potato Salad, 202
    Italian-Seasoned Potatoes, 227
    mashing, 225
    Oven-Baked Potato Pie, 224
    Oven-Roasted Potatoes, 228
    Parmesan Potato Packets, 204
    Potato Cakes, 225
    Potato Salad, 58
    Red Potato and Green Bean Salad, 57
    Santa Fe Potato Salad, 56
    Savory Mashed New Potatoes, 226
Potato Salad, 58
Pot Roast in Foil, 111
Pot Roast with Vegetables, 112–13
puddings
    Sunday Pudding, 285
    Sweet Potato Pudding, 229
Puffy Apple Pancake, 256
pumpkin
    Frosty Pumpkin Pie, 303
    Pumpkin Muffins, 99
Pumpkin Muffins, 99

puree, definition of, 15

quiches
    Broccoli Rice Quiche, 243
Quick and Easy Chili, 35
Quick Chicken a la King, 146
Quick Lemon Pie, 300

Ranch Chicken, 142
Ranch Bread, 88
raspberries
    Fresh Fruit with Raspberry Dip, 46
    Raspberry Banana Sherbet, 293
    Raspberry Danish Dessert, 295
    Raspberry Tapioca Salad, 51
Raspberry Banana Sherbet, 293
Raspberry Danish Dessert, 295
Raspberry Tapioca Salad, 51
Raspberry Vinaigrette, 77
Red Pepper Sauce, 194
Red Pork Chops, 167
Red Potato and Green Bean Salad, 57
rice
    Broccoli Rice Quiche, 243
    cooking, 241
    Fried Rice, 242
    Haystacks, 130
    Mexican Rice, 241
    Pork Chops with Brown Rice, 168
    Rice and Mushrooms, 240
    Rice-Cheese Dish, 239
    Tex-Mex Chicken and Rice Casserole, 138
Rice and Mushrooms, 240
Rice-Cheese Dish, 239
roast, definition of, 15
Roast Beef Sandwiches, 120
Roast Pork with Cherry Sauce, 170
rolls
    Cinnamon Pull-Aparts, 81
    Frosted Half-time Rolls, 89
    Italian Pull-Aparts, 82
    Orange Rolls, 90
    Seasoned Rolls, 86
    Two-Hour Rolls, 91

salad dressings
    for Apple Avocado Salad, 62
    for Bacon and Tomato Salad, 64
    Basic Vinaigrette, 76
    for Bow-Tie Pasta and Chicken Salad, 75
    for Caesar Salad, 61
    for Cilantro, Chicken, and Black Bean Salad, 71
    Citrus Dressing for Fresh Fruits, 78
    for Garden Chicken Salad, 70
    Lemon Vinaigrette, 77
    Oriental Dressing, 68–69
    Poppy Seed Dressing, 76
    Raspberry Vinaigrette, 77
    for Red Potato and Green Bean Salad, 57
    for Santa Fe Potato Salad, 56
    for Spinach Salad, 63
    for Spring Salad, 65
    for Strawberry and Melon Salad, 47
salads, fruit
    Carrot Apple Salad, 54
    Cherry Pie Salad, 48
    Cinnamon Pears, 49
    Cranberry Salad, 50
    Fresh Fruit with Raspberry Dip, 46
    Raspberry Tapioca Salad, 51
    Spring Salad with Orange Dressing, 65
    Strawberry and Melon Salad with Lime Dressing, 47
    Summer Fruit Salad, 45
salads, green
    Apple Avocado Salad, 62
    Bacon, Cauliflower, and Lettuce Salad, 55
    Bacon and Tomato Salad, 64
    Caesar Salad, 61
    California Salad, 59
    Iceberg Salad with Cashews, 60
    Spinach Salad, 63
    Spring Salad with Orange Dressing, 65
salads, main dish
    Bow-Tie Pasta and Chicken Salad, 75
    Chicken Salad Supreme, 67

Index

  Chinese Chicken Salad, 68–69
  Cilantro, Chicken, and Black Bean
    Salad, 71
  Garden Chicken Salad, 70
  Mexican Chow Mein, 73
  Pasta-Vegetable Salad, 74
  Taco Salad, 72
salads, pasta
  Bow-Tie Pasta and Chicken Salad, 75
  Pasta-Vegetable Salad, 74
salads, potato
  Hot Bacon Potato Salad, 202
  Potato Salad, 58
  Santa Fe Potato Salad, 56
salads, vegetable
  Carrot Apple Salad, 54
  Coleslaw, 66
  Corn Salad, 53
  Pasta-Vegetable Salad, 74
  Red Potato and Green Bean Salad, 57
  Tomato Salad, 52
salmon
  Baked Salmon, 155
  Chili-Crusted Salmon and Roasted
    Scalloped Potatoes, 157
  Dill Salmon, 192
  Mediterranean-Style Salmon, 156
  Salmon with Papaya-Mango-Pineapple
    Salsa, 154
  Teriyaki Salmon, 193
Salmon with Papaya-Mango-Pineapple
  Salsa, 154
Salsa, 196
Salsa Beef, 118
Salsa Chicken Enchiladas, 129
Salsa Fish, 190
salsas
  Nectarine Salsa, 159
  Salsa, 196
  Tomato Relish, 184–85
Salt Lake City Dessert, 291
sandwiches
  California Burgers, 189
  Chili Burgers, 188
  Roast Beef Sandwiches, 120
  Sloppy Joes, 108
  Stir-Fry Steak Sandwiches, 119
  Super Hamburgers, 187
Santa Fe Potato Salad, 56
sauces
  Barbecue Sauce, 198
  Cheese Sauce, 173
  Chocolate Sauce, 287
  for Egg Burritos, 257
  Fruit Sauce, 78
  Lemon Sauce, 141
  Mustard Sauce, 158
  Orange Sauce, 217
  for Raspberry Danish Dessert, 295
  Red Pepper Sauce, 194
  Simple Spaghetti Sauce, 253
  Spaghetti Sauce, 252
  Speedy Mock Hollandaise, 234
  Sweet and Sour Sauce, 133
  for vegetables, 213
  Velvet Fudge Sauce, 297
  White Sauce, 134–35
sauté, definition of, 15
Sautéed Halibut with Nectarine Salsa, 159
Savory Mashed New Potatoes, 226
Scout Dinners, 105
Sea Bass or Haddock with Black Bean
  Relish, 197
seafood. *See* fish
Seasoned Rolls, 86
sherbets
  Orange Sherbet Dessert, 294
  Raspberry Banana Sherbet, 293
shred, definition of, 15
shrimp
  Angel Hair Pasta and Shrimp, 153
  Grilled Shrimp, 191
  Shrimp Linguini, 152
  Shrimp Stroganoff, 151
Shrimp Linguini, 152
Shrimp Stroganoff, 151
sift, definition of, 15
simmer, definition of, 15
Simple Spaghetti Sauce, 253
Skillet Tomatoes and Zucchini, 232

Index

Sloppy Joes, 108
Snickerdoodles, 280
Sopa de Tortilla con Naranja, 31
soups
    Bean and Salsa Soup, 39
    Cheesy Vegetable Soup, 32
    Chili, 36
    Chunky Baked Potato Soup, 41
    Clam Chowder, 34
    Easy "Homemade" Soup, 29
    Easy Minestrone Soup, 40
    Hearty Cream of Chicken Soup, 25
    Old-Fashioned Chicken Noodle Soup, 26–27
    Oven Stew, 38
    Quick and Easy Chili, 35
    Sopa de Tortilla con Naranja, 31
    Taco Soup, 30
    Tomato Basil Soup, 42
    Tortilla Soup with Orange, 31
    Vegetable Beef Soup, 28
    Vegetable Cheese Soup, 33
    White Chili, 37
Spaghetti Sauce, 252
Speedy Mock Hollandaise, 234
Spiced Peach Cake, 268
Spinach Salad, 63
Spring Salad with Orange Dressing, 65
squash
    Summer Squash, 230
    Zucchini Carrot Casserole, 231
steam, definition of, 15
stews
    Oven Stew, 38
stir, definition of, 15
stir-fry, definition of, 16
Stir-Fry Steak Sandwiches, 119
stocks
    Chicken Broth, 26–27
strawberries
    Fresh Strawberry Pie, 304
    Strawberry and Melon Salad with Lime Dressing, 47
    Strawberry and Melon Salad with Lime Dressing, 47

Summer Fruit Salad, 45
Summer Squash, 230
Sunday Pudding, 285
Super Hamburgers, 187
Sweet and Sour Chicken Kabobs, 177
Sweet and Sour Sauce, 133
sweetbreads
    Banana Nut Bread or Muffins, 95
Sweet Potato Pudding, 229
Swiss Chicken, 126
swordfish
    Grilled Swordfish or Halibut a la Orange, 195
    Grilled Swordfish with Red Pepper Sauce, 194

Taco Salad, 72
Taco Soup, 30
tapioca
    Raspberry Tapioca Salad, 51
Tennessee-Style Cornbread, 94
Teriyaki Salmon, 193
Texas Sheet Cake, 265
Tex-Mex Chicken and Rice Casserole, 138
Thyme Butter, 221
Tomato Basil Soup, 42
tomatoes
    Bacon and Tomato Salad, 64
    New York Steak with Tomato Relish and Black-Eyed Peas, 184–85
    Skillet Tomatoes and Zucchini, 232
    Tomato Basil Soup, 42
    Tomato Salad, 52
    Tomato Relish, 184–85
Tomato Salad, 52
toppings
    for Apple or Peach Crisp, 288
    for Easy Apple Pie, 299
    Fruit Topping, 254
tortillas
    Flour Tortillas, 93
Tortilla Soup with Orange, 31
toss, definition of, 16
trifles
    Angel's Delight, 292

Index

Brownie Trifle, 286
tuna
    Cheddar Tuna Pie, 164
Tutti Frutti Ice Cream, 306
Two-Hour Rolls, 91

Vegetable Beef Soup, 28
Vegetable Cheese Soup, 33
Vegetable Lasagna, 249
vegetables
    Cheesy Vegetable Soup, 32
    Chop Suey, 117
    Easy "Homemade" Soup, 29
    Glaze for Vegetables, 235
    Oriental Vegetables, 233
    Oven Stew, 38
    Pot Roast with Vegetables, 112–13
    roasting, 235
    steaming, 211
Vegetable Beef Soup, 28
Vegetable Cheese Soup, 33

Vegetable Lasagna, 249
See also specific vegetables
Velvet Fudge Sauce, 297
vinaigrettes
    Basic Vinaigrette, 76
    Lemon Vinaigrette, 77
    Raspberry Vinaigrette, 77

whip, definition of, 16
White Bread, 92
White Chili, 37
White Sauce, 134–35

yogurt
    Fruit and Yogurt Ice Cream, 309

zucchini
    Skillet Tomatoes and Zucchini, 232
    Summer Squash, 230
    Zucchini Carrot Casserole, 231
Zucchini Carrot Casserole, 231

RECIPE IDEAS

RECIPE IDEAS

RECIPE IDEAS

RECIPE IDEAS

RECIPE IDEAS

RECIPE IDEAS

RECIPE IDEAS

EQUIVALENCY CHART

LIQUID MEASURES

1 gal = 4 qt = 8 pt = 16 cups = 128 fl oz

½ gal = 2 qt = 4 pt = 8 cups = 64 fl oz

¼ gal = 1 qt = 2 pt = 4 cups = 32 fl oz

½ qt = 1 pt = 2 cups = 16 fl oz

¼ qt = 1/2 pt = 1 cup = 8 fl oz

DRY MEASURES

1 cup = 16 Tbsp = 48 tsp = 250mL

¾ cup = 12 Tbsp = 36 tsp = 175mL

⅔ cup = 10⅔ Tbsp = 32 tsp = 150mL

½ cup = 8 Tbsp = 24 tsp = 125mL

⅓ cup = 5⅓ Tbsp = 16 tsp = 75mL

¼ cup = 4 Tbsp = 12 tsp = 50mL

⅛ cup = 2 Tbsp = 6 tsp = 30mL

1 Tbsp = 3 tsp = 15mL